CHANAKYA

**The Great Indian Visionary, Economist, and Strategist:
His Legacy and Relevance in Modern Times**

Prof. (Dr.) Jai Paul Dudeja

CONTENTS

SECTION-1
INTRODUCTION AND OVERVIEW OF CHANAKYA

SECTION-2
LIFE STORIES OF CHANAKYA (MULTIPLE VERSIONS)

SECTION-3
CONTRIBUTIONS OF CHANAKYA

TESTIMONIAL FROM
PROF. (DR.) ANAND RANGANATHAN

Professor at Jawaharlal Nehru University, New Delhi.

**SCIENTIST, AUTHOR, A POPULAR TV COMMENTATOR,
CONSULTING EDITOR OF 'SWARAJYA',
WINNER OF MULTIPLE AWARDS AND HONOURS**

It is a pleasure for me to write a brief Testimonial on Prof. (Dr.) Jai Paul Dudeja's book on "Chanakya: The Great Indian Visionary, Economist, and Strategist: His Legacy and Relevance in Modern Times".

Born in 375 BCE on the Indian soil, Chanakya (also known as Kautilya and Vishnugupta), lived a life, whose contributions and legacy are relevant even today, not only in India but in the whole world. Chanakya was a great visionary, philosopher, teacher, economist, a Statesman, and Strategist. He was the prime minister and political advisor of Emperor Chandragupta and also that of his son Bindusara.

The two famous books authored by Chanakya are: **Neeti-shastra and Arthashastra**, which are the guiding principles even today for the commoners and the heads of the states.

'Chanakya Neeti' is this great thinker's practical wisdom for the people of his time. These teachings are so fundamental that their relevance is almost ever-lasting. Written in simple and lucid language with clear thoughts, these observations have not only withstood the test of time but many of phrases have become the oft-quoted proverbs (called 'Chanakya's quotes')

Chanakya's magnum opus, **the Arthashastra** ("The Science of Material Gain"), is regarded as the first authoritative text on political science, foreign policy, diplomacy and economics. In this treatise, he wrote about the entire spectrum of economic wealth, strategies to manage the affair of the kingdom and its people, both in peace and war.

Chanakya was the first thinker of the ancient times who nurtured the sense of nationalism and inculcated in the minds of the people that they owed their basic allegiance to the Rajya (State of Nation) as Rajadharma. Chankya's legacy is as relevant today as in the past.

Prof. Dudeja, in his signature style of a popular teacher, has covered this subject on CHANAKYA, in a clear and interesting way, which will be appreciated by all the readers in India and other countries.

This book can also be treated as a guideline for the heads of respective nations for the efficient conduct of their respective governments.

I congratulate Prof. (Dr.) Jai Paul Dudeja for writing such an excellent book on this important topic.

– Anand Ranganathan, Author and Scientist

PREFACE

Dear Readers,

I am extremely happy to see this book titled, **"Chanakya: The Great Indian Visionary, Economist, and Strategist: His Legacy and Relevance in Modern Times"**, in your hands. It is my firm belief that you have chosen to read this book with a specific aim in mind, and I assure you that you will not be disappointed with it.

Between 375 and 283 BCE, a legend by the name, Chanakya (also known as Kautilya and Vishnugupta), lived a life on the Indian soil, whose contributions and legacy are relevant even today, not only in India but in the whole world. Chanakya was a great visionary, philosopher, teacher, economist, a statesman, and a strategist. He was the prime minister and political advisor of Emperor Chandragupta and also that of his son Bindusara. It is said that Chanakya was insulted by Dhanananda, the then king of Pataliputra, which led Chanakya to take a vow to dethrone him; which he did with the help of Chandragupta. Besides being the person responsible to pick up Chandragupta as a child, Chanakya nurtured him and was responsible for making him the king of the largest empire in India of that time. The two famous books authored by Chanakya are: Neeti-shastra and Arthashastra, which are the guiding principles even today for the commoners and the heads of the states.

The present book describes the life, contributions, and relevance of Chanakya, the legendary. It is hoped that the readers will take inspiration from this ancient Indian and learn a lot from his contributions.

This book is divided into three sections, consisting of 17 chapters in all.

The value of this book has been enhanced by a generous **TESTIMONIAL from Dr. Anand Ranganathan**, Professor at Jawaharlal Nehru University, New Delhi, Scientist, Author, A popular TV commentator, Consulting editor of 'SWARAJYA', Winner of multiple awards and honors,

The author sincerely believes that a book of this nature will be appreciated by all the common readers and statesmen across the globe who wish to know more of Chanakya, his legacy, contributions and the relevance in today's times and apply the same in their personal life and in the society.

The author would open heartedly love to receive any encouraging/ critical comments as well as feedback from the dear readers at his Email ID: drjpdudeja@gmail.com

Sincerely

2025 **Prof. (Dr.) Jai Paul Dudeja**

ACKNOWLEDGEMENTS

The seeds of my interest in the continual quest for new and ancient knowledge were lovingly sown by my revered parents: **Late (Dr.) Shanti Sawrup Dudeja and (Late) Mrs. Jai Devi Dudeja**. I am sure that they are watching me every moment from wherever they are in the other world and continuously sending their blessings to me.

I have greatly benefitted in going through the books, reports, research papers and articles, referred to in the **'Bibliography'** in this Book. I gratefully acknowledge these authors for enhancing my understanding on the subject matter of this book.

I wish to place on record my sincere thanks and appreciation to **Prof. (Dr.) Anand Ranganathan**, for providing a generous **TESTIMONIAL** for this book.

Last but not the least, my greatest admiration is reserved for **Mrs. Rita Dudeja**, my wife and my best friend. She is the source of inspiration for me and a co-traveller on the path of trust and truth.

2025   **Prof. (Dr.) Jai Paul Dudeja**

PROFILE OF THE AUTHOR

Born in June 1948, Prof. (Dr.) Jai Paul Dudeja holds a brilliant academic record. He did his Master's degree in Physics from Birla Institute of Technology and Science (BITS), Pilani (India), and Ph.D. degree in Physics from the Indian Institute of Technology (IIT), Delhi. He has been in regular employment as a Scientist, Professor, Dean, Director, Principal and a Senior Administrator in various educational institutions, universities, laboratories, public and private organizations. He superannuated as a Senior Scientist and Additional Director in May 2008 from the Defence Research and Development Organisation (DRDO), Government of India. After DRDO, he served for over 11 years, till his last posting as a Director at Amity University Gurgaon, from where he retired in Nov 2019.

Till date, Dr. Dudeja has published/presented about 90 research papers in various national and international journals/conferences. Besides this, he has authored the following **thirty books** on science, technology, spirituality, mysticism, and consciousness:

1. Gayatri Mantra: A GPS to Enlightenment
2. Maha Mrityunjaya Mantra: An Invincible Armour for Conquering Death
3. Ajapa-Japa Sohum-Humsa Mantra: An Eternal Mantra for Inner Consciousness
4. The Third Eye: A Spiritual Laser for Stimulating Inner Awakening
5. Quantum Physics of Consciousness and Non-Duality in Eastern Philosophy

6. Quantum Science of Love, Healing, Happiness, and Bliss in Ancient Wisdom
7. Chakras Healing and Kundalini Awakening by Yogic Techniques,
8. Meditation Practices across the Globe and their Beneficial Effects.
9. Comparative Analysis of Hindu, Buddhist, and Jain Philosophies
10. Mantras for Happiness
11. Om Namah Shivaya: A Powerful Mantra for Mastering Five Elements
12. Trataka: A Concentrated Gazing Technique for Mystical Powers
13. Walking Meditation: Techniques and Benefits
14. Quantum Science of Ganesha Consciousness
15. Tantra Science
16. Quantum Brain, Mind, and Thinking
17. Profound Meditation Techniques in Tibetan Buddhism
18. REIKI: A Holistic Energy Healing Technique
19. Shaktipāt: Instant Transmission of Spiritual Energy from a Siddha Guru to the Disciple
20. Vāstu Shāstra: Ancient Indian Science of Architecture
21. Vedantic Thoughts on Māyā, Mithyā, and the Brahman
22. Siddhis (Supernatural Powers): A Guide for Understanding and Attaining These
23. Near-Death Experience: Scientific Interpretation (Inspired by True Story of a Friend)
24. Universe before the Big Bang: A Deeper Insight into Cosmology
25. Spiritual Intelligence: Significance, Applications, Measurement, and Development Techniques
26. Mind-Reading and Artificial Intelligence: Past, Present and Future (Science, Technology, Opportunity, Risks and Regulations)
27. Climate Change: A Global Challenge (Causes, Adverse Effects, Monitoring, Adaptation, And Mitigation).

28. Converging, Emerging, Innovative, Disruptive, and Critical Technologies for Modern and Future Warfare

29. A Guidebook on Healthy and Unhealthy Foods and Diets: With Description of Over 80 Foods, Diets and Cuisines in the World

30. Maa Saraswati: The Goddess of Knowledge, Wisdom, Creativity, Speech, Arts, and Music.

Dr. Dudeja has delivered many invited lectures in the international conferences in India and abroad.

He has been recognized as the "World's Who's Who in Science & Engineering".

INTRODUCTION AND OVERVIEW OF CHANAKYA

CHAPTER 1

CHANAKYA: INTRODUCTION AND OVERVIEW

1.1 WHO WAS CHANAKYA?

Acharya Chanakya, also known as Vishnugupta and Kautilya, was an outstanding economist and philosopher, as well as a stateman. His magnum opus, the **Arthashastra** ("The Science of Material Gain"), is regarded as the first authoritative text on political science and economics. In this treatise, he wrote about the entire spectrum of economic wealth, strategies to manage the affair of the kingdom and its people, both in peace and war. Chanakya was one of the greatest teachers who taught 'Arthashastra', an ancient Indian treatise on statecraft, economic policy and military strategy he had mastered in this field.

Chanakya was an epoch-making personality. It was the time when India was emerging out of the 'Dark Age'. The old values were losing their relevance and the new were yet to be established. It was an age of confusion, which permeated every walk of the society. The Dharma, so far a guiding and uniting force, was being subjected to the contradictory interpretations. The factionalism and fundamentalism were raising their ugly heads and entering into the vitality of the social and religious norms. Taking the advantage of his confusion, Alexander of Macedon invaded India with the help of the selfish rulers of some border states. Chanakya witnessed and felt the severe trauma of this major invasion by a real foreigner. Earlier all the invaders, who attacked India eventually settled in this country. But Alexander's invasion was an attack of totally an alien culture and army which had strong tradition and strength of their own glorious past. But, ironically, this shattering jolt helped efface the prevailing confusion in India and expedited the emergence of a new system, which was in essence authored by Chanakya.

Chanakya was the first thinker of the ancient times who nurtured the sense of nationalism and inculcated in the minds of the people that they owed their basic allegiance to the Rajya (State of Nation) and not to the Dharma. In contradiction to the earlier concept he made the State paramount.

Chanakya is touted as the "Pioneer Economist of India". Chanakya was the political adviser and Prime Minister of Emperor Chandragupta (321 BCE -297 BCE). Chanakya was a professor at the University of Takshashila (located in present day Pakistan) and was an expert in commerce, warfare, economics, etc.

Another famous work of Chankya is **'Chanakya Neeti'**. Both these works of Chanakya/ Kautilya, are followed even today as these provide a lot of inputs, guidance and inspirations for the people, kings, leaders, political masters. **"Neeti-shastra"**, a treatise on the ideal way of life shows his in-depth study of the Indian way of life.

Chanakysa had seen that in the absence of any omnipotent religious authority the misconstrued faiths were shattering the very structure of society and morality. What was needed the total change or renovation of the system. But, there were no guiding beacons to enlighten the people about this new system. Then he wrote two significant books the 'Arthashastra' (known as Kautilya's Arthashastra) and a collection of his observation on various practical aspects of life entitled 'Chanakya-Neeti'.

1.2 LIFE OF CHANAKYA

1.2.1 Birth and Death of Chanakya

According to Jain Legends, Chanakya was born in 375 BCE in Chanaka village in Golla region, South India. He lived for 92 years and died in Pataliputra (modern-day Patna), India.

According to the Buddhist version, he was born around 350 BC within the Brahmin clan known as Kutila of Takshashila. He is also known as "Machiavelli" from India.

1.2.2 Childhood of Chanakya

Rishi Chanak named his son as "Chanakya". Chanakya was born to a poor Brahmin family. He was a victim of poverty throughout his childhood due to of his economic hardship. There were times when Chanakya could not even manage to buy food and would go to go to bed hungry.

When Chanakya was born, he had a full set of teeth, which is a sign that he would become a king or an emperor. But since he was born in a Brahmin family, it was considered inappropriate. Thus, his teeth were broken and it was predicted that he would make another person a king and rule through him.

According to another version about Chanakya's full set of teeth, An astrologer predicted that this feature indicated he would become a king but would be separated from his mother. Upon hearing this, Chanakya knocked out his own teeth with a stone, declaring he would never live apart from his mother nor desire kingship.

Being a teacher himself, Rishi Chanak knew the importance of education. Taxila (Takshashila) was one of the world centers for education.

At a very early age little Chanakya started studying Vedas. The Vedas; considered to be the toughest scriptures to study were completely studied and memorized by Chanakya in his infancy. He was also attracted to studies in politics. In politics, Chanakya's acumen and shrewdness was visible right from childhood. He was a student of politics right from childhood. Known as a masterful political strategist, he knew how to put his own people in the opposite camp and spy the enemy without its knowledge before destroying the enemy.. Chanakya was an ace player in turning the tables in his favor irrespective of the circumstances. He never budged to pressure tactics by the ruthless politicians. In this way after studying religion and politics, he turned his attention to economics, which remained his lifelong friend.

1.2.3   Life of Chanakya as a Student

Takshashila, (later corrupted as Taxila),one of the topmost centers of education at that time in India became Chanakya's breeding ground of acquiring knowledge in the practical and theoretical aspect. The teachers were highly knowledgeable who used to teach sons of kings. It is said that a certain teacher had 101 students and all of them were princes! The university at Taxila was well versed in teaching the subjects using the best of practical knowledge acquired by the teachers. The age of entering the university was sixteen. The branches of studies most sought after in around India ranged from law, medicine, warfare and other indigenous forms of learning. The four Vedas, archery, hunting, elephant-lore and 18 arts were taught at the university of Taxila. So prominent was the place where Chanakya received his education that it goes to show the making of the genius. The very requirements of admission filtered out the outlawed and people with lesser credentials.

Chanakya was well-versed in Greek and Persian too.

After acquiring vast knowledge in various branches of study he wanted everybody to get benefited. He believed in the broadcasting of knowledge and not in the storage of it. So famous was Chanakya in the vicinity of the university that he had many nicknames. He was called variously by different people, namely – Vishnugupta, Kautilya and Chanakya. The whole nation was bewildered by the cleverness and wit of this seemingly small boy who went on to single handedly unify the country with the sheer power of his character. He lived his life working to his capacity in pursuit of his vision of a happy strong and prosperous India.

1.2.4   Taxila (Takshashila) University

At a time when the Dark Ages were looming large, the existence of a university of Taxila's grandeur really makes India stand apart way ahead of the European countries who struggled with ignorance and total information blackout. For the Indian subcontinent Taxila stood as a light house of higher knowledge and pride of India. Now Taxila is situated in Pakistan at a place called Rawalpindi. The university accommodated more than 10,000 students at a time. The university offered courses spanning a period of more than eight years. The students were admitted after graduating from their own countries. Aspiring students opted for elective subjects going for in-depth studies in specialized branches of learning. After graduating from the university, the students were recognized as the best scholars in the subcontinent. This university became a cultural heritage as the time passed. Taxila was the junction where people of different origins mingled with each other and exchanged knowledge of their countries. The university was famous as "Taxila" university, named after the city where it was situated. The king and rich people of the region used to donate lavishly for the development of this university. In the religious scriptures also, Taxila is mentioned as the place where the king of snakes, **Vasuki** selected Taxila for the dissemination of knowledge on earth.

Here it would be advisable to mention briefly the range of subjects taught in the university of Taxila. (1) Science, (2) Philosophy, (3) Ayurveda, (4) Grammar of various languages, (5) Mathematics, (6) Economics, (7) Astrology, (8) Geography, (9) Astronomy, (10) Surgical science, (11) Agricultural sciences, (12) Archery, and (13) Ancient and Modern Sciences.

The university also used to conduct researches on these and various other subjects.

After finishing his studies from, Chankya was made as the Professor (Acharya) of Political Science and Economics at Takshashila and much later, was appointed as an advisor to the Emperor Chandragupta.

Chanakya began his teachings by sharing an insightful anecdote. 'Once, a young farmer planted a mango tree. He watered it daily, ensuring its growth. Years later, when the tree was big and bore juicy fruits, the farmer said, 'Just as I nurtured this tree, so should you nurture your friendships and dreams. They will grow and provide sweet rewards in due time.'

Continuing his lessons, Chanakya discussed the essence of leadership. He said, 'A good leader is like a shepherd. He guides and protects his followers, just as a shepherd does with his flock. A true leader puts others before himself and always acts with integrity.'

Once upon a time in ancient India, there lived a wise man named Chanakya. He was a strategist and philosopher known for his timeless wisdom. One day, a group of young boys came to him seeking guidance. Chanakya smiled and said, 'Listen carefully, for I shall share with you the wisdom that will guide you through life.'

1.2.4   Teachings of Acharya Chanakya

Chanakya began his teachings by sharing an insightful anecdote. 'Once, a young farmer planted a mango tree. He watered it daily, ensuring its growth. Years later, when the tree was big and bore juicy fruits, the farmer said, 'Just as I nurtured this tree, so should you nurture your friendships and dreams. They will grow and provide sweet rewards in due time.'

Continuing his lessons, Chanakya discussed the essence of leadership. He said, 'A good leader is like a shepherd. He guides and protects his followers, just as a shepherd does with his flock. A true leader puts others before himself and always acts with integrity.'

Chanakya then emphasized character development. 'Just as gold shines even when tested by fire, a person's true character is revealed during challenging times. Build your character by practicing honesty, compassion, and perseverance. These virtues will make you strong and resilient.'

Chanakya shared another valuable lesson. 'Success is not defined by wealth or position but by the impact you have on others. Strive to make a positive difference in people's lives. Leave behind a legacy of kindness, generosity, and love.'

Next, Chanakya talked about the importance of diplomacy. He shared a story of two neighbouring kings who were constantly at odds. One day, they sought Chanakya's advice. He said, 'Instead of conflict, seek common ground. Understand each other's perspectives and find ways to collaborate. Diplomacy can bring peace and prosperity.'

1.3 EVENTS AFTER CHANAKYA BECAME ACHARYA (PROFESSOR)

Chanakya was a person who had a great character and talent as well as being an exceptional teacher. Chanakya was famous due to his innovative concepts and brilliant policies.

However, because of a couple of events, the course of events that the whole life of Acharya Chanakya. The events that changed the destiny of Chanakya's circumstances altered Chanakya's lifestyle and path.

The following were the two notable events in Chanakya's life:

(i) The first event was Alexander's invasion into India and the annexed state by the smaller states.

(ii) In the second instance, Kautilya was mocked and insulted by the king Dhana Nanda of Pataliputra; leading Chanakya to vow to overthrow his empire one day.

1.3.1 Commotion in Taxila

Gandhar Republic was not able to come out of the shock of the comprehensive defeat at the hands of the province of Porus, when a new contingency stared in the eyes of Taxila. Thousands of refugees poured in Taxila as a result of the widespread attacks of the armies of **Alexander.** These people were not productive for the state as they didn't come to Taxila to acquire knowledge or in search of jobs. They didn't have money or any kind of assets to buy themselves the essential commodities. To resolve the problem, a meeting was convened by the rulers of the neighbouring countries and the king of Taxila. The knowledgeable people who gathered to give their opinions on the problem faced by Taxila, gave out their suggestions. At the end of the meeting, it was decided that the refugees must be given cover under humanitarian grounds. So, in line with the decision taken, a stretch of land outside Taxila was allotted for the refugees. They were allowed to enter Taxila after proving their identity with the sentry. In this way what appeared to be a calamity was appeased without much ado. The incident was just a precursor to a series of events which reverberated across India as a result of the invasions of Alexander.

1.3.2   Move towards Pataliputra

Though Chanakya was just a professor (Acharya) in the Taxila University which seemed to be far away from the happenings in the country, he actually was able to influence the governments in a big way. His students looked at him as an ideal teacher who inspired and exemplified great knowledge. His students respected him and were ready to fight at any moment at his orders. Two of his students who have been mentioned at various instances were Bhadrabhatt and Purushdutt. In the events that unfolded in the life of Chanakya, these two played a pivotal role in the achievement of his goals. It is rumoured that they acted as spies for Chanakya, collecting information about his enemies.

Somehow, Chanakya came to know that there was a chance of foreign invasion. Europe's great warrior Salukes was readying his armies to attack the weakened republics of India. There were grave designs threatening the unity and integrity of the nation. In such a scenario, the ruler of Pataliputra, Mahanand was squeezing the common man of his wealth with an object of enriching his own exchequer. Chanakya was aware of the internal and external threats of the country. On the one hand, the rulers of the neighbouring countries were looking for the slightest of chance to annex the prosperous regions of the country and on the other hand, foreign invaders started moving towards the country with an expectation of easily smothering the country. These thoughts gave Chanakya sleepless nights. He envisioned his country clutched in the chains of slavery and defeated because of internal squabbles and differences. So, he decided on the historical day, thus saying:

"Now the time has come to leave the university. The scrupulous rulers of the country must be uprooted and there is a need to strengthen the country politically and economically. My first and foremost duty is to save the country of the foreign invaders and salvage this dangerous proposition."

With these thoughts in mind, he left Taxila University for Pataliputra which paved the way for watershed changes in the politics of India and Pataliputra.

1.3.3 Pataliputra – The city of Fortunes

Pataliputra, (presently known as Patna) has been historically a very important city politically and strategically. Like Delhi, Pataliputra has seen the ups and downs of development and great reversals. The well-known Chinese traveller Fahian, who visited the city in 399 BC described it as prosperous city endowed with rich natural resources. At the same time, another Chinese traveller Huen sang described it as a city of rubbles and ruins.

Shishunagvanshi established the city on the southern bank of the Ganges. It was addressed with different names at different times. To. Illustrate, a few names were: Pushpapur, Pushpanagar, Pataliputra and Patna.

The city was industrious in producing essential commodities and luxurious goods for the rich. When Chanakya entered the city, it was known for respecting knowledgeable people and scholars. The intellectuals from across the country were warmly invited for the intercourse of new ideas and development of the state. It was virtually the city of fortunes as it recognized the true talent and rewarded richly for the work done by an individual. No wonder Chanakya decided to start his glorious campaign from Pataliputra.

"I will destroy you"

Dhanananda, the ruler of Pataliputra was unscrupulous and cruel by nature. He was always busy gathering money without thinking about consequences. He was always dissatisfied with the amount of money he had. Collecting taxes exorbitantly, he was a villain in the public eye. There was public outrage on the taxes which were collected on unwanted things. The main aim of collecting taxes was to serve the selfish interests of the king. There were taxes on hides, tax on wood and tax even on stone! The amount of money which Dhanananda had was unimaginable.

When Chanakya arrived at Pataliputra, there was a change in the way he ran his kingdom. He gave gifts to the poor and was on the way of becoming lenient in administration. He had formed a trust or committee to administer his gifts and charities. The committee was headed by scholars and influential people of the society. It is said that the president had the powers to make up to ten million gold coins.

Since Chanakya was a great scholar from Taxila, he was included in the committee for charity. Chanakya later on became the president of the 'Sungha' (Trust). The Sungha used to help the king in the distribution of the money allotted for charity to the different sections of the society. In the process of delegation of the funds for charity, the president of the trust had to meet the king frequently. When Chanakya met the king for the first time, he was disgusted at the ugly appearance of Chanakya. As time passed, the king developed contempt for Chanakya. There was no refinement in words and conduct. To further fuel the differences between Dhanananda and Chanakya, the courtiers dissuaded the king from having a cordial relationship with Chanakya. Chanakya acted like a thorough professional and avoided praising the king. He always spoke bluntly and tersely. The king did not like the way Chanakya behaved with him. The king removed Chanakya from the post of president without any reasons. Chanakya was enraged at the proposition of being exploited by the less knowledgeable king. So, he erupted like a volcano on the king, and said, "Arrogance in you has eroded the respect which I had for you. You have removed me from the presidentship for no fault of mine. You can't act in a way detrimental to the demeanour of a king. You think there is none to question you? You have removed me from my rightful place and **I will dethrone you! "**

1.4 CHANAKYA MEETS CHANDRAGUPTA

Just after getting humiliated from the king, Chanakya scampered through the streets of Pataliputra. In a hurried walk, he stumbled upon a stump of grass and was about to fall. Chanakya the great scholar had his own style of handling things. He looked at the roots of the grass and quickly got into action. Though he was angry, he never let his anger to get out of control. He directed the anger in the right direction. Calmly, he sat down in the burning sun, removed that grass from the roots from the earth. After making sure that not even a single strand of grass is left, he resumed his journey.

While Chanakya was engrossed in removing the grass from the ground, a young man was closely watching the act of Chanakya. The young man was Chandragupta, the would be emperor of the Mauryan Empire. He looked bright. Looking at the determination of Chanakya, he was impressed and wanted to talk to the knowledgeable man.

He went to Chanakya, addressed him respectfully, and took him into the choultry (a resting place, inn, or shelter for travelers). Chanakya asked him about his family background beginning his talk by asking, "Who are you? You seem to be worried."

The young man stepped forward with great reverence and said, "Sir, my name is Chandragupta. Yes, you are correct I am in great trouble but should I trouble you with my worries?"

Chanakya calmed down the young man by saying, "You can tell me about your troubles with freewill and without any ambiguities. If I am capable enough, I'll definitely help you."

"I am the grandson of king Sarvarthasiddhi, He had two wives, Sunanda Devi and Mura Devi. Sunanda got nine sons called the Navanandas. Mura, had only one which was my father. The Nandas tried to kill my father time and again. We were more than hundred brothers. The Nandas out of jealousy, tried to kill all of us. Somehow, I survived and I am totally disgusted with my life. I want to take revenge on the Nandas who are ruling over the country presently."

Chanakya who was freshly wounded by the Nandas found a companion to destroy the distraught king. Chanakya was greatly moved by the tale of woe. He was emotionally charged listening to the story of Chandragupta and vowed to destroy the Nandas and get Chandragupta his rightful place as a king of Pataliputra. Chanakya said "I will get you the kingship, Chandragupta. From that day on Chanakya and Chandragupta worked in tandem to destroy the corrupt and unscrupulous rule of the Nandas.

Chandragupta has not been well documented. The place of birth, family background and several details regarding his life are not available. Several things have been said and written about his family and parents. Probably, he belonged to the Moria community. He might have got the name Chandragupta Maurya afterwards and his royal lineage was known as the Maurya dynasty. His mother was perhaps the daughter of a village headman. His father was the king of a forest area called Pippatavana, who died in a war. Chandragupta came to Pataliputra along with his mother.

As a boy Chandragupta was a born leader. Even as a boy, he was accepted as a leader by all. As a boy he used to mimic the king' court. His bravery and shrewdness were visible right from childhood. As Chanakya was moving along the streets of Pataliputra, he saw little Chandragupta enacting the king. Sitting on the large throne, the little boy shouted against injustice and corrupt practices of the kings and people in general. Looking at the bright face of Chandragupta, he was impressed at the intellect and wisdom in the boy's voice. For seven or eight years Chandragupta had his education there, and that too, with selected teachers shortlisted by Chanakya himself. The art of warfare and the art of governance were mastered by Chandragupta with equal expertise.

1.5 THE GREEK INVADER, ALEXANDER AND CHANAKYA-CHANDRAGUPTA

The relationship between Chandragupta and Chanakya bloomed through the years developing into a strong force for their enemies. Most of the historical events took place right under the eyes of Chanakya and Chandragupta. The troops of Alexander and the umpteen number of invaders who ravaged the subcontinent for decades around India. It is said that Chandragupta met Alexander. The bold and arrogant talk by Chandragupta enraged Alexander as a result of which Chandragupta was arrested. Chanakya's training to Chandragupta was over by now and he thought it to be the right occasion to let Chandragupta taste the practical aspect of warfare. Chanakya closely observed the movement and strategies employed by Alexander. He also became aware of the weaknesses of the Indian rulers.

1.5.1 Freedom from the Greeks

The rustic boy that Chandragupta was, now had matured into a sound military commander. The source of strength for Chandragupta and his army was the power of mind and the towering personality of Chanakya. In that war of independence for northern India, Chandragupta was the physical instrument, while its thinking brain was Chanakya.

The deterioration of the prowess of Alexander happened because of the weakening of Satraps or the commanding officers. Niccosar, a Satrap was killed even when Alexander was alive. Another formidable Satrap called Philip, was killed weakening Alexander like never before. After Alexander's death in Babylon, all his Satraps were either killed or dislodged, one by one. Alexander's lieutenants divided his empire among themselves in 321 BC. No realm east of the Indus – the River Sindhu was mentioned in that settlement. It meant that the Greeks themselves had accepted that this region had gone out of their rule.

Chanakya strategically supported Chandragupta in defeating the successors of Alexander the Great in Afghanistan.

1.6   DEFEAT OF NANDA KING

Before defeating the Nandas, Chanakya had to employ various strategies before victory. Chanakya firstly tested the policy of attacking the core of the city. The policy met with defeats again and again. With the change in strategy, Chanakya and Chandragupta began the attack on the borders of the Magadha Empire. Again, there were mistakes. The troops were not stationed in the areas conquered. So, when they marched forward, the people of the conquered areas joined together again and encircled their army. Thus, those who had been defeated had to be fought again and again

Chandragupta and Chanakya learnt lessons from these mistakes. They now stationed troops in the conquered regions. So those enemies would not raise and cause any trouble. Chanakya with his cleverness had earlier won the friendship of king Parvataka (or Porus Second). Now Parvataka, his brother Vairochaka and son Malayeketu came with their armies to help them. The Nanda king had the support of a big army. The other equally important support was the guidance of his very able minister, Amatya Rakshasa. This minister was very intelligent and had unlimited loyalty to the king. Chanakya knew that getting Amatya out of his way was the only way of defeating King Nanda. Chanakya devised a plan which involved planting of spies in the enemy camp. In a very short span of time, the weaknesses of the Nandas became visible. Parallelly, the Nandas and Amatya Rakshasa made plans to counter any attacks by Chanakya.

Details are not available regarding the war between the Nandas on the one hand and Chandragupta and Chanakya on the other. But it was a keen and bitter fight. The Nanda king died. His sons and relatives also died. Even Amatya Rakshasa was helpless. Chandragupta was victorious proving the foresight of Chanakya regarding his abilities. The old king and his wife retired to the forest. It is said that after sometime Chanakya had the old king and his wife killed, because he thought that if Amatya Rakshasa made them take a son by the rights of adoption, there would be claimants to the throne. He wanted the lineage of the Nandas should be totally eliminated.

Chanakya is one of the greatest mentors of India — and highly underrated. Under his supervision, Chandragupta Maurya — a commoner by birth — established the Mauryan Empire. At its peak, the empire rose among the most prominent empires across the globe and perhaps the largest ever in the Indian subcontinent.

From Myanmar to Afghanistan and Kashmir to mid-Tamil Nadu, the Mauryan Empire expanded across 5 million square km.

One currency, one system, one law. It was the "complete" empire!

However, Chandragupta's bloodline did not make him a king (not a nepotism product). He was a commoner by birth.

1.7   THE TRUE SIDE OF CHANAKYA AS A PERSON

The momentous life of Chanakya reminds us of a revengeful saga where the individual is obsessed by the idea of taking revenge. But personal revenge was not the aim of Chanakya. He wanted that the kingdom should be secure and that the administration should go on smoothly, bringing happiness to the people. He thought that there were two ways of ensuring the happiness of the people. Firstly, Amatya Rakshasa had to be made Chandragupta's minister; Secondly, a book must be written, laying down how a king should conduct himself, how he should protect himself and the kingdom from the enemies, how to ensure law and order, and so on.

One day, a Chinese traveller visited Chanakya while he was engrossed in official work. After finishing, Chanakya extinguished the lamp he was using and lit another before greeting the traveller. Curious, the traveller asked about the change of lamps. Chanakya explained,

"The oil in the first lamp was state property, used for official work. Now that we are speaking privately, I am using oil bought with my personal funds. This is not a custom but a principle."

Despite being the chief advisor to the king, Chanakya lived modestly in a small hut. One night, a thief broke in, searching for valuables. Finding nothing but a bundle of new woolen clothes meant for distribution to the poor, the thief attempted to steal them. Chanakya caught him and asked why he had stolen the wool. The thief replied, "Why do you, a king's advisor, use old, torn wool when you have new ones?" Chanakya replied, "These new clothes are meant for the poor. I have no right to use them. I use only what belongs to me, even if it is old."

Chanakya often shared wisdom passed down by his mother. One parable highlights the importance of perception: A venomous snake in a village bit anyone it saw, terrorizing the community. A monk, witnessing this, warned the snake to stop harming people. The snake agreed and refrained from biting. When the monk returned, he saw the snake, now weak and beaten by children. The snake lamented, "I followed your advice, and this is the result." The monk replied, "I told you not to bite, but I did not tell you to appear weak. Even a harmless snake should project strength to survive."

By writing **"Arthashastra" and "Neeti-shastra"**, Chanakya has become a never-ending phenomenon. He truly guided the generations with his wisdom. It would ideally suit the closing of the life of Chanakya with a couple of quotations by Chanakya:

"The secret task of a king is to strive for the welfare of his people incessantly. The administration of the kingdom is his religious duty. His greatest gift would be to treat all as equals."

"The happiness of the commoners is the happiness of the king. Their welfare is his welfare. A king should never think of his personal interest or welfare, but should try to find his joy in the joy of his subjects."

These words were written 2300 years ago by Chanakya, the expert statesman and wise sage. And Chanakya is also another name for courage and perseverance.

1.8 KAUTILYA'S SAPTANG THEORY OF STATE

The term "Saptang" signifies seven integral components or elements. According to this doctrine, a well-governed kingdom comprises these essential elements that foster stability and prosperity:

(i) **Swami (The Ruler):** The central figure responsible for decision-making, law enforcement, kingdom protection, and citizen welfare.

(ii) **Amatya (The Minister):** Advisors pivotal in governance, tasked not only with counsel but also with maintaining confidentiality in their deliberations.

(iii) **Janapada (The People and the Territory**): Encompasses loyal citizens, fertile lands rich in resources, and a populace dedicated to their homeland and religious practices.

(iv) **Durga (Fortification):** Defensive structures crucial for safeguarding against external threats and ensuring internal stability.

(v) **Kosha (The Treasury):** Economic backbone comprising financial resources, revenue management, and funding for state activities.

(vi) **Danda (The Army):** Military forces essential for defending the state and maintaining law and order.

(vii) **Mitra (Alliance):** Diplomatic ties and strategic alliances vital for enhancing the state's security and prosperity through trade and international relations.

1.9 LEGACY AND INFLUENCE OF CHANAKYA

Chanakya's legacy extends beyond his lifetime, leaving an indelible mark on Indian civilization and political thought. His profound insights into governance, statecraft, and ethics continue to resonate with scholars, politicians, and leaders worldwide. Here are some aspects of his enduring legacy and influence:

(i) **The Arthashastra:** Chanakya's masterwork, the Arthashastra, is a cornerstone in political science and administration. It provides extensive insights into governance, economics, diplomacy, and military strategy and maintains its significance through its practical approach to statecraft.

(ii) **Philosophical Contributions:** Chanakya's ethics, morality, and leadership teachings have impacted Indian philosophy and culture. His emphasis on the state's welfare (Rajadharma) and rulers' ethical conduct continues to shape discussions on governance and public administration.

Founding of Takshashila University: Chanakya's role in founding Takshashila University, one of ancient India's oldest centres of learning, underscores his commitment to education and scholarship. Takshashila became a renowned seat of learning, attracting students and scholars from across the Indian subcontinent and beyond.

(iii) **Political Strategy and Diplomacy:** Chanakya's strategic acumen and diplomatic prowess inspire leaders grappling with complex geopolitical challenges. His emphasis on alliances, espionage, and statecraft remains relevant in contemporary international relations.

(iv) **Chanakya Neeti:** Chanakya's aphorisms, collected in works such as the Chanakya Neeti, offer practical wisdom and guidance for individuals seeking success and prosperity in various spheres of life. His maxims on leadership, ambition, and personal conduct continue to be quoted and revered for their timeless relevance.

(v) **Role in Indian History:** As the architect of the Maurya Empire and the mentor to Emperor Chandragupta Maurya, Chanakya occupies a central place in Indian history. His contributions to the unification of India and the establishment of a He is held in high regard in the records of Indian civilization due to his strong empire.

(vi) **Cultural Depictions and Reverence:** Chanakya's life and teachings have been depicted in various literary works, dramas, and films, further cementing his status as a legendary figure in

Indian culture. Portrayals often depict him as a wise advisor guiding rulers with wisdom and foresight.

1.10 SOME TIMELESS ADVICE FROM CHANAKYA

(i)   Behind all friendships lies self-interest. Friendship cannot exist without it.

(ii) Never share your secrets with others; doing so may lead to your ruin.

(iii) Self-respect can guide the selfish, madness can be controlled by giving freedom, and the intelligent can be influenced by truth.

(iv) Before undertaking a task, ask yourself: Why am I doing this? What will be the result? Will I succeed? Proceed only if the answers satisfy you.

(v)   Once you start a task, do not let success or failure deter you. Complete what you begin, and you will find happiness and satisfaction.

(vi) A ruler's ultimate goal should be the welfare of the people. They must govern with fairness and treat all citizens equally.

(vii) A ruler's focus should be the happiness of the common man, not their personal comfort.

CHAPTER 2

LEGENDS OF CHANAKYA-CHANDRAGUPTA

2.1 FOUR VERSIONS OF THE LEGENDS PF CHANAKYA-CHANDRAGUPTA

There is no documented historical information about Chanakya: narratives about him come from legendary accounts. There are four distinct accounts of the ancient Chanakya-Chandragupta katha (legend):

(i) **Buddhist version:** Mahavamsa (5th-6th cent. CE) and its commentary Vamsatthappakasini (Pali language);

(ii) **Jain version:** Parishishtaparvan (12th cent. CE) by Hemachandra, based on 1st-8th century sources;

(iii) **Kashmiri version:** Kathasaritsagara (11th cent. CE) by Somadeva, Brihat-Katha-Manjari by Ksemendra; and

(iv) **Vishakhadatta's version:** Mudrarakshasa (4th-8th cent. CE), a Sanskrit play by Vishakhadatta; largely fictional.

In all the four versions, Chanakya feels insulted by the Nanda king, and vows to destroy him. After dethroning the Nanda, he installs Chandragupta as the new king.

The legend of Chanakya and Chandragupta is detailed in the Pali-language Buddhist chronicles of Sri Lanka. It is not mentioned in Dipavamsa, the oldest of these chronicles. The earliest Buddhist source to mention the legend is Mahavamsa, which is generally dated between fifth and sixth centuries CE. Vamsatthappakasini (also known as Mahvamsa Tika), a commentary on Mahavamsa, provides some more details about the legend. Its author is unknown, and it is dated variously from sixth century CE to 13th century CE. Some other texts provide additional details about the legend; for example, the Maha-Bodhi-Vamsa and the Atthakatha give the names of the nine Nanda kings said to have preceded Chandragupta.

2.2   BUDDHIST VERSION OF CHANAKYA-CHANDRAGUPTA LEGEND

The legend of Chanakya and Chandragupta is detailed in the Pali-language Buddhist chronicles of Sri Lanka. It is not mentioned in Dipavamsa, the oldest of these chronicles. The earliest Buddhist source to mention the legend is **Mahavamsa**, which is generally dated between fifth and sixth centuries CE. Vamsatthappakasini (also known as Mahvamsa Tika), a commentary on Mahavamsa, provides some more details about the legend. Its author is unknown, and it is dated variously from sixth century CE to 13th century CE. Some other texts provide additional details about the legend; for example, the Maha-Bodhi-Vamsa and the Atthakatha give the names of the nine Nanda kings said to have preceded Chandragupta.

According to the Buddhist legend, the Nanda emperors who preceded Chandragupta were robbers-turned-rulers. Chanakya was a Brahmin from Takshashila. He was well-versed in three Vedas and politics. He was born with canine teeth, which were believed to be a mark of royalty. His mother feared that he would neglect her after becoming an emperor. To pacify her, Chanakya broke his canine teeth.

Chanakya had an ugly appearance, accentuated by his broken teeth and crooked feet. One day, the Emperor **Dhana Nanda** (of Pataliputra) organized an alms-giving ceremony for Brahmins. Chanakya went to Pushpapura to attend this ceremony. Disgusted by his appearance, the emperor ordered him to be thrown out of the assembly. Chanakya broke his sacred thread in anger, and cursed the emperor. The emperor ordered his arrest, but Chanakya escaped in the disguise of an Ājīvika. He befriended Dhananada's son **Pabbata**, and instigated him to seize the throne. With the help of a signet ring given by the prince, Chanakya fled the palace through a secret door.

Chanakya escaped to the Vinjha forest. There, he made 800 million gold coins, using a secret technique that allowed him to turn 1 coin into 8 coins. After hiding this money, he started searching for a person worthy of replacing Dhana Nanda. One day, he saw a group of children playing: the young Chandragupta played the role of an emperor, while other boys pretended to be vassals, ministers, or robbers. The "robbers" were brought before Chandragupta, who ordered their limbs to be cut off, but then miraculously re-attached them. Chandragupta had been born in a royal family, but was brought up by a hunter after his father was killed by an usurper, and the devatas caused his mother to abandon him. Astonished by the boy's miraculous powers, Chanakya paid 1000 gold coins to his foster-father, and took Chandragupta away, promising to teach him a trade.

Chanakya had two potential successors to Dhana Nanda: **Pabbata** (Dhana Nanda's son) and **Chandragupta**. He gave each of them an amulet to be worn around the neck with a woolen thread. One day, he decided to test them. While Chandragupta was asleep, he asked Pabbata to remove Chandragupta's woolen thread without breaking it and without waking up Chandragupta. Pabbata failed to accomplish this task. Sometime later, when Pabbata was sleeping, Chanakya challenged Chandragupta to complete the same task. Chandragupta retrieved the woolen thread by cutting off Pabbata's head. For the next seven years, Chanakya trained Chandragupta for imperial duties. When Chandragupta became an adult, Chanakya dug up his hidden treasure of gold coins, and assembled an army.

The army of Chanadragupta and Chanakya invaded Dhana Nanda's empire, but disbanded after facing a severe defeat. While wandering in disguise, the two men once listened to the conversation between a woman and her son. The mother was scolding her child for burning himself by eating from the middle of a bowl of porridge rather than the cooler edge. The woman scolded him, saying that he was eating food like Chandragupta, who attacked the central part of the empire (Pataliputra) instead of conquering the border villages first. Chanakya and Chandragupta realized their mistake. They assembled a new army, and started conquering the border villages. Gradually, they advanced to the empire's capital Pataliputra, where they killed the Emperor Dhana Nanda. Chanakya ordered a fisherman to find the place where Dhana Nanda had hidden his treasure. As soon as the fishermen informed Chanakya about its location, Chanakya had him killed. Chanakya anointed Chandragupta as the new emperor, and tasked a man named Paṇiyatappa with eliminating rebels and robbers from the empire.

When Bindusara was in his youth, Chandragupta gave up the throne and followed the Jain saint Bhadrabahu to present-day Karnataka and settled in the place of Shravana Belagola. He lived as an ascetic for some years and died of voluntary starvation according to Jain tradition. Chanakya meanwhile stayed in the court as an advisor to Bindusara.

Chanakya started mixing small doses of poison in the new emperor's food **to make him immune to poisoning attempts by the enemies.** Chandragupta, who was not aware of this, once shared the food with his **pregnant empress Durdhara**, who was seven days away from delivery. Chanakya arrived just as the empress ate the poisoned morsel. Realizing that she was going to die, Chanakya decided to save the unborn child. He cut off the empress's head and cut open her belly with a sword to take out the fetus. Over the next seven days, he placed the fetus in the belly of a goat freshly killed each day. After seven days, Chandragupta's son was "born". He was named **Bindusara** because his body was spotted with drops (**bindu**) of goat's blood.

The earliest Buddhist legends do not mention Chanakya in their description of the Mauryan dynasty after this point. Dhammapala's commentary on Theragatha, however, mentions a legend about

Chanakya and a Brahmin named Subandhu. According to this account, Chanakya was afraid that the wise Subandhu would surpass him at Chandragupta's court. So, he got Chandragupta to imprison Subandhu, whose son Tekicchakani escaped and became a Buddhist monk. The 16th-century Tibetan Buddhist author Taranatha mentions Chanakya as one of Bindusara's "great lords". According to him, Chanakya destroyed the nobles and kings of 16 towns and made Bindusara the master of all the territory between the eastern and the western seas (Arabian Sea and the Bay of Bengal).

The real cause of Chanakya's death is unknown and disputed. According to a legend, Subandhu, one of Bindusara's ministers, did not like Chanakya. One day he told Bindusara that Chanakya was responsible for the murder of his mother. Bindusara asked the nurses, who confirmed the story of his birth. Bindusara was horrified and enraged. When Chanakya, who was an old man by this time, learned that the King was angry with him, he decided to end his life. As per the Jain tradition, he decided to starve himself to death. By this time, the King learned the full story: Chanakya was not directly responsible for his mother's death, which was an accident. He asked Subandhu to convince Chanakya to give up his plan to kill himself. However, Subandhu, pretending to conduct a ceremony for Chanakya, burnt Chanakya alive.

Despite founding the Mauryan Empire and guiding Chandragupta to power, Chanakya met his demise at the hands of his own people, fulfilling the adage "those who seek revenge risk their own demise."

2.3 JAIN VERSION OF CHANAKYA-CHANDRAGUPTA LEGEND (12TH CENTURY CE, BASED ON 1ST-8TH CENTURY CE)

The Chandragupta-Chanakya legend is mentioned in several commentaries of the Shvetambara canon. The most well-known version of the Jain legend is contained in the Sthaviravali-Charita or Parishishta-Parvan, written by the 12th-century writer

Hemachandra. Hemachandra's account is based on the Prakrit kathanaka literature (legends and anecdotes) composed between the late first century CE and mid-8th century CE. These legends are contained in the commentaries (churnis and tikas) on canonical texts such as Uttaradhyayana and Avashyaka Niryukti.

It is believed that the Jain version is older and more consistent than the Buddhist version of the legend.

Narrative

According to the Jain account, Chanakya was born to two lay Jains (shravaka) named Chanin and Chaneshvari. His birthplace was the Chanaka village in Golla vishaya (district). The identity of "Golla" is not certain, but Hemachandra states that Chanakya was a Dramila, implying that he was a native of South India.

Chanakya was born with a full set of teeth. According to the monks, this was a sign that he would become a king in the future. Chanin (Chanakya's father) did not want his son to become haughty (arrogant), so he broke Chanakya's teeth. The monks prophesied that the baby would go on to become a power behind the throne. Chanakya grew up to be a learned shravaka, and married a Brahmin woman. Her relatives mocked her for being married to a poor man. This motivated Chanakya to visit Pataliputra, and seek donations from the Emperor Nanda, who was famous for his generosity towards Brahmins. While waiting for the emperor at the imperial court, Chanakya sat on the emperor's throne. A dasi (slave woman) courteously offered Chanakya the next seat, but Chanakya kept his kamandal (water pot) on it, while remaining seated on the throne. The servant offered him a choice of four more seats, but each time, he kept his various items on the seats, refusing to budge from the throne. Finally, the annoyed servant kicked him off the throne. Enraged, Chanakya vowed to uproot Nanda and his entire establishment, like "a great wind uproots a tree".

Chanakya knew that he was prophesied to become a power behind the throne. So, he started searching for a person worthy of being a king. While wandering, he did a favour for the pregnant daughter of a village chief, on the condition that her child would belong to him. Chandragupta was born to this lady. When Chandragupta grew up, Chanakya came to his village and saw him playing "king" among a group of boys. To test him, Chanakya asked him for a donation. The boy told Chanakya to take the cows nearby, declaring that nobody would disobey his order. This display of power convinced Chanakya that Chandragupta was the one worthy of being a king.

Chanakya took Chandragupta to conquer Pataliputra, the capital of Nanda. He assembled an army using the wealth he had acquired through alchemy. The army suffered a severe defeat, forcing Chanakya and Chandragupta to flee the battlefield. They reached a lake while being pursued by an enemy officer. Chanakya asked Chandragupta to jump into the lake, and disguised himself as a meditating ascetic. When the enemy soldier reached the lake, he asked the 'ascetic' if he had seen Chandragupta. Chanakya pointed at the lake. As the soldier removed his armor to jump into the lake, Chanakya took his sword and killed him. When Chandragupta came out of the water, Chanakya asked him, "What went through your mind, when I disclosed your location to the enemy?" Chandragupta replied that he trusted his master to make the best decision. This convinced Chanakya that Chandragupta would remain under his influence even after becoming the king. On another occasion, Chanakya similarly escaped the enemy by chasing away a washerman, and disguising himself as one. Once, he cut open the belly of a Brahmin who had just eaten food, and took out the food to feed a hungry Chandragupta.

One day, Chanakya and Chandragupta overheard a woman scolding her son. The child had burnt his finger by putting it in the middle of a bowl of hot gruel. The woman told her son that by not starting from the cooler edges, he was being foolish like Chanakya, who attacked the capital before conquering the bordering regions. Chanakya realized his mistake, and made a new plan to defeat Nanda. He formed an alliance with Parvataka, the king of a mountain kingdom called Himavatkuta, offering him half of Nanda's empire.

After securing Parvataka's help, Chanakya and Chandragupta started besieging the cities other than Pataliputra. One particular city offered a strong resistance. Chanakya entered this city disguised as a Shaivite mendicant, and declared that the siege would end if the idols of the seven mothers were removed from the town's temple. As soon as the superstitious defenders removed the idols from the temple, Chanakya ordered his army to end the siege. When the defenders started celebrating their victory, Chanakya's army launched a surprise attack and captured the town.

Gradually, Chanakya and Chandragupta subdued all the regions outside the capital. Finally, they captured Pataliputra and Chandragupta became the emperor. They allowed the Emperor Nanda to go into exile, with all the goods he could take on a cart. As Nanda and his family were leaving the city on a cart, his daughter saw Chandragupta, and fell in love with the new emperor. She chose him as her husband by svayamvara tradition. As she was getting off the cart, nine spokes of the cart's wheel broke. Interpreting this as an omen, Chanakya declared that Chandragupta's dynasty would last for nine generations.

Meanwhile, Parvataka fell in love with one of Nanda's visha kanyas (poison girl, assassin). Chanakya approved the marriage, and Parvataka collapsed when he touched the girl during the wedding. Chanakya asked Chandragupta not to call a physician. Thus, Parvataka died and Chandragupta became the sole ruler of Nanda's territories.

Chanakya then started consolidating the power by eliminating Nanda's loyalists, who had been harassing people in various parts of the empire. Chanakya learned about a weaver who would burn any part of his house infested with cockroaches. Chanakya assigned the responsibility of crushing the rebels to this weaver. Soon, the empire was free of insurgents. Chanakya also burned a village that had refused him food in the past. He filled the imperial treasury by inviting rich merchants to his home, getting them drunk and gambling with a loaded dice.

Once, the empire suffered a 12-year long famine. Two young Jain monks started eating from the emperor's plate, after making themselves invisible with a magic ointment. Chanakya sensed their presence by covering the palace floor with a powder, and tracing their footprints. At the next meal, he caught them by filling the dining room with thick smoke, which caused the monks' eyes to water, washing off the ointment. Chanakya complained about the young monks' behavior to the head monk Acharya Susthita. The Acharya blamed people for not being charitable towards monks, so Chanakya started giving generous alms to the monks.

Meanwhile, Chandragupta had been patronizing the non-Jain monks. Chanakya decided to prove to him that these men were not worthy of his patronage. He covered the floor of the palace area near the women's rooms with powder and left the non-Jain monks there. Their footprints showed that they had sneaked up to the windows of the women's rooms to peep inside. The Jain monks, who were assessed using the same method, stayed away from the women's rooms. After seeing this, Chandragupta appointed the Jain monks as his spiritual counsellors.

Chanakya used to mix small doses of poison in Chandragupta's food to make him immune to poisoning attempts. The emperor, unaware of this, once shared his food with Empress Durdhara. Chanakya entered the room at the instant she died. He cut open the dead empress's belly and took out the baby. The baby, who had been touched by a drop ("bindu") of the poison, was named **Bindusara**.

After Chandragupta abdicated the throne to become a Jain monk, Chanakya appointed Bindusara as the new emperor. Chanakya asked Bindusara to appoint a man named Subandhu as one of his ministers. However, Subandhu wanted to become a higher minister and grew jealous of Chanakya. So, he told Bindusara that Chanakya was responsible for the death of his mother. Bindusara confirmed the allegations with the nurses, who told him that Chanakya had cut open the belly of his mother. Bindusara became enraged, and started hating Chanakya. As a result, Chanakya, who had grown very old by this time, retired and decided to starve himself to death. Meanwhile, Bindusara learned the detailed circumstances of his birth, and implored Chanakya to resume his ministerial duties. After failing to pacify Chanakya, the emperor ordered Subandhu to convince Chanakya to give up his suicide plan. Subandhu, while pretending to appease Chanakya, burned him to death. Subandhu then took possession of Chanakya's home. Chanakya had anticipated this, and before retiring, he had set up a cursed trap for Subandhu. He had left behind a chest with a hundred locks. Subandhu broke the locks, hoping to find precious jewels. He found a sweet-smelling perfume and immediately inhaled it. But then his eyes fell on a birch bark note with a curse written on it. The note declared that anybody who smelled this perfume will have to either become a monk or face death. Subandhu tested the perfume on another man, and then fed him luxurious food (something that the monks abstain from). The man died, and then Subandhu was forced to become a monk to avoid death.

According to another Jain text – the Rajavali-Katha – Chanakya accompanied Chandragupta to forest for retirement, once Bindusara became the emperor.

2.4 KASHMIRI VERSION OF CHANAKYA-CHANDRAGUPTA LEGEND (11TH CENT. CE)

Brihatkatha-Manjari by Kshemendra and Kathasaritsagara by Somadeva are two 11th-century Kashmiri Sanskrit collections of legends. Both are based on a now-lost Prakrit-language Brihatkatha-Sarit-Sagara, which was based on the now-lost Paishachi-language Brihatkatha (before 3rd cent. CE) by Gunadhya. The Chanakya-Chandragupta legend in these collections features another character, named **Shakatala**.

Kashmiri narrative

The Kashmiri version of the legend goes like this: Vararuchi (identified with Katyayana), Indradatta and Vyadi were three disciples of the sage Varsha. Once, on behalf of their guru Varsha, they travelled to Ayodhya to seek a gurudakshina (guru's fee) from Emperor Nanda. As they arrived to meet Nanda, the emperor died. Using his yogic powers, Indradatta entered Nanda's body and granted Vararuchi's request for 10 million gold dinars (gold coins). The imperial minister **Shakatala** realized what was happening, and had Indradatta's body burnt. But before he could take any action against the fake emperor (Indradatta in Nanda's body, also called Yogananda), the emperor had him arrested. Shakatala and his 100 sons were imprisoned and were given food sufficient only for one person. Shakatala's 100 sons starved to death, so that their father could live to take revenge.

Meanwhile, the fake emperor appointed Vararuchi as his minister. As the emperor's character kept deteriorating, a disgusted Vararuchi retired to a forest as an ascetic. Shakatala was then restored as the minister, but kept planning his revenge. One day, Shakatala came across Chanakya, a Brahmin who was uprooting all the grass in his path, because one blade of the grass had pricked his foot. Shakatala realized that he could use a man so vengeful to destroy the fake emperor. He invited Chanakya to the emperor's assembly, promising him 100,000 gold coins for presiding over a ritual ceremony.

Shakatala hosted Chanakya in his own house and treated him with great respect. But the day Chanakya arrived at the imperial court, Shakatala got another Brahmin named **Subandhu** to preside over the ceremony. Chanakya felt insulted, but Shakatala blamed the emperor for this dishonor. Chanakya then untied his **topknot (sikha),** and vowed not to re-tie it until the emperor was destroyed. The emperor ordered his arrest, but he escaped to Shakatala's house. There, using materials supplied by Shakatala, he performed a magic ritual which made the emperor sick. The king died of a fever after 7 days.

Shakatala then executed Hiranyagupta, the son of the fake emperor. He anointed Chandragupta, the son of the real emperor Nanda, as the new emperor (in Kshemendra's version, it is Chanakya who installs Chandragupta as the new emperor). Shakatala also appointed Chanakya as the imperial priest (rajpurohita). Having achieved his revenge, he then retired to the forest as an ascetic.

2.5   MUDRARAKSHASA VERSION OF CHANAKYA-CHANDRAGUPTA LEGEND (4TH-8TH CENT. CE)

Mudrarakshasa ("The signet ring of Rakshasa") is a Sanskrit play by Vishakhadatta. Its date is uncertain, but it mentions the Huna, who invaded northern India during the Gupta period. Therefore, it could not have been composed before the Gupta era. It is dated variously from the late fourth century to the eighth century. The Mudrarakshasa legend contains narratives not found in other versions of the Chanakya-Chandragupta legend. Because of this difference, it is suggested that it the most of fictional or legendary, without any historical basis.

Mudrarakshasa narrative (4th-8th cent. CE)

According to the Mudrarakshasa version, the Emperor Nanda once removed Chanakya from the "first seat of the empire" (this possibly refers to Chanakya's expulsion from the emperor's assembly). For this reason, Chanakya vowed not to tie his **top knot (shikha)** until the complete destruction of Nanda. Chanakya made a plan to dethrone Nanda, and replace him with Chandragupta, his son by a lesser empress. Chanakya engineered Chandragupta's alliance with another powerful king Parvateshvara (or Parvata), and the two rulers agreed to divide Nanda's territory after subjugating him. Their allied army included Bahlika, Kirata, Parasika, Kamboja, Shaka, and Yavana soldiers. The army invaded Pataliputra (Kusumapura) and defeated the Nandas. **Parvata is identified with King Porus by some scholars.**

Nanda's prime minister Rakshasa escaped Pataliputra, and continued resisting the invaders. He sent a vishakanya (poison girl) to assassinate Chandragupta. Chanakya had this girl assassinate Parvata instead, with the blame going to Rakshasa. However, Parvata's son Malayaketu learned the truth about his father's death and defected to Rakshasa's camp. Chanakya's spy Bhagurayana accompanied Malayaketu, pretending to be his friend.

Rakshasa continued to plot Chandragupta's death, but all his plans were foiled by Chanakya. For example, once Rakshasa arranged for assassins to be transported to Chandragupta's bedroom via a tunnel. Chanakya became aware of them by noticing a trail of ants carrying the leftovers of their food. He then arranged for the assassins to be burned to death.

Meanwhile, Parvata's brother Vairodhaka became the ruler of his emperor. Chanakya convinced him that Rakshasa was responsible for killing his brother, and agreed to share half of Nanda's emperor with him. Secretly, however, Chanakya hatched a plan to get Vairodhaka killed. He knew that the chief architect of Pataliputra was a Rakshasa loyalist. He asked this architect to build a triumphal arch for Chandragupta's procession to the imperial palace. He arranged the procession to be held at midnight citing astrological reasons, but actually to ensure poor visibility. He then invited Vairodhaka to lead the procession on Chandragupta's elephant, and accompanied by Chandragupta's bodyguards. As expected, Rakshasa's loyalists arranged for the arch to fall on who they thought was Chandragupta. Vairodhaka was killed, and once again, the assassination was blamed on Rakshasa.

Malayaketu and Rakshasa then formed an alliance with five kings: Chiravarman of Kauluta (Kulu), Meghaksha of Parasika, Narasimha of Malaya, Pushkaraksha of Kashmira, and Sindhusena of Saindhava. This allied army also included soldiers from Chedi, Gandhara, Hunas, Khasa, Magadha, Shaka, and Yavana territories.

In Pataliputra, Chanakya's agent informed him that three Rakshasa loyalists remained in the capital: the Jain monk Jiva-siddhi, the scribe Shakata-dasa and the jewelers' guild chief Chandana-dasa. Of these, Jiva-siddhi was actually a spy of Chanakya, unknown to his other spies. Chandana-dasa sheltered Rakshasa's wife, who once unknowingly dropped her husband's signet-ring (mudra). Chanakya's agent got hold of this signet-ring, and brought it to Chanakya. Using this signet ring, Chanakya sent a letter to Malayaketu warning him that his allies were treacherous. Chanakya also asked some of Chandragupta's princes to fake defection to Malayaketu's camp. In addition, Chanakya ordered Shakata-dasa's murder, but had him 'rescued' by Siddharthaka, a spy pretending to be an agent of Chandana-dasa. Chanakya's spy then took Shakata-dasa to Rakshasa.

When Shakata-dasa and his 'rescuer' Siddharthaka reached Rakshasa, Siddharthaka presented him the signet-ring, claiming to have found it at Chandana-dasa's home. As a reward, Rakshasa gave him some jewels that Malayaketu had gifted him. Sometime after this, another of Chanakya's agents, disguised as a jeweler, sold Parvata's jewels to Rakshasa.

Sometime later, Rakshasa sent his spies disguised as musicians to Chandragupta's court. But Chanakya knew all about Rakshasa's plans, thanks to his spies. In front of Rakshasa's spies, Chanakya and Chandragupta feigned an angry argument. Chandragupta pretended to dismiss Chanakya, and declared that Rakshasa would make a better minister. Meanwhile, Malayaketu had a conversation with Chanakya's spy Bhagurayana while approaching Rakshasa's house. Bhagurayana made Malayaketu distrustful of Rakshasa, by saying that Rakshasa hated only Chanakya, and would be willing to serve Nanda's son Chandragupta. Shortly after this, a messenger came to Rakshasa's house and informed him that Chandragupta had dismissed Chanakya while praising him. This convinced Malayaketu that Rakashasa could not be trusted.

Malayaketu then decided to invade Pataliputra without Rakshasa by his side. He consulted the Jain monk Jiva-siddhi to decide an auspicious time for beginning the march. Jiva-siddhi, a spy of Chanakya, told him that he could start immediately. Jiva-siddhi also convinced him that Rakshasa was responsible for his father's death, but Bhagurayana persuaded him not to harm Rakshasa. Shortly after, Chanakya's spy Siddharthaka pretended to get caught with a fake letter addressed to Chandragupta by Rakshasa. Wearing the jewels given by Rakshasa, he pretended to be an agent of Rakshasa. The letter, sealed with Rakshasa's signet-ring, informed Chandragupta that Rakshasa only wished to replace Chanakya as the prime minister. It also stated that five of Malayaketu's allies were willing to defect to Chandragupta in return for land and wealth. An angry Malayaketu summoned Rakshasa, who arrived wearing Parvata's jewels that Chanakya's agent had sold him. When Malayaketu saw Rakshasa wearing his father's jewels, he was convinced that there was indeed a treacherous plan against him. He executed his five allies in a brutal manner.

The rest of Malayaketu's allies deserted him, disgusted at his treatment of the five slayed allies. Rakshasa managed to escape, tracked by Chanakya's spies. One of Chanakya's spies, disguised as a friend of Chandana-dasa, got in touch with him. He told Rakshasa that Chandana-dasa was about to be executed for refusing to divulge the location of Rakshasa's family. On hearing this, Rakshasa rushed to Pataliputra to surrender and save the life of his loyal friend Chandana-dasa. When he reached Pataliputra, Chanakya, pleased with his loyalty to Chandana-dasa, offered him clemency. Rakshasa pledged allegiance to Chandragupta and agreed to be his prime minister, in return for release of Chandana-dasa and a pardon for Malayaketu. **Chanakya then bound his top knot (shikha), having achieved his objective, and retired.**

LIFE STORIES OF CHANAKYA
(MULTIPLE VERSIONS)

CHAPTER 3

CONTRIBUTIONS AND LEGACY OF CHANAKYA

3.1   LEGACY OF CHANAKYA

The legacy of Chanakya is profound and multifaceted, influencing various aspects of political thought, governance, and strategy both in ancient India and in contemporary contexts. Who was Chanakya in the context of his lasting legacy? He is regarded as one of the greatest political thinkers in Indian history, and his ideas continue to resonate in modern political discourse. Ultimately, understanding who was Chanakya provides valuable insights into the principles of governance and the importance of the welfare of the state and its citizens.

3.2   CONTRIBUTIONS OF CHANAKYA

Following are the two significant and famous book by Chanakya:

3.2.1   Chanakya Neeti or Neeti-Shastra

Neeti-Shastra covers a broad spectrum of subjects such as leadership, governance, administration, diplomacy, warfare, economics, personal growth, and social behaviour. It offers insights into effective decision-making, integrity, human psychology, power dynamics, financial management, and relationship building.

Chanakya Neeti shlokas are useful shlokas composed by Chanakya (Vishnugupta), for our day-to-day life and environment. These shlokas give us very valuable insight into society and political life. Even today these shlokas have exactly the same value and relevance in our life as it was more than 2300 years back.

Chanakya Neeti is a collection of aphorisms, said to be selected by Chanakya from the various shastras. The topics discussed are ethics, morality, governance and several others.

Chanakya Neeti underscores the significance of wisdom, knowledge, strategic planning, ethical conduct, and the quest for excellence.

As a comprehensive guide, it provides valuable insights for individuals seeking advice on life, governance, and personal development. Its enduring relevance and practical wisdom make it a respected source of knowledge, valued in both historical contexts and contemporary society.

3.2.2   Arthashastra (or Kautilya Arthashastra)

The Arthashastra served as Chanakya's training manual, transforming Chandragupta from a citizen to a monarch. Its precepts not only helped Chandragupta seize power but also maintain it, passing the legacy to his son, Bindusara, and grandson, Ashoka the Great.

The Arthashastra draws from the Charvaka philosophical school, which rejects supernatural explanations in favour of a materialistic worldview.

Charvaka's foundation likely contributed to the practical, hands-on nature of the Arthashastra.

Despite being written over 2,000 years ago, Chanakya's teachings remain applicable in modern life, spanning leadership, management, conflict resolution, and diplomacy.

3.3   INTRODUCTION TO KAUTILYA ARTHASHASTRA

Kautilya's Arthashastra is an Ancient Indian Sanskrit treatise on statecraft, politics, economic policy and military strategy. The text is likely the work of several authors over centuries, starting as a compilation of Arthashastras, texts which date from the 2nd c. BCE to the 1st c. CE. These treatises were compiled and amended in a new treatise, in the 1st century CE by either an anonymous author or Kautilya, though earlier and later dates have also been proposed. While often regarded as created by a single author, it is argued that this compilation, possibly titled Daṇḍanīti, served as the basis for a major expansion and redaction in the 2nd or 3rd century CE by either Kautilya or an anonymous author, when several books, dialogical comments, and the disharmonious chapter-division were added, and a stronger Brahmanical ideology was brought in. The text thus became a proper Arthashastra, and was retitled to Kautilya's Arthashastra.

Two names for the text's compiler or redactor are used in the text, **Kautilya) and Vishnugupta.** Chanakya (375–283 BCE), the counsellor of Chandragupta Maurya, is implied in a later interpolation, reinforced by Gupta-era and medieval traditions, **which explicitly identified Kautilya with Chanakya.** This identification started during the Gupta reign (c. 240–c. 579), strengthening the Gupta's ideological presentation as heirs of the Mauryas. The Arthashastra was influential until the 12th century, when it disappeared. It was rediscovered in 1905 by R. Shamasastry, who published it in 1909. The first English translation, also by Shamasastry, was published in 1915.

The Sanskrit title, Arthashastra, can be translated as 'treatise on "political science"' or "economic science" or simply "statecraft", as the word artha is polysemous in Sanskrit; the word has a broad scope. It includes books on the nature of government, law, civil and criminal court systems, ethics, economics, markets and trade, the methods for screening ministers, diplomacy, theories on war, nature of peace, and the duties and obligations of a king. The text incorporates Hindu philosophy, includes ancient economic and cultural details on agriculture, mineralogy, mining and metals, animal husbandry, medicine, forests and wildlife.

The Arthashastra explores issues of social welfare, the collective ethics that hold a society together, advising the king that in times and in areas devastated by famine, epidemic and such acts of nature, or by war, he should initiate public projects such as creating irrigation waterways and building forts around major strategic holdings and towns and exempt taxes on those affected. The text was influenced by Hindu texts such as the sections on kings, governance and legal procedures included in **Manusmriti**.

3.3.1   Structure, Dating, and Authorship of Arthashastra

The authorship and date of writing are unknown, and there is evidence that the surviving manuscripts are not original, and are based on texts which were modified and edited in their history, but were most likely completed in the available form between the 1st and 3rd century CE. It is stated that the surviving manuscripts of the Arthashastra are the product of a transmission that has involved at least three major overlapping divisions or layers, which together **consist of 15 books, 150 chapters and 180 topics.**

3.3.2   History of the Arthashastra Manuscript

The Arthasastra is mentioned and dozens of its verses have been found on fragments of manuscript treatises buried in ancient Buddhist monasteries of northwest China, Afghanistan and northwest Pakistan. This includes the Spitzer Manuscript (c. 200 CE) discovered near Kizil in China and the birch bark scrolls now a part of the Bajaur Collection (1st to 2nd century CE) discovered in the ruins of a Khyber Pakhtunkhwa Buddhist site in 1999.

The text was considered lost by colonial era scholars, until **a manuscript was discovered in 1905. A copy of the Arthashastra in Sanskrit, written on palm leaves, was presented by a Tamil Brahmin from Thanjavur to the newly opened Mysore Oriental Library** headed by Benjamin Lewis Rice. The text was identified by the librarian **Rudrapatna Shamasastry** as the Arthashastra. During 1905–1909, Shamasastry published English translations of the text in installments, in journals Indian Antiquary and Mysore Review.

During 1923–1924, Julius Jolly and Richard Schmidt published a new edition of the text, which was based on a Malayalam script manuscript in the Bavarian State Library. In the 1950s, fragmented sections of a north Indian version of Arthashastra were discovered in the form of a Devanagari manuscript in a Jain library in Patan, Gujarat. A new edition based on this manuscript was published by Muni Jina Vijay in 1959. In 1960, **R. P. Kangle** published a critical edition of the text, based on all the available manuscripts. Numerous translations and interpretations of the text have been published since then.

The text written in Sanskrit of the 1st millennium BCE Sanskrit, which is coded, dense and capable of many interpretations, especially as English and Sanskrit are very different languages, both grammatically and syntactically. Patrick Olivelle, whose translation was published in 2013 by Oxford University Press, said it was the "most difficult translation project I have ever undertaken." Parts of the text are still opaque after a century of modern scholarship.

3.3.3 Translation of Arthashastra

Different scholars have translated the word "Arthashastra" in different ways.

R.P. Kangle: "Artha is the sustenance or livelihood of men, and Arthasastra is the science of the means to "Artha science of politics";

A.L. Basham: A "treatise on polity"

D.D. Kosambi: "Science of material gain"

G.P. Singh: "Science of polity"

Roger Boesche: "Science of political economy"

Patrick Olivelle: "Science of politics"

Artha (prosperity, wealth, purpose, meaning, economic security) is one of the four aims of human life in Hinduism (Puruṣārtha), the others being dharma (laws, duties, rights, virtues, right way of living), kama (pleasure, emotions, sex) and moksha (spiritual liberation). Shāstra is the Sanskrit word for "rules" or "science".

Dr. R. Shamashastry, the translator of the English version of Kautilya's Artha-Shastra, quotes a prediction from the Vishnu Purana fourth canto, twenty-fourth chapter, regarding the appearance of Chanakya Pandit. This prediction, incidentally, was scribed fifty centuries ago, nearly 2,700 years before this political heavyweight and man of destiny was to appear. The prediction informs us: "(First) Mahapadma then his sons - only nine in number - will be the lords of the earth for a hundred years. A brahmana named Kautilya will slay these Nandas. On their death, the Mauryas will enjoy the earth. Kautilya himself will install Chandragupta on the throne. His son will be Bindusara and his son will be Ashokavardhana." Similar prophecies are also repeated in the Bhagavata, Vayu and Matsya Puranas.

3.3.4   Structure of Arthashastra Manuscript

The first chapter of the first book is a table of contents, while the last chapter of the last book is a short 73 verse epilogue asserting that all thirty-two Yukti—elements of correct reasoning methods were deployed to create the text; both were probably later added to the original text.

A notable structure of the treatise is that while all chapters are primarily prose, each transitions into a poetic verse towards its end, as a marker, a style that is found in many ancient Hindu Sanskrit texts where the changing poetic meter or style of writing is used as a syntax code to silently signal that the chapter or section is ending. All 150 chapters of the text also end with a colophon stating the title of the book it belongs in, the topics contained in that book (like an index), the total number of titles in the book and the books in the text. Finally, the Arthashastra text numbers it 180 topics consecutively, and does not restart from one when a new chapter or a new book starts. The topics are unevenly divided over the chapters, with some chapters containing multiple topics, and some topics spread over multiple chapters; a peculiarity which betrays extensive redaction, with the division into chapters as a later addition.

The division into 15, 150, and 180 of books, chapters and topics, respectively, was probably not accidental, because ancient authors of major Hindu texts favor certain numbers, such as 18 Parvas in the epic Mahabharata. The largest book is the second, with 1,285 sentences, while the smallest is eleventh, with 56 sentences. The entire book has about 5,300 sentences on politics, governance, welfare, economics, protecting key officials and king, gathering intelligence about hostile states, forming strategic alliances, and conduct of war, exclusive of its table of contents and the last epilogue-style book.

3.3.5 Organisation of Arthashastra

The English translation of Arthashastra, which ascribes itself to the famous Brahman Kautilya (also named Vishnugupta and Chanakya) and dates from the period 321-296 B.C. The topics of the text include internal and foreign affairs, civil, military, commercial, fiscal, judicial, tables of weights, measures of length and divisions of time.

Following are the 15 books and the associated chapters in Arthashastra:

Book 1 - Concerning Discipline

Chapter 1 - The Life of a King

Chapter 2 - Determination of the Place of Ānvīkṣakī

Chapter 3 - Determination of the Place of the Triple Vedas

Chapter 4 - Vārtā and Daṇḍanīti

Chapter 5 - Association with the Aged

Chapter 6 - The Shaking Off of the Aggregate of the Six Enemies

Chapter 7 - The Life of a Saintly King

Chapter 8 - Creation of Ministers

Chapter 9 - The Creation of Councilors and Priests

Chapter 3 - The Application of Medicines and Mantras

Chapter 4 - Remedies Against the Injuries of One's Own Army

Book 15 – The Plan of a Treatise

Chapter 1 – Paragraphical Divisions of the Treatise

3.4   SOME KEY ELEMENTS OF CHANAKYA'S LEGACY

(i)   Political Philosophy

Chanakya's most significant contribution is his work, the '**Arthashastra**,' which serves as a foundational text in political science and economics. It outlines principles of statecraft, governance, and military strategy, emphasizing the importance of pragmatism and realpolitik. His ideas on power dynamics, diplomacy, and state management continue to be studied and applied in modern political theory.

(ii)   Strategic Thinking

Chanakya is often regarded as one of the earliest proponents of strategic thinking. His emphasis on planning, foresight, and adaptability in governance has influenced military leaders, politicians, and business strategists alike. His teachings encourage leaders to be shrewd and resourceful in navigating complex political landscapes."

(iii) Leadership and Governance

Chanakya's principles of leadership stress the importance of a strong, decisive governance. He advocated for the welfare of the state and its citizens, emphasizing that a ruler should be wise, just, and capable of making tough decisions for the greater good. His ideas on ethical leadership and the responsibilities of rulers remain relevant today. His teachings encourage leaders to be shrewd and resourceful in navigating complex political landscapes.

(iv) Economic Insights

In the "Arthashastra," Chanakya discusses various aspects of economics, including taxation, trade, and resource management. His insights into economic policies and practices have influenced economic thought in India and beyond, highlighting the interconnectedness of politics and economics.

(v) Educational Influence

Chanakya's teachings are incorporated into various educational curricula, particularly in the fields of political science, management, and leadership studies. His teachings encourage leaders to be shrewd and resourceful strategies and philosophies are taught in business schools and political science programs, emphasizing their relevance in contemporary contexts.

(vi) Symbol of Wisdom

Chanakya's most significant contribution is his work, the 'Arthashastra,' which serves as a foundational text in political science and economics. His name is synonymous with cleverness and strategic thinking, and he is frequently referenced in discussions about leadership and governance.

(vii) Modern Applications

Chanakya's principles are applied in various fields today, including business management, military strategy, and political campaigns. His emphasis on strategy, negotiation, and understanding human behaviour resonates with modern leaders and decision-makers.

(viii) Cultural Impact

Chanakya's life and teachings have inspired numerous works of literature, films, and television series, making him a prominent figure in Indian culture. His character is often depicted as a wise and cunning strategist, symbolizing intelligence and resourcefulness.

Chanakya's contributions were temporarily lost to history after the decline of the Gupta Empire in the 6th century CE and were only rediscovered in the early 20th century.

CHAPTER 4

NEETI-SHASTRA

4.1 INTRODUCTION TO CHANAKYA NEETI

'Chanakya Neeti' is, in fact, this great thinker's pithy observation to impart the practical wisdom to the people of his time. But these teachings are so fundamental that its relevance is almost ever-lasting. Enshrined in the simple sense. Written in simple lucid language with clear thoughts, these observations have not only withstood the test of time but many of phrases, like and have become the oft-quoted proverbs of our attempt has been to bring out their full meaning and interpret them in the context of the modern times so that their undecaying relevance may be fully appreciated. To bring home the fundamentality of these sayings, we have also compared them with the prevailing modern concept. The need for these rather lengthy explanations was felt owing to the occasional terseness of these observations. Sometimes Chanakya even contradicts his own, earlier observations, perhaps to reveal the fundamental truth by sheer contradiction. At times even some of the immoral teachings are the part of this book. But they appear immoral only at the prima facie viewing. While telling what we should learn from the other beings, Chanakya says:

Prattutthaanam cha Yuddham cha Samvibhaagashcha Bandhushu

That is, "Learn from the cock the following four things: getting up at the right time, fighting bitterly, making your brothers flee and usurping their share also!" Although, apparently it appears down right immoral, this teaching is rooted in the instinct of self-preservation which is natural. It is in this context that some of such unethical teachings are to be understood.

Although Chanakya is painted as a scheming manipulator who could stoop to even the meanest level to serve his purpose, a few of his shlokas negate this concept and present Chanakya as a sort hearted and imaginative poet. He says:

Bandhanaani Khal Santi Bahuni Prem Rajju Krit Bandhanmannyat
Daarubhed Nipunoapi Shadanghri Nishkriyo Bhavati Pankaj Koshe.

Meaning: There are many bondages but that of love is entirely different. The black-bee, which penetrates through even wood, gets inertly enclosed in the fold of the lotus flowers.

Who can consider the author of this Shloka to be a hard-hearted man?

There might be certain aphorisms which might appear objectionable to some persons, especially those who discuss the role of women in our society. Chanakya shares the same thoughts as these were prevalent during this time or are still prevalent in certain sections of our society. The entire Hindu thought gives only two positions to women: either they are adorable or they are like any other pleasure source to enjoy. The sense of companionship, which is clearly an occidental concept, is missing for obvious reasons. Well, nobody can be perfect in the world. Even the greatest thinkers of the world had some kind of views of their own. A man is a product of the social set up. No doubt, Chanakya tried to affect a change but even he could not get rid himself of some diehard idiosyncrasies.

4.2   ABOUT THE BOOK ON CHANAKYA NEETI

Chanakya Neeti is a policy book composed by Acharya Chanakya There are 17 chapters in this policy book. Chanakya Neeti has an important place in Sanskrit Neeti books. In order to make life happy and purposeful in a formulaic style, many topics have been described in Chanakya Neeti.

Acharya Chanakya has collected verses and formulas in his policy book Chanakya Neeti by studying the heritage and religious texts of his ancestors. By studying Chanakya Neeti common man can identify success in life, right and wrong, unfair, moral or immoral, religion or unrighteousness, wisdom or foolishness, beneficial or harmful, good or bad, useful or useless. Chanakya has laid a lot of emphasis on education in these sources. They say that education is the real salvation of a person. There are also some prejudiced things in the book, which may not stand the test of the modern world. But generally, the formulas are very logical.

4.3 BENEFITS OF CHANAKYA NEETI

Chanakya Neeti provides many life skills and solutions for problems.

Following are some of the benefits of Chanakya Neeti:

(i)   **Leadership Skills:** Chanakya Neeti is a wonderful leadership guide, which helps people to develop skills in leadership.

The Art of Building Relationships: According to Chanakya Neeti, the art of maintaining relationships becomes easy.

Management of Wealth: Chanakya Neeti explains in detail how to accumulate wealth and how to manage it effectively.

(ii) **Good Conduct:** According to Chanakya Neeti i, people are taught about good conduct, which makes them more successful in society.

(iii) **Solutions of Problems:** Chanakya Neeti is a guide to solving many problems. It helps people seek a better future.

Apart from all these benefits, Chanakya Neeti is an important scripture, which helps people to lead a better life.

In presenting this work, two old English versions of Chanakya Neeti -shastra have been referred, which were published at the close of the last century. However, these apparently were translated by mere scholars (not devotees) who seem to have missed many subtleties of Chanakya's vast wit and wisdom. Another unedited and unpublished manuscript Chanakya Neeti -shastra with both English translation and Latinized transliteration produced by the Vrindavana ISKCON Centre was also referred to. It was however the learned Vaishnava pandit and Sanskrit scholar Sri V. **Badarayana Murthy**, of the South Indian Madhva School, who helped the modern world see the depth and import of these verses from the original Devanagari.

The spiritual master His Divine Grace A.C. Bhaktivedanta Swami Prabhupada had expressed a desire that Sri Chanakya Neeti-shastra be properly translated into English.

4.4 SOME CHANAKYA-NEETI SUTRAS/APHORISMS

mūrkhaśiṣyopadeśena duṣṭastrībharaṇena ca.
duḥkhitaiḥ samprayogeṇa paṇḍito'pyavasīdati. . 01-04

Meaning: Even a pandit comes to grief by giving instruction to a foolish disciple, by maintaining a wicked wife, and by excessive familiarity with the miserable.

duṣṭā bhāryā śaṭhaṃ mitraṃ bhṛtyaścottaradāyakaḥ.
sasarpe ca gṛhe vāso mṛtyureva na saṃśayaḥ. . 01-05

Meaning: A wicked wife, a false friend, a saucy servant and living in a house with a serpent in it are nothing but death.

āpadarthe dhanaṃ rakṣecchrīmatāṃ kuta āpadaḥ.
kadāciccalate lakṣmīḥ sañcito'pi vinaśyati. . 01-07

Meaning: Save your wealth against future calamity. Do not say, "What fear has a rich man of calamity?" When riches begin to forsake one, even the accumulated stock dwindles away.

yasmindeśe na sammāno na vṛttirna ca bāndhavāḥ.
na ca vidyāgamo'pyasti vāsaṃ tatra na kārayet. . 01-08

Meaning: Do not inhabit a country where you are not respected, cannot earn your livelihood, have no friends, or cannot acquire knowledge.

lokayātrā bhayaṃ lajjā dākṣiṇyaṃ tyāgaśīlatā.
pañca yatra na vidyante na kuryāttatra saṃsthitim. . 01-10

Meaning: Wise men should never go into a country where there are no means of earning one's livelihood, where the people have no dread of anybody, have no sense of shame, no intelligence, or a charitable disposition.

jānīyātpreṣaṇe bhṛtyānbāndhavān vyasanāgame.
mitraṃ cāpattikāleṣu bhāryāṃ ca vibhavakṣaye. . 01-11

Meaning: Test a servant while in the discharge of his duty, a relative in difficulty, a friend in adversity, and a wife in misfortune.

āture vyasane prāpte durbhikṣe śatrusaṅkaṭe.
rājadvāre śmaśāne ca yastiṣṭhati sa bāndhavaḥ. . 01-12

Meaning: He is a true friend who does not forsake us in time of need, misfortune, famine, or war, in a king's court, or at the crematorium (smashana).

yo dhruvāṇi parityajya adhruvaṃ pariṣevate.
dhruvāṇi tasya naśyanti cādhruvaṃ naṣṭameva hi. . 01-13

Meaning: He who forgoes the certain for the uncertain, has his certain also destroyed. The uncertain even otherwise would be destroyed on its own.

varayetkulajāṃ prājño virūpāmapi kanyakām.
rūpaśīlāṃ na nīcasya vivāhaḥ sadṛśe kule. . 01-14

Meaning: A wise man should marry a virgin of a respectable family even if she is deformed. He should not marry one of a low-class family, though beautiful. Marriage in a family of equal status is preferable.

yasya putro vaśībhūto bhāryā chandānugāminī.
vibhave yaśca santuṣṭastasya svarga ihaiva hi. . 02-03

Meaning: He whose son is obedient to him, whose wife's conduct is in accordance with his wishes, and who is content with his riches, has his heaven here on earth.

te putrā ye piturbhaktāḥ sa pitā yastu poṣakaḥ.
tanmitraṃ yatra viśvāsaḥ sā bhāryā yatra nirvṛtiḥ. . 02-04

Meaning: They alone are sons who are devoted to their father. He is a father who supports his sons. He is a friend in whom we can confide, and she only is a wife in whose company the husband feels contented and peaceful.

parokṣe kāryahantāraṃ pratyakṣe priyavādinam.
varjayettādṛśaṃ mitraṃ viṣakumbhaṃ payomukham. . 02-05

Meaning: Avoid him who talks sweetly before you but tries to ruin you behind your back, for he is like a pitcher of poison with milk on top.

na viśvasetkumitre ca mitre cāpi na viśvaset.
kadācitkupitaṃ mitraṃ sarvaṃ guhyaṃ prakāśayet. . 02-06

Meaning: Do not put your trust in a bad companion nor even trust an ordinary friend, for if he should get angry with you, he may bring all your secrets to light.

mātā śatruḥ pitā vairī yābhyāṃ bālā na pāṭhitāḥ.
sabhāmadhye na śobhante haṃsamadhye bako yathā. . 02-11

Meaning: Those parents who do not educate their sons are their enemies; for as is a crane among swans, so are ignorant so are ignorant sons in a public assembly.

ślokena vā tadardhena tadardhārdhākṣareṇa vā |
abandhyaṃ divasaṃ kuryāddānādhyayanakarmabhiḥ ||
– (Chanakya Neeti, 2.13)

Meaning: Let not a single day pass without your learning a verse, half a verse, or a fourth of it, or even one letter of it; nor without attending to charity, study and other pious activity.

kāntāviyogaḥ svajanāpamānaṃ
ṛṇasya śeṣaṃ kunṛpasya sevā.
dāridryabhāvādvimukhaṃ ca mitraṃ
vināgninā pañca dahanti kāyam. . 02-14

Meaning: Separation from the wife, disgrace from one's own people, an enemy saved in battle, service to a wicked king, poverty, and a mismanaged assembly: these six kinds of evils, if afflicting a person, burn him even without fire.

nadītīre ca ye vṛkṣāḥ paragehesu kāminī.
mantrahīnāśca rājānaḥ śīghraṃ naśyantyasaṃśayam. . 02-15

Meaning: Trees on a river bank, a woman in another man's house, and kings without counsellors go without doubt to swift destruction.

nirdhanaṃ puruṣaṃ veśyā prajā bhagnaṃ nṛpaṃ tyajet.
khagā vītaphalaṃ vṛkṣaṃ bhuktvā cābhyāgato gṛham. . 02-17

Meaning: The prostitute has to forsake a man who has no money, the subject a king that cannot defend him, the birds a tree that bears no fruit, and the guests a house after they have finished their meals.

durjanasya ca sarpasya varaṃ sarpo na durjanaḥ.
sarpo daṃśati kāle tu durjanastu pade pade. . 03-04

Meaning: Of a rascal and a serpent, the serpent is the better of the two, for he strikes only at the time he is destined to kill, while the former at every step.

pralaye bhinnamaryādā bhavanti kila sāgarāḥ |
sāgarā bhedamicchanti pralaye'pi na sādhavaḥ ||
— *(Chanakya Neeti, 3.6)*

Meaning: At the time of the Pralaya (universal destruction) the oceans are to exceed their limits and seek to change, but a saintly man never changes.

merchant prahartavyaḥ pratyakṣo dvipadaḥ paśuḥ.
bhidyate vākya-śalyena adṛśaṃ kaṇṭakaṃ yathā. . 03-07

Meaning: Do not keep company with a fool for as we can see he is a two-legged beast. Like an unseen thorn he pierces the heart with his sharp words.

rūpayauvanasampannā viśālakulasambhavāḥ |
vidyāhīnā na śobhante nirgandhāḥ kiṃśukā yathā ||
— *(Chanakya Neeti, 3.8)*

Meaning: Though one can be endowed with beauty and youth and born in noble families, yet without education they are like the Palasa flower which is void of sweet fragrance.

ekenāpi suvṛkṣeṇa puṣpitena sugandhinā.
vāsitaṃ tadvanaṃ sarvaṃ suputreṇa kulaṃ yathā. . 03-14

Meaning: As a whole forest becomes fragrant by the existence of a single tree with sweet-smelling blossoms in it, so a family becomes famous by the birth of a virtuous son.

kiṃ jātairbahubhiḥ putraiḥ śokasantāpakārakaiḥ.
varamekaḥ kulālambī yatra viśrāmyate kulam. . 03-17

Meaning: What is the use of having many sons if they cause grief and vexation? It is better to have only one son from whom the whole family can derive support and peace- fulness.

lālayetpañcavarṣāṇi daśavarṣāṇi tāḍayet.
prāpte tu ṣoḍaśe varṣe putre mitravadācaret. . 03-18

Meaning: Fondle a son until he is five years of age, and use the stick for another ten years, but when he has attained his sixteenth year treat him as a friend.

mūrkhā yatra na pūjyante dhānyaṃ yatra susañcitam.
dāmpatye kalaho nāsti tatra śrīḥ svayamāgatā. . 03-21

Meaning: Lakshmi, the Goddess of wealth, comes of Her own accord where fools are not respected, grain is well stored up, and the husband and wife do not quarrel.

kāmadhenugunā vidyā hyakāle phaladāyinī |
pravāse mātṛsadṛśī vidyā guptaṃ dhanaṃ smṛtam ||
— *(Chanakya Neeti, 4.5)*

Meaning: Learning is like a cow of desire (*Kamadhenu*). It, like her, yields in all seasons. Like a mother, it feeds you on your journey, therefore learning is a hidden treasure.

eko'pi guṇavānputro nirguṇena śatena kim.
ekaścandrastamo hanti na ca tārāḥ sahasraśaḥ. . 04-06

Meaning: A single son endowed with good qualities, is far better than a hundred devoid of them. For the moon, though one, dispels the darkness, which the stars, though numerous, cannot.

mūrkhaścirāyurjāto'pi tasmājjātamṛto varaḥ.
mṛtaḥ sa cālpaduḥkhāya yāvajjīvaṃ jaḍo dahet. . 04-07

Meaning: A still-born son is superior to a foolish son endowed with a long life. The first causes grief, but a moment, while the latter like a blazing fire consumes his parents in grief for life.

kugrāmavāsaḥ kulahīnasevā
kubhojanaṃ krodhamukhī ca bhāryā.
putraśca mūrkho vidhavā ca kanyā
vināgninā ṣaṭpradahanti kāyam. . 04-08

Meaning: Residing in a small village devoid of proper living facilities, serving a person born of a low family, unwholesome food, a frowning wife, a foolish son, and a widowed daughter burn the body without fire.

sā bhāryā yā śucirdakṣā sā bhāryā yā pativratā.
sā bhāryā yā patiprītā sā bhāryā satyavādinī. . 04-13

Meaning: She is a true wife who is clean, expert, chaste, pleasing to the husband, and truthful.

anabhyāse viṣaṃ śāstram |
– (Chanakya Neeti, 4.15)

Meaning: Knowledge without practice is like poison.

kaḥ kālaḥ kāni mitrāṇi ko deśaḥ kau vyayāgamau |
kaścāhaṃ kā ca me śaktiriti cintyaṃ muhurmuhuḥ ||
– (Chanakya Neeti, 4.18)

Meaning: Consider again and again the following: the right time, the right friends, the right place, the right means of income, the right ways of spending, and from whom you derive your power.

yathā caturbhiḥ kanakaṃ parīkṣyate
nigharṣaṇacchedanatāpatāḍanaiḥ |
tathā caturbhiḥ puruṣaḥ parīkṣyate
tyāgena śīlena guṇena karmaṇā ||

– (Chanakya Neeti, 5.2)

Meaning: As gold is tested in four ways by rubbing, cutting, heating and beating – so a man should be tested by these four things: his renunciation, his conduct, his qualities, and his actions.

ekodarasamudbhūtā ekanakṣatrajātakāḥ.
na bhavanti samāḥ śīle yathā badarakaṇṭakāḥ. . 05-04

Meaning: Though persons be born from the same womb and under the same stars, they do not become alike in dis- position as the thousand fruits of the badari tree.

mūrkhāṇāṃ paṇḍitā dveṣyā adhanānāṃ mahādhanāḥ.
parāṃganā kulastrīṇāṃ subhagānāṃ ca durbhagāḥ. . 05-06

Meaning: The learned are envied by the foolish; rich men by the poor; chaste women by adulteresses; and beautiful ladies by ugly ones.

abhyāsāddhāryate vidyā kulaṃ śīlena dhāryate.
guṇena jñāyate tvāryaḥ kopo netreṇa gamyate. . 05-08

Meaning: Learning is retained through putting into practice; family prestige is maintained through good behaviour; a respectable person is recognised by his excellent qualities; and anger is seen in the eyes.

anyathā vedaśāstrāṇi jñānapāṇḍityamanyathā.
anyathā tatpadaṃ śāntaṃ lokāḥ kliśyanti cāhnyathā. . 05-10

Meaning: Those who blaspheme Vedic wisdom, who ridicule the life style recommended in the shastras, and who deride men of peaceful temperament, come to grief unnecessarily.

dāridryanāśanam dānaṃ śīlam durgatināśanam |
ajñānanāśinī prajñā bhāvanā bhayanāśinī ||

– (Chanakya Neeti, 5.11)

Meaning: Charity puts end to poverty; righteous conduct to misery; discretion to ignorance; and scrutiny to fear.

nāsti kāmasamo vyādhirnāsti mohasamo ripuḥ.
nāsti kopasamo vahnirnāsti jñānātparaṃ sukham. . 05-12

Meaning: There is no disease (so destructive) as lust; no enemy like infatuation; no fire like wrath; and no happiness like spiritual knowledge.

janmamṛtyū hi yātyeko bhunaktyekaḥ śubhāśubham I
narakeṣu patatyekaeko yāti parāṃ gatim II
– (Chanakya Neeti, 5.13)

Meaning: A person is born alone and dies alone; and experiences the good and bad consequences of their karma alone; and goes alone to hell or the Supreme abode.

vṛthā vṛṣṭiḥ samudreṣu vṛthā tṛptasya bhojanam.
vṛthā dānaṃ samarthasya vṛthā dīpo divāpi ca. . 05-16

Meaning: Rain which falls upon the sea is useless; so is food for one who is satiated; in vain is a gift for one who is wealthy; and a burning lamp during the daytime is use- less.

satyena dhāryate pṛthvī satyena tapate raviḥ I
satyena vāti vāyuśca sarvaṃ satye pratiṣṭhitam II
– (Chanakya Neeti, 5.19)

Meaning: The earth is supported by the power of truth; it is the power of truth that makes the sun shine and the winds blow; indeed all things rest upon truth.

rājapatnī guroḥ patnī mitrapatnī tathaiva ca.
patnīmātā svamātā ca pañcaitā mātaraḥ smṛtāḥ. . 05-23

Meaning: These five should be considered as mothers; the king's wife, the preceptor's wife, the friend's wife, your wife's mother, and your own mother.

pakṣiṇaḥ kākaścaṇḍālaḥ paśūnāṃ caiva kukkuraḥ.
munīnāṃ pāpaścaṇḍālaḥ sarvacāṇḍālanindakaḥ. . 06-02

Meaning: Among birds the crow is vile; among beasts the dog; the ascetic whose sins is abominable, but he who blasphemes others is the worst chandala.

yasyārthāstasya mitrāṇi yasyārthāstasya bāndhavāḥ.
yasyārthāḥ sa pumāṁlloke yasyārthāḥ sa ca paṇḍitaḥ. . 06-05

Meaning: He who has wealth has friends. He who is wealthy has relatives. The rich one alone is called a man, and the affluent alone are respected as pandits.

kālaḥ pacati bhūtāni kālaḥ saṃharate prajāḥ |
kālaḥ supteṣu jāgarti kālo hi duratikramaḥ ||
– (Chanakya Neeti, 6.7)

Meaning: Time perfects all living beings as well as kills them; it alone is awake when all others are asleep. Time is insurmountable, rest upon truth.

lubdhamarthena gṛhṇīyāt stabdhamañjalikarmaṇā.
mūrkhaṃ chando'nuvṛttyā ca yathārthatvena paṇḍitam. . 06-12

Meaning: Conciliate a covetous man by means of a gift, an obstinate man with folded hands in salutation, a fool by humoring him, and a learned man by truthful words.

varaṃ na rājyaṃ na kurājarājyaṃ
varaṃ na mitraṃ na kumitramitram.
varaṃ na śiṣyo na kuśiṣyaśiṣyo
varaṃ na dāra na kudaradāraḥ. . 06-13

Meaning: It is better to be without a kingdom than to rule over a petty one; better to be without a friend than to befriend a rascal; better to be without a disciple than to have a stupid one; and better to be without a wife than to have a bad one.

arthanāśaṃ manastāpaṃ gṛhe duścaritāni ca.
vañcanaṃ cāpamānaṃ ca matimānna prakāśayet. . 07-01

Meaning: A wise man should not reveal his loss of wealth, the vexation of his mind, the misconduct of his own wife, base words spoken by others, and disgrace that has befallen him.

dhanadhānyaprayogeṣu vidyāsaṅgrahaṇe tathā.
āhāre vyavahāre ca tyaktalajjaḥ sukhī bhavet. . 07-02

Meaning: He who gives up shyness in monetary dealings, in acquiring knowledge, in eating and in business, becomes happy.

saṃtoṣastriṣu kartavyaḥ svadāre bhojane dhane l
triṣu caiva na kartavyo'dhyayane japadānayoḥ ll
— *(Chanakya Neeti, 7.4)*

Meaning: One should be satisfied with one's wife (spouse), food, and money. One should never be satisfied with one's study, chanting, and charity.

tuṣyanti bhojane viprā mayūrā ghanagarjite.
sādhavaḥ parasampattau khalāḥ paravipattiṣu. . 07-09

Meaning: Brahmanas find satisfaction in a good meal, peacocks in the peal of thunder, a sadhu in seeing the prosperity of others, and the wicked in the misery of others.

nātyantaṃ saralairbhāvyaṃ gatvā paśya vanasthalīm l
chidyante saralāstatra kubjāstiṣṭhanti pādapāḥ ll
— *(Chanakya Neeti, 7.12)*

Meaning: Do not be very upright in your dealings, as you would see in forest, the straight trees are cut down while the crooked ones are left standing.

śunaḥ pucchamiva vyarthaṃ jīvitaṃ vidyayā vinā.
na guhyagopane śaktaṃ na ca daṃśanivāraṇe. . 07-19

Meaning: The following qualities of the denizens of hell may characterize men on earth; extreme wrath, harsh speech, enmity with one's relations, the company with the base, and service to men of low extraction.

adhamā dhanamicchanti dhanamānau ca madhyamāḥ.
uttamā mānamicchanti māno hi mahatāṃ dhanam. . 08-01

Meaning: Low class men desire wealth; middle class men both wealth and respect; but the noble, honour only; hence honour is the noble man's true wealth.

> *dīpo bhakṣayate dhvāntaṃ kajjalaṃ ca prasūyate |*
> *yadannaṃ bhakṣayennityaṃ jāyate tādṛśī prajā ||*
> — *(Chanakya Neeti, 8.3)*

Meaning: The lamp consumes darkness and produces dark soot. Similarly, what food we eat affects what we produce (offsprings).

> *vittaṃ dehi guṇānviteṣu matimannānyatra dehi kvacit*
> *prāptaṃ vārinidherjalaṃ ghanamukhe mādhuryayuktaṃ sadā.*
> *jīvānsthāvarajaṃgamāṃśca sakalānsaṃjīvya bhūmaṇḍalaṃ*
> *bhūyaḥ paśya tadeva koṭiguṇitaṃ gacchantamambhonidhim. . 08-04*

Meaning: O wise man! Give your wealth only to the worthy and never to others. The water of the sea received by the clouds is always sweet. The rain water enlivens all living beings of the earth both movable (insects, animals, humans, etc.) and immovable (plants, trees, etc.), and then returns to the ocean it value multiplied a million-fold.

> *tailābhyaṅge citādhūme maithune kṣaurakarmaṇi.*
> *tāvadbhavati cāṇḍālo yāvatsnānaṃ na cācaret. . 08-06*

Meaning: After having rubbed oil on the body, after encountering the smoke from a funeral pyre, after sexual intercourse, and after being shaved, one remains a chandala until he bathes.

> *ajīrṇe bheṣajaṃ vāri jīrṇe vāri balapradam.*
> *bhojane cāmṛtaṃ vāri bhojanānte viṣāpaham. . 08-07*

Meaning: Water is the medicine for indigestion; it is invigorating when the food that is eaten, is well digested; it is like nectar when drunk in the middle of a dinner; and it is like poison when taken at the end of a meal.

> *hataṃ jñānaṃ kriyāhīnaṃ hataścājñānato naraḥ.*
> *hataṃ nirṇāyakaṃ sainyaṃ striyo naṣṭā hyabhartṛkāḥ. . 08-08*

Meaning: Knowledge is lost without putting it into practice; a man is lost due to ignorance; an army is lost without a commander; and a woman is lost without a husband.

krodho vaivasvato rājā tṛṣṇā vaitaraṇī nadī |
vidyā kāmadudhā dhenuḥ saṃtoṣo nandanaṃ vanam ||
— (Chanakya Neeti, 8.14)

Meaning: Anger is a personification of Yama (the demigod of death); Thirst is like the hellish river Vaitarani; Knowledge is like a Kamadhenu (the cow of plenty), and Contentment is like Nandanavana (the garden of Indra).

asantuṣṭā dvijā naṣṭāḥ santuṣṭāśca mahībhṛtaḥ.
salajjā gaṇikā naṣṭā nirlajjāśca kulāṅganā. . 08-18

Meaning: Discontented brahmanas, contented kings, shy prostitutes, and immodest housewives are ruined.

vidvānpraśasyate loke vidvān sarvatra pūjyate.
vidyayā labhate sarvaṃ vidyā sarvatra pūjyate. . 08-20

Meaning: A learned man is honoured by the people. A learned man commands respect everywhere for his learning. Indeed, learning is honoured everywhere.

māṃsabhakṣyaiḥ surāpānairmukhaiścākṣaravarjitaiḥ.
paśubhiḥ puruṣākārairbhārākrāntā hi medinī. . 08-22

Meaning: The earth is encumbered with the weight of the flesh-eaters, wine-bibblers, dolts and blockheads, who are beasts in the form of men.

annahīno dahedrāṣṭraṃ mantrahīnaśca ṛtvijaḥ.
yajamānaṃ dānahīno nāsti yajñasamo ripuḥ. . 08-23

Meaning: There is no enemy like a yajna (sacrifice) which consumes the kingdom when not attended by feeding on a large scale; consumes the priest when the chanting is not done properly; and consumes the yajaman (the respon- sible person) when the gifts are not made.

parasparasya marmāṇi ye bhāṣante narādhamāḥ.
ta eva vilayaṃ yānti valmīkodarasarpavat. . 09-02

Meaning: Those base men who speak of the secret faults of others destroy themselves like serpents who stray onto anthills.

sarvauṣadhīnāmamṛtā pradhānā
sarveṣu saukhyeṣvaśanaṃ pradhānam.
sarvendriyāṇāṃ nayanaṃ pradhānaṃ
sarveṣu gātreṣu śiraḥ pradhānam. . 09-04

Meaning: Nectar (amrita) is the best among medicines; eating good food is the best of all types of material happiness; the eye is the chief among all organs; and the head occupies the chief position among all parts of the body.

ahiṃ nṛpaṃ ca śārdūlaṃ vṛddhaṃ ca bālakaṃ tathā.
paraśvānaṃ ca mūrkhaṃ ca sapta suptānna bodhayet. . 09-07

Meaning: The serpent, the king, the tiger, the stinging wasp, the small child, the dog owned by other people, and the fool: these seven ought not to be awakened from sleep.

nirviṣeṇāpi sarpeṇa kartavyā mahatī phaṇā.
viṣamastu na cāpyastu ghaṭāṭopo bhayaṅkaraḥ. . 09-10

Meaning: The serpent may, without being poisonous, raise high its hood, but the show of terror is enough to frighten people – whether he be venomous or not.

svahastagrathitā mālā svahastaghṛṣṭacandanam.
svahastalikhitaṃ stotraṃ śakrasyāpi śriyaṃ haret. . 09-12

Meaning: By preparing a garland for a Deity with one's own hand; by grinding sandal paste for the Lord with one's own hand; and by writing sacred texts with one's own hand – one becomes blessed with opulence equal to that of Indra.

sukhārthī cettyajedvidyāṃ vidyārthī cettyajetsukham.
sukhārthinaḥ kuto vidyā sukhaṃ vidyārthinaḥ kutaḥ. . 10-03

Meaning: He who desires sense gratification must give up all thoughts of acquiring knowledge; and he who seeks knowledge must not hope for sense gratification. How can he who seeks sense gratification acquire knowledge, and he who possesses knowledge enjoy mundane sense pleasure?

raṅkaṃ karoti rājānaṃ rājānaṃ raṅkameva ca.
dhaninaṃ nirdhanaṃ caiva nirdhanaṃ dhaninaṃ vidhiḥ. . 10-05

Meaning: Fate makes a beggar a king and a king a beggar. It makes a rich man poor and a poor man rich.

lubdhānāṃ yācakaḥ śatrurmūrkhānāṃ bodhako ripuḥ.
jārastrīṇāṃ patiḥ śatruścaurāṇāṃ candramā ripuḥ. . 10-06

Meaning: The beggar is a miser's enemy; the wise counsellor is the fool's enemy; her husband is an adulterous wife's enemy; and the moon is the enemy of the thief.

antaḥsāravihīnānāmupadeśo na jāyate.
malayācalasaṃsargānna veṇuścandanāyate. . 10-08

Meaning: Those that are empty-minded cannot be benefited by instruction. Bamboo does not acquire the quality of sandalwood by being associated with the Malaya Mountain.

annāddaśaguṇaṃ piṣṭaṃ piṣṭāddaśaguṇaṃ payaḥ |
payasō'ṣṭaguṇaṃ māṃsāṃ māṃsāddaśaguṇaṃ ghṛtam || 10-19 ||

Meaning: Flour has ten times the essence than rice. Milk has ten times the essence than flour. Meat has ten times essence than milk. Ghee has ten times the essence than meat.

śōkēna rōgā vardhantē payasā vardhatē tanuḥ |
ghṛtēna vardhatē vīryaṃ māṃsānmāṃsam pravardhatē || 10-20 ||

Meaning: Sickness increases through worries, body becomes healthier through milk, virility and energy increases through ghee, meat becomes stronger through meat (by consuming meat, meat may become stronger, but the full body becomes healthier only through eating vegetables).

> *vajreṇāpi hatāḥ patanti girayaḥ kiṃ vajramātraṃ nagā-*
> *stejo yasya virājate sa balavānsthūleṣu kaḥ pratyayaḥ. . 11-03*

Meaning: The elephant has a huge body but is controlled by the ankusha (goad): yet, is the goad as large as the elephant? A lighted candle banishes darkness: is the candle as vast as the darkness. A mountain is broken even by a thunderbolt: is the thunderbolt therefore as big as the mountain? No, he whose power prevails is really mighty; what is there in bulk?

> *na durjanaḥ sādhudaśāmupaiti*
> *bahuprakārairapi śikṣyamāṇaḥ.*
> *āmūlasiktaḥ payasā ghṛtena*
> *na nimbavṛkṣo madhuratvameti. . 11-06*

Meaning: The wicked man will not attain sanctity even if he is instructed in different ways, and the neem tree will not become sweet even if it is sprinkled from the top to the roots with milk and ghee.

> *antargatamalo duṣṭastīrthasnānaśatairapi.*
> *na śudhyati yathā bhāṇḍaṃ surāyā dāhitaṃ ca sat. . 11-07*

Meaning: Mental dirt cannot be washed away even by one- hundred baths in the sacred waters, just as a wine pot cannot be purified even by evaporating all the wine by fire.

> *ekāhāreṇa santuṣṭaḥ ṣaṭkarmanirataḥ sadā.*
> *ṛtukālābhigāmī ca sa vipro dvija ucyate. . 11-12*

Meaning: He alone is a true brahmana (dvija or "twice-born") who is satisfied with one meal a day, who has the six samskaras (or acts of purification such as garbhadhana, etc.) performed for him, and who cohabits with his wife only once in a month on an auspicious day after her menses.

> *vāpīkūpataḍāgānāmārāmasuraveśmanām.*
> *ucchedane nirāśaṅkaḥ sa vipro mleccha ucyate. . 11-16*

Meaning: The brahmana who destroys a pond, a well, a tank, a garden and a temple is called a mleccha.

devadravyaṃ gurudravyaṃ paradārābhimarśanam.
nirvāhaḥ sarvabhūteṣu vipraścāṇḍāla ucyate. . 11-17

Meaning: The brahmana who steals the property of the Deities and the spiritual preceptor, who cohabits with another's wife, and who maintains himself by eating anything and everything is called a chandala.

mātṛvatparadāreṣu paradravyeṣu loṣṭravat.
ātmavatsarvabhūteṣu yaḥ paśyati sa paṇḍitaḥ. . 12-14

Meaning: He who regards another's wife as his mother, the wealth that does not belong to him as a lump of mud, and the pleasure and pain of all other living beings as his own – truly sees things in the right perspective, and he is a true pandit.

vidyā mitraṃ pravāse ca bhāryā mitraṃ gṛheṣu ca.
vyādhitasyauṣadhaṃ mitraṃ dharmo mitraṃ mṛtasya ca. . 12-17

Meaning: Realised learning (vidya) is our friend while travel- ling, the wife is a friend at home, medicine is the friend of a sick man, and meritorious deeds are the friends at death.

anālokya vyayaṃ kartā anāthaḥ kalahapriyaḥ.
āturaḥ sarvakṣetreṣu naraḥ śīghraṃ vinaśyati. . 12-19

Meaning: The unthinking spender, the homeless urchin, the quarrel monger, the man who neglects his wife and is heedless in his actions – all these will soon come to ruination.

gate śoko na kartavyo bhaviṣyaṃ naiva cintayet |
vartamānena kālena vartayanti vicakṣaṇāḥ ||
(Chanakya Neeti, 13.2)

Meaning: We should not (unduly) grieve for what is past, and not worry about what is yet to come; the wise live in the present.

rājñi dharmiṇi dharmiṣṭhāḥ pāpe pāpāḥ same samāḥ.
rājānamanuvartante yathā rājā tathā prajāḥ. . 13-08

Meaning: If the king is virtuous, then the subjects are also virtuous. If the king is sinful, then the subjects also become sinful. If he is mediocre, then the subjects are mediocre. The subjects follow the example of the king. In short, as is the king so are the subjects.

yugānte pracalenmeruḥ kalpānte sapta sāgarāḥ.
sādhavaḥ pratipannārthānna calanti kadācana. . 13-21

Meaning: At the end of the yuga, Mount Meru may be shaken; at the end of the kalpa, the waters of the seven oceans may be disturbed; but a sadhu will never swerve from the spiritual path.

jale tailaṃ khale guhyaṃ pātre dānaṃ manāgapi.
prājñe śāstraṃ svayaṃ yāti vistāraṃ vastuśaktitaḥ. . 14-05

Meaning: Oil on water, a secret communicated to a base man, a gift given to a worthy receiver, and scriptural instruction given to an intelligent man spread out by virtue of their nature.

agnirāpaḥ striyo mūrkhāḥ sarpā rājakulāni ca.
nityaṃ yatnena sevyāni sadyaḥ prāṇaharāṇi ṣaṭ. . 14-12

Meaning: We should always deal cautiously with fire, water, women, foolish people, serpents, and members of a royal family; for they may, when the occasion presents itself, at once bring about our death.

susiddhamauṣadhaṃ dharmaṃ gṛhacchidraṃ ca maithunam.
kubhuktaṃ kuśrutaṃ caiva matimānna prakāśayet. . 14-17

Meaning: A wise man should not divulge the formula of a medicine which he has well prepared; an act of charity which he has performed; domestic conflicts; private affairs with his wife; poorly prepared food he may have been offered; or slang he may have heard.

tyaja durjanasaṃsargaṃ bhaja sādhusamāgamam.
kuru puṇyamahorātraṃ smara nityamanityataḥ. . 14-20

Meaning: Eschew wicked company and associate with saintly persons. Acquire virtue day and night, and always meditate on that which is eternal forgetting that which is temporary.

kucailinaṃ dantamalopadhāriṇam
bahvāśinaṃ niṣṭhurabhāṣiṇam ca.
sūryodaye cāstamite śayānaṃ
vimuñcati śrīryadi cakrapāṇiḥ. . 15-04

Meaning: He who wears unclean garments, has dirty teeth, as a glutton, speaks unkindly and sleeps after sunrise – al- though he may be the greatest personality – will lose the favour of Lakshmi.

dūrāgataṃ pathi śrāntaṃ vṛthā ca gṛhamāgatam.
anarcayitvā yo bhuṅkte sa vai cāṇḍāla ucyate. . 15-11

Meaning: He is a chandala who eats his dinner without entertaining the stranger who has come to his house quite accidentally, having travelled from a long distance and is exhausted/tired.

guṇairuttamatāṃ yāti noccairāsanasaṃsthitaḥ |
prāsādaśikharastho'pi kākaḥ kiṃ garuḍāyate || 16-06

Meaning: Greatness comes from good qualities and not from a high position. A crow doesn't become a Garuda (the chief of the feathered race) just by sitting on the top of a palace.

araṃ prāṇaparityāgo mānabhaṅgena jīvanāt.
prāṇatyāge kṣaṇaṃ duḥkhaṃ mānabhaṅge dine dine. . 16-16

Meaning: It is better to die than to preserve this life by incurring disgrace. The loss of life causes but a moment's grief, but disgrace brings grief every day of one's life.

pustakasthā tu yā vidyā parahastagataṃ dhanam.
kāryakāle samutpanne na sā vidyā na taddhanam. . 16-20

Meaning: One whose knowledge is confined to books and whose wealth is in the possession of others, can use neither his knowledge nor wealth when the need for them arises.

yaddūraṃ yaddurārādhyaṃ yacca dūre vyavasthitam.
tatsarvaṃ tapasā sādhyaṃ tapo hi duratikramam. . 17-03

Meaning: That thing which is distant, that thing which appears impossible, and that which is far beyond our reach, can be easily attained through tapasya (religious austerity), for nothing can surpass austerity.

takṣakasya viṣaṃ dante makṣikāyāstu mastake.
vṛścikasya viṣaṃ pucche sarvāṅge durjane viṣam. . 17-08

Meaning: There is poison in the fang of the serpent, in the mouth of the fly and in the sting of a scorpion; but the wicked man is saturated with it.

patyurājñāṃ vinā nārī hyupoṣya vratacāriṇī.
āyuṣyaṃ harate bhartuḥ sā nārī narakaṃ vrajet. . 17-09

Meaning: The woman who fasts and observes religious vows without the permission of her husband shortens his life, and goes to hell.

dānena pāṇirna tu kaṅkaṇena
snānena śuddhirna tu candanena.
mānena tṛptirna tu bhojanena
jñānena muktirna tu muṇḍanena. . 17-12

Meaning: The hand is not so well adorned by ornaments as by charitable offerings; one does not become clean by smearing sandalwood paste upon the body as by taking a bath; one does not become so much satisfied by dinner as by having respect shown to him; and salvation is not attained by self-adornment as by cultivation of spiritual knowledge.

āhāranidrābhayamaithunāni
samāni caitāni nṛṇāṃ paśūnām.
jñānaṃ narāṇāmadhiko viśeṣo
jñānena hīnāḥ paśubhiḥ samānāḥ. . 17-17

Meaning: Men have eating, sleeping, fearing and mating in common with the lower animals. That in which men excel the beasts is discretionary knowledge; hence, indiscreet men who are without knowledge should be regarded as beasts.

rājā veśyā yamaścāgnistaskaro bālayācakau.
paraduḥkhaṃ na jānanti aṣṭamo grāmakaṇṭakaḥ. . 17-19

Meaning: A king, a prostitute, Lord Yamaraja, fire, a thief, a young boy, and a beggar cannot understand the suffering of others. The eighth of this category is the tax collector.

4.5 SOME MORE APHORISMS FROM CHANAKYA NEETI

Vittam Dehi gunaaniviteshu Matimaannaannyatra Dehi Kvachit Praaptam Vaaritidherjalam Dhanyachaam Maadhuryayuktam Sadaa. Jeevaah Sthaavar Jangamaashcha Sakalaa Sajeevya Bhoomadalam Bhooyah Pashya Tadaiv Kotigunitam Gachaanttyammbhonidhim.

O wise! Give riches to the virtuous only, never to the undeserving, to those who lack good qualities. The clouds derive water from the seas and then making it sweet and then rain on the earth to make the beings of the earth survive. Then this water returns to the sea many million times more than the water the seas had given to the clouds.

Chanakya says that if one gives money to someone who is wise, intelligent and full of virtues, the receiver is able to multiply it many times over and this way, not only the receiver but the whole society is benefited. Giving the analogy of the seawater-cloud-rain-sea cycle, he explains his point very cogently. If the seas give water to cloud (the virtuous, deserving receiver), it makes it sweet and then rains it over the earth to help all beings survive there. Then through rivers this rain water, multiplied million times over by the clouds, returns to the seas, and during the process keeping the earth lush and green and its beings rejuvenated.

Kimtayaa Kriyate Laxammyaa Yaa Vadhooriv Kevalaa.
Yaa Tu Veshyaiv Saamaanmyapathikairapi Bhujjyate.

What are the uses of the riches kept inside the house like the bride of an orthodox and traditional family? And those riches which like the prostitutes are enjoyed by all have no usefulness either.

The miser keeps his wealth secretly hidden in the vaults which serve no purpose of the society. And the riches with the fools are like the prostitute enjoyed by others, especially the low category people.

In that case also the wealth is not well spent. This way, obliquely Chanakya says that riches should be spent in the welfare of the virtuous who help the society and they should neither be amassed in a miserly way nor spent extravagantly.

Atikleshen Ye Chaarthaah Dharmasyaati Kramentu.
Shatroonaam Pranipaaten Te Hyaarthah Na Bhavantu Me.

I don't crave for such a wealth which is extorted by saddening someone, by irreligious and immoral means or by seeking shelter of the enemies.

In the modern context this could be interpreted as an unwillingness to get such a wealth as may be received by immoral means, by torturing anyone or from the enemy of one's faith or country, i.e., the black money or the money received through the smuggling activities or through the treacherous deal with the enemies.

Aputrasya Griha Shoonnyam Dishah Shoonnyaasttvabaandhavaah.
Moorkhassya Hridayam Shoonnyam Sarvashoonmyam Daridrataa.

A home is vacuous for the one who has lost his son (or who has no son); all the quarters of the world are vacuous for him who has lost a brother (or who has no brothers); for the fool his heart is vacuous (i.e., he has no plans, no occupation) but for the pauper everything is meaningless or vacuous.

Here the vacuousness should be deemed to be absence of any hope. Obviously, a home has no hope for the sonless person; for the brotherless person, there is no hope to get support from any quarter of the world; a fool devoid of any capability to plan for future is hopeless and for a man without any resource of any kind, the whole existence is barren of any hope.

Varam Vanam Vyaaghragajendra Sevitam Drumaalayam
Pakkvaphalaambusevanam.
Trineshu Shayaa Shatjeernavallkalam Na Bandhumaddhye Dhanheena Jeevanam.

It is imprudent to stay in a jungle teeming with panthers and elephants; to dwell beneath the trees and survive by eating wild fruits and drinking (unchecked) water; to sleep on the bed made of wild straw and wear clothes made of the bark of the trees. But, if one is forced to dwell among his close relations as a pauper, it is better to go and stay in the jungles under the conditions explained above rather than stay there. Meaning that if a person is poor and moneyless; he had better stay in a jungle suffering the wildest conditions rather than stay as a pauper among his relations.

Anaagat vidhaataa Cha Prattutpannamatistathaa.
Dvaavetau Sukhameveta Yaddbhavishyo Vinashyati.

He who is aware of the future troubles and possesses sharp intelligence remains happy. In contradistinction to this stage, he who remains inactive, waiting for the good days to come destroys his own life.

A far-sighted and intelligent person is able to tackle the troubles far more efficiently than that fatalist sluggard who eventually gets destroyed by his lack of foresight and inactivity.

CHAPTER 5

KAUTILYA'S ARTHASHASHASTRA

BOOK 1: CONCERNING THE DISCIPLINE

Arthashastra is a science to the extent that it provides a practical manual for the means and manner of territorial acquisition and, once acquired, proper maintenance and protection of that territory. It is an art to the extent that the practitioner must rely on experience and wisdom, informed by the general rules and guidelines Kautilya provides, for application in specific contexts. In this way, Arthashastra provides a strategy for governments to protect their territories, gain the territories of others, and maintain all these territories properly and well. It encompasses both the administration and foreign policy of the state. It is the art and science of statecraft; of politics and administration.

The primary theme of Arthashastra is ruling well. Artha is a word with many forms or meaning. For instance, it is used to denote material well-being, livelihood, and economically productive activity. At the level of the state, government plays an important role in ensuring the material well-being of the nation and its people. Therefore, Arthashastra includes guidance on the productive enterprises, taxation, revenue collection, budget, and is in this manner the part of economics. The significance of successful economically-oriented political activities is critical to the state treasury (Kosha) or economy of the state. Therefore, Kautilya in Arthashastra enumerates the importance of maintaining the right balance between the welfare of the people and augmenting the resources of the state. As a result, an efficient administration ensuring law and order and upholding the fabric of society is a prerequisite for successful governance of the state. Kautilya, thus advocates that the ruler, to ensure protection of the state from external aggression (raksha), maintenance of law within the state (palana), and safeguarding the welfare of the people (yogashema), takes an active interest in economic affairs. Preceding the admonition of Machiavelli by nearly two millennia, that the state which fails to grow ultimately withers and dies, Kautilya insists that the prosperity of the state and its inhabitants cannot be maintained unless new territory is acquired by settlement of virgin lands, by alliance, or by conquest. In a political environment with many kings, being content with one's own territory makes one vulnerable to the expansionist ambitions of the other kings. To deal with the aspirations of other kings, employment of numerous peaceful or hostile means (referred to as foreign policy, below) is advocated by Kautilya. Since conquest provided the primary means for acquisition (labha) of new territory, preparing for, and waging war constituted an integral part of Kautilya's Arthashastra. Understanding war as more than mere combat, as a complex and interconnected set of activities across layers of human interaction, Kautilya set down the guidelines of a complete governing system. Thus, Arthashastra is an art of governance that includes administration (law order and justice), economy (taxation, revenue, and expenditure), and foreign policy (defense and war). It is important to note that Kautilyan society followed traditional Hindu form, and was comprised mainly of four classes and various sub-classes. The Brahmins were priests involved in sacred knowledge. Kshatriyas were warriors, incorporated into the military, for the protection of the country. Vaishyas were associated with agriculture, cattle rearing, and subsequently trade and commerce. Shudras were the backbone of the productive capacity of the country, serving as agriculturists, artisans, and craftsmen. Shudras constituted the labor community and also functioned as artists for entertainment of the public. While Kautilya advocated the protection of class system, he regarded the state as superior to religion, also insisting that a large conquering army must include men who were Vaishyas and Shudras to augment the Kshatriyas. Kautilya promoted the state power, over the demands of class and religion. —Artha is the sustenance or livelihood (vrtitih) of men; it means: the earth inhabited by men. Arthashastra is thus an extension of artha to the highest levels of society; it is —the science which is the means of the acquisition and protection of the earth. In India, since time immemorial, artha has been considered one of three realms of human existence: Dharma, Artha, and Kama. These denote legal relations, political and economic relations, and individual and social relations. Artha concerns the earth where people live and seek their individual material well-being. Arthashastra is the science concerned with providing and extending general well-being on earth. Since state activity alone can make such general well-being possible, the protection of earth (territory) and its acquisition—essential duties of proper state activity—is integral to the science. Accordingly, Arthashastra has a twofold aim: it provides guidance to the ruler to protect (palana) his territory and, secondly, it shows how territory should be acquired (labha). Therefore, Arthashastra is a science dealing with state affairs in the internal and external spheres; it is the science of statecraft or of politics, administration, and diplomacy.

The Arthashastra is concerned with the security and foreign policy needs of a state interacting with numerous other states, what we would term today a multipolar state system. From his theoretical concepts and analysis of the interactions of such a system, Kautilya offers four devices or models to provide practical advice for specific situations. These are relative power, deviations from the ideal, classification by type of motivation, and the influence of the intangible and the unpredictable.

To sum up, Kautilya's Arthashastra is an anthology of political wisdom and theory—the essence of an art of statecraft. According to Kautilya, the focus of statecraft should always be the safety and comfort of the people of the state—the word artha simply denotes the material well-being of the individuals. Kautilya argues that the wealth of the nation is in its territory and the people who follow a variety of specific occupations.1 Consequently, the state has an important role in maintaining both the physical size of the state and the skills and interests of its population, and it is the highest duty of the king to provide security to the people while preserving the wealth of the people. To do so, state leadership is required to ensure maintenance of law and order and to uphold the fabric of the society. In other words, the state provides internal security and maintains social order for the people of the state.

As we have noted earlier that the Kautilya's Arthashastra consists of 15 books and 150 chapters; in this, and the following chapters, we shall give the English translations of some selected books and chapters.

5.1   ARTHASHASTRA, BOOK 1, CHAPTER 6:

Shaking Off of the Aggregate of the Six Enemies

Restraint of the organs of sense, on which success in study and discipline depends, can be enforced by abandoning lust, anger, greed, vanity, haughtiness (mada), and overjoy (harsha).

Absence of discrepancy in the perception of sound, touch, colour, flavour, and scent by means of the ear, the skin, the eyes, the tongue, and the nose, is what is meant by the restraint of the organs of sense. Strict observance of the precepts of sciences also means the same; for the sole aim of all the sciences is nothing but restraint of the organs of sense.

Whosoever is of reverse character, whoever has not his organs of sense under his control, will soon perish, though possessed of the whole earth bounded by the four quarters.

For example: Bhoja, known also by the name Dāṇḍakya, making a lascivious attempt on a Brāhman maiden, perished along with his kingdom and relations.

So also Karāla, the Vaideha. Likewise Janamejaya under the influence of anger against Brahmanas, as well as Tālajaṅgha against the family of Bhṛgus.

Aila in his attempt under the influence of greed to make exactions from Brahmanas, as well as Ajabindu, the Sauvīra (in a similar attempt).

Rāvaṇa, unwilling under the influence of vanity to restore a stranger's wife, as well as Duryodhana, to part with a portion of his kingdom; Dambhodbhava as well as Arjuna of Haihaya dynasty being so haughty as to despise all people.

Vātāpi, in his attempt under the influence of overjoy to attack Agastya, as well as the corporation of the Vṛṣnis in their attempt against Dvaipāyana.

Thus, these and other several kings, falling a prey to the aggregate of the six enemies, and having failed to restrain their organs of sense, perished together with their kingdom and relations. Having driven out the aggregate of the six enemies, Ambarīṣa of Jāmadagnya, famous for his restraint of the organs of sense, as well as Nābhāga, long enjoyed the earth.

5.2 ARTHASHASTRA. BOOK 1, CHAPTER 7: LIFE OF A SAINTLY KING

Hence, by overthrowing the aggregate of the six enemies (mentioned above), he shall restrain the organs of sense; acquire wisdom by keeping company with the aged; see through his spies; establish safety and security by being ever active; maintain his subjects in the observance of their respective duties by exercising authority; keep up his personal discipline by receiving lessons in the science; and endear himself to the people by bringing them in contact with wealth and doing good to them.

Thus, with his organs of sense under his control, he shall keep away from hurting the woman and property of others; avoid not only lustfulness, even in dream, but also falsehood, haughtiness, and evil proclivities; and keep away from unrighteous and uneconomical transactions.

Not violating righteousness and economy, he shall enjoy his desires. He shall never be devoid of happiness. He may enjoy in an equal degree the three pursuits of life, charity, wealth, and desire, which are inter-dependent upon each other. Any one of these three, when enjoyed to an excess, hurts not only the other two, but also itself.

Kauṭilya holds that wealth, and wealth alone, is important, inasmuch as charity and desire depend upon wealth for their realisation.

Those teachers and ministers who keep him from falling a prey to dangers, and who, by striking the hours of the day as determined by measuring shadows, warn him of his careless proceedings even in secret, shall invariably be respected.

Sovereignty is possible only with assistance. A single wheel can never move. Hence, he (the king) shall employ ministers and hear their opinion.

5.3   ARTHASHASTRA, BOOK 1, CHAPTER 10: CHARACTER OF MINISTERS

Assisted by his prime minister and his high priest, the king shall, by offering temptations, examine the character of ministers appointed in government departments of ordinary nature.

The king shall dismiss a priest who, when ordered, refuses to teach the Vedas to an outcaste person or to officiate in a sacrificial performance undertaken by an outcaste person.

Then the dismissed priest shall, through the medium of spies under the guise of classmates, instigate each minister, one after another, saying on oath, "This king is unrighteous; well, let us set up in his place another king who is righteous, or who is born of the same family as of this king, or who is kept imprisoned, or a neighbouring king of his family and of self-sufficiency, or a wild chief, or an upstart; this attempt is to the liking of all of us; what dost thou think?"

If any one or all of the ministers refuse to acquiesce in such a measure, he or they shall be considered pure. This is what is called religious allurement.

A commander of the army, dismissed from service for receiving condemnable things, may, through the agency of spies under the guise of classmates, incite each minister to murder the king in view of acquiring immense wealth, each minister being asked, "This attempt is to the liking of all of us; what dost thou think?"

If they refuse to agree, they are to be considered pure. This is what is termed monetary allurement.

A woman-spy, under the guise of an ascetic and highly esteemed in the harem of the king, may allure each prime minister, one after another, saying, "The queen is enamoured of thee and has made arrangements for thy entrance into her chamber; besides this, there is also the certainty of large acquisitions of wealth."

If they discard the proposal, they are pure. This is what is styled love allurement.

With the intention of sailing on a commercial vessel, a minister may induce all other ministers to follow him. Apprehensive of danger, the king may arrest them all. A spy, under the guise of a fraudulent disciple, pretending to have suffered imprisonment, may incite each of the ministers thus deprived of wealth and rank, saying, "The king has betaken himself to an unwise course; well, having murdered him, let us put another in his stead. We all like this; what dost thou think?"

If they refuse to agree, they are pure. This is what is termed allurement under fear.

Of these tried ministers, those whose character has been tested under religious allurements shall be employed in civil and criminal courts; those whose purity has been tested under monetary allurements shall be employed in the work of a revenue collector and chamberlain; those who have been tried under love allurements shall be appointed to superintend the pleasure grounds, both external and internal; those who have been tested by allurements under fear shall be appointed to immediate service; and those whose character has been tested under all kinds of allurements shall be employed as prime ministers, while those who are proved impure under one or all of these allurements shall be appointed in mines, timber and elephant forests, and factories.

Teachers have decided that, in accordance with ascertained purity, the king shall employ in corresponding works those ministers whose character has been tested under the three pursuits of life, religion, wealth and love, and under fear.

Never, in the view of Kauṭilya, shall the king make himself or his queen an object of testing the character of his councillors, nor shall he vitiate the pure, like water with poison.

Sometimes the prescribed medicine may fail to reach the person of moral disease; the mind of the valiant, though naturally kept steadfast, may not, when once vitiated and repelled under the four kinds of allurements, return to and recover its original form.

Hence, having set up an external object as the butt for all the four kinds of allurements, the king shall, through the agency of spies, find out the pure or impure character of his ministers.

5.4 ARTHASHASTRA, BOOK 1, CHAPTER 11: INSTITUTION OF SPIES

Assisted by the council of his ministers tried under espionage, the king shall proceed to create spies: Spies under the guise of a fraudulent disciple, a recluse, a householder, a merchant, an ascetic practising austerities, a classmate or a colleague, a fire-brand, a poisoner, and a mendicant woman. A skilful person capable of guessing the mind of others is a fraudulent disciple. Having encouraged such a spy with honour and money rewards, the minister shall tell him, "Sworn to the king and myself, thou shalt inform us of whatever wickedness thou findest in others."

One, who is initiated in asceticism and is possessed of foresight and pure character is a recluse. This spy, provided with much money and many disciples, shall carry on agriculture, cattle-rearing, and trade on the lands allotted to him for the purpose. Out of the produce and profits thus acquired, he shall provide all ascetics with subsistence, clothing and lodging, and send on espionage such among those under his protection as are desirous to earn a livelihood, ordering each one of them to detect a particular kind of crime committed in connection with the king's wealth, and to report of it when they come to receive their subsistence and wages. All the ascetics (under the recluse) shall severally send their followers on similar errands.

A cultivator, fallen from his profession, but possessed of foresight and pure character, is termed a householder spy. This spy shall carry on the cultivation of lands allotted to him for the purpose, and maintain cultivators, etc.—as before.

A trader, fallen from his profession, but possessed of foresight and pure character, is a merchant spy. This spy shall carry on the manufacture of merchandise on lands allotted to him for the purpose, etc.—as before.

A man with shaved head or braided hair and desirous to earn livelihood is a spy under the guise of an ascetic practising austerities. Such a spy surrounded by a host of disciples with shaved head or braided hair may take his abode in the suburbs of a city, and pretend as a persons

barely living on a handful of vegetables or meadow grass taken once in the interval of a month or two, but he may take in secret his favourite foodstuffs.

Merchant spies pretending to be his disciples may worship him as one possessed of preternatural powers. His other disciples may widely proclaim that "this ascetic is an accomplished expert of preternatural powers."

Regarding those persons who, desirous of knowing their future, throng to him, he may, through palmistry, foretell such future events as he can ascertain by the nods and signs of his disciples concerning the works of highborn people of the country—viz. small profits, destruction by fire, fear from robbers, the execution of the seditious, rewards for the good, forecast of foreign affairs, saying, "This will happen to-day, that to-morrow, and that this king will do." Such assertions of the ascetic, his disciples shall corroborate (by adducing facts and figures).

He shall also foretell not only the rewards which persons possessed of foresight, eloquence, and bravery are likely to receive at the hands of the king, but also probable changes in the appointments of ministers.

The king's minister shall direct his affairs in conformity to the forecast made by the ascetic. He shall appease with offer of wealth and honour those who have had some well-known cause to be disaffected, and impose punishments in secret on those who are for no reason disaffected or who are plotting against the king.

Honoured by the king with awards of money and titles, these five institutes of espionage, shall ascertain the purity of character of the king's servants.

5.5 ARTHASHASTRA, BOOK 1, CHAPTER 14: WINNING OVER FACTIONS

Those who are deluded with false promise of large rewards; those of whom one party, though equally skilful as another party in artistic work or in turning out productive or beneficial works, is slighted by bestowing larger rewards on its rival party; those who are harassed by courtiers; those who are invited to be slighted; those who are harassed by banishment; those who, in spite of their large outlay of money, have failed in their undertakings; those who are prevented from the exercise of their rights or from taking possession of their inheritance; those who have fallen from their rank and honours in government service; those who are shoved to the corner by their own kinsmen; those whose women are violently assaulted; those who are thrown in jail; those who are punished in secret; those who are warned of their misdeeds; those whose property has been wholly confiscated; those who have long suffered from imprisonment; those whose relatives are banished—all these come under the group of provoked persons.

He, who has fallen a victim to misfortune by his own misdeeds; he who is offended (by the king); he whose sinful deeds are brought to light; he who is alarmed at the award of punishment on a man of like guilt; he whose lands have been confiscated; he whose rebellious spirit is put down by coercive measures; he who, as a superintendent of all government departments, has suddenly amassed a large amount of wealth; he who, as a relative of such a rich man, aspires to inherit his wealth; he who is disliked by the king; and he who hates the king—ail these come under the group of persons alarmed.

He who is impoverished; he who has lost much wealth; he who is niggardly; he who is addicted to evil propensities; and he who is engaged in dangerous transactions—all these constitute the group of ambitious persons.

He who is self-sufficient; he who is fond of honour; he who is intolerant of his rival's honour; he who is esteemed low; he who is of a fiery spirit; he who is foolhardy as well as he who is not content with what he has been enjoying—all these come under the group of haughty persons.

Of these, he who clings to a particular faction shall be so deluded by spies with shaved head or braided hair as to believe that he is intriguing with that part. Partisans under provocation, for example, may be won over by telling that "Just as an elephant in rut and mounted over by a driver under intoxication tramples under its foot whatever it comes across, so this king, dispossessed of the eye of science, blindly attempts to oppress both citizens and country people; it is possible to restrain him by setting up a rival elephant against him; so, have forbearance enough (to wait)."

Likewise alarmed persons may be won over by telling that "Just as a hidden snake bites and emits poison over whatever alarms it, so this king, apprehensive of danger from thee, will ere long emit the poison of his resentment on thee; so, thou mayest better go elsewhere."

Similarly, ambitious persons may be won over by telling that "Just as a cow reared by dog-keepers gives milk to dogs, but not to Brahmanas, so this king gives milk (rewards) to those who are devoid of valour, foresight, eloquence and bravery, but not to those who are possessed of noble character; so, the other king, who is possessed of power to discriminate men from men, may be courted."

In like manner haughty persons may be won over by telling that "Just as a reservoir of water belonging to Cāṇḍālas is serviceable only to Cāṇḍālas, but not to others, so this king of low birth confers his patronage only on low-born people, but not on Aryas like thee; so, the other king, who is possessed of power to distinguish between men and men, may be courted."

All these disaffected persons, when acquiescing to the above proposals, may be made under a solemn compact to form a combination together with the spies to achieve their end.

Likewise, friends of a foreign king may also be won over by means of persuasion and rewards, while implacable enemies may be brought round by sowing dissensions, by threats, and by pointing out the defects of their master.

5.6 ARTHASHASTRA, BOOK 1, CHAPTER 16: MISSION OF ENVOYS

Whoever has succeeded as a councillor is an envoy.

Whoever possesses ministerial qualifications is a charge d'affaires.

Whoever possesses the same qualifications less by one quarter is an agent entrusted with a definite mission.

Whoever possesses the same qualifications less by one-half is a conveyer of royal writs.

Having made excellent arrangements for carriage, conveyance, servants and subsistence, he (an envoy) shall start on his mission, thinking that "The enemy shall be told thus: the enemy will say thus; this shall be the reply to him; and thus, he shall be imposed upon."

The envoy shall make friendship with the enemy's officers such as those in charge of wild tracts, of boundaries, of cities, and of country parts. He shall also contrast the military stations, sinews of war, and strongholds of the enemy with those of his own master. He shall ascertain the size and area of forts and of the state, as well as strongholds of precious things and assailable and unassailable points.

Having obtained permission, he shall enter into the capital of the enemy, and state the object of the mission as exactly as entrusted to him, even at the cost of his own life.

Brightness in the tone, face and eyes of the enemy; respectful reception of the mission; enquiry about the health of friends; taking part in the narration of virtues; giving a seat close to the throne; respectful treatment of the envoy; remembrance of friends; closing the mission with satisfaction—all these shall be noted as indicating the good graces of the enemy, and the reverse his displeasure.

A displeased enemy may be told:

"Messengers are the mouthpieces of kings, not only of thyself, but of all; hence messengers who, in the face of weapons raised against them, have to express their mission as exactly as they are entrusted with, do not, though outcastes, deserve death; where is then reason to put messengers of Brāhman caste to death? This is another's speech. This (i.e. delivery of that speech verbatim) is the duty of messengers."

Not puffed up with the respects shown to him, he shall stay there till he is allowed to depart. He shall not care for the mightiness of the enemy; shall strictly avoid women and liquor; shall take bed single; for it is well known that the intentions of envoys are ascertained while they are asleep or under the influence of liquor.

He shall, through the agency of ascetic and merchant spies or through their disciples, or through spies under the disguise of physicians, and heretics, or through recipients of salaries from two states, ascertain the nature of the intrigue prevalent among parties favourably disposed to his own master, as well as the conspiracy of hostile factions, and understand the loyalty or disloyalty of the people to the enemy, besides any assailable points.

If there is no possibility of carrying on any such conversation (conversation with the people regarding their loyalty), he may try to gather such information by observing the talk of beggars, intoxicated and insane persons, or of persons babbling in sleep, or by observing the signs made in places of pilgrimage and temples, or by deciphering paintings and secret writings.

Whatever information he thus gathers, he shall try to test by intrigues.

He shall not check the estimate which the enemy makes of the elements of sovereignty of his own master; but he shall only say in reply, "All is known to thee." Nor shall he disclose the means employed (by his master) to achieve an end in view.

If he has not succeeded in his mission, but is still detained, he shall proceed to infer thus:

"Whether seeing the imminent danger into which my master is likely to fall and desirous of averting his own danger; whether in view of inciting against my master an enemy threatening in the rear or a king whose dominion in the rear is separated by other intervening states; whether in view of causing internal rebellion in my masters' state, or of inciting a wild chief against my master; whether in view of destroying my master by employing a friend or a king whose dominion stretches out in the rear of my master's state; whether with the intention of averting the internal trouble in his own state or of preventing a foreign invasion or the inroads of a wild chief; whether in view of causing the approaching time of my master's expedition to lapse; whether with the desire of collecting raw materials and merchandise, or of repairing his fortifications, or of recruiting a strong army capable to fight; whether waiting for the time and opportunity necessary for the complete training of his own army; or whether in view of making a desirable alliance in order to avert the present contempt brought about by his own carelessness, this king detains me thus."

Then he may stay or get out as he deems it desirable; or he may demand a speedy settlement of his mission.

Or having intimated an unfavourable order to the enemy, and pretending apprehension of imprisonment or death, he may return even without permission; otherwise, he may be punished.

Transmission of missions, maintenance of treaties, issue of ultimatum, gaining of friends, intrigue, sowing dissension among friends, fetching secret force; carrying away by stealth relatives and gems, gathering information about the movements of spies, bravery, breaking of treaties of peace, winning over the favour of the envoy and government officers of the enemy—these are the duties of an envoy.

The king shall employ his own envoys to carry on works of the above description, and guard himself against (the mischief of) foreign envoys by employing counter envoys, spies, and visible and invisible watchmen.

5.7   ARTHASHASTRA, BOOK 1, CHAPTER 19: DUTIES OF A KING

If a king is energetic, his subjects will be equally energetic. If he is reckless, they will not only be reckless likewise, but also eat into his works. Besides, a reckless king will easily fall into the hands of his enemies. Hence the king shall ever be wakeful.

He shall divide both the day and the night into eight nālikās (11 hours), or according to the length of the shadow (cast by a gnomon standing in the sun): the shadow of three puruṣās (36 aṅgulās or finches), of one puruṣa (12 inches), of four aṅgulās (3 inches), and absence of shadow denoting midday are the four one-eighth divisions of the forenoon; like divisions (in the reverse order) in the afternoon.

Of these divisions, during the first one-eighth part of the day, he shall post watchmen and attend to the accounts of receipts and expenditure; during the second part, he shall look to the affairs of both citizens and country people; during the third, he shall not only bathe and dine, but also study; during the fourth, he shall not only receive revenue in gold but also attend to the appointments of superintendents; during the fifth, he shall correspond in writs with the assembly of his ministers, and receive the secret information gathered by his spies; during the sixth, he may engage himself in his favourite amusements or in self-deliberation; during the seventh, he shall superintend elephants, horses, chariots, and infantry; and during the eighth part, he shall consider various plans of military operations with his commander-in-chief.

At the close of the day, he shall observe the evening prayer.

During the first one-eighth part of the night, he shall receive secret emissaries; during the second, he shall attend to bathing and supper and study; during the third, he shall enter the bedchamber amid the sound of trumpets and enjoy sleep during the fourth and fifth parts; having been awakened by the sound of trumpets during the sixth part, he shall recall to his mind the injunctions of sciences as well as the day's duties; during the seventh, he shall sit considering administrative measures and send out spies; and during the eighth division of the night, he shall receive benedictions from sacrificial priests, teachers and the high priest, and having seen his physician, chief cook and astrologer, and having saluted, both a cow. with its calf and a bull by circumambulating round them, he shall get into his court.

Or in conformity to his capacity, he may alter the time-table and attend to his duties.

When in the court, he shall never cause his petitioners to wait at the door, for when a king makes himself inaccessible to his people and entrusts his work to his immediate officers, he may be sure to engender confusion in business, and to cause thereby public disaffection, and himself a prey to his enemies.

He shall, therefore, personally attend to the business of gods, of heretics, of Brāhmans learned in the Vedas, of cattle, of sacred places, of minors, the aged, the afflicted, and the helpless, and of women;—all this in order (of enumeration) or according to the urgency or pressure of those works.

All urgent calls he shall hear at once, but never put off; for when postponed, they will prove too hard or impossible to accomplish.

Having seated himself in the room where the sacred fire has been kept, he shall attend to the business of physicians and ascetics practising austerities; and that in company with his high priest and teacher and after preliminary salutation (to the petitioners).

Accompanied by persons proficient in the three sciences (trividyā) but not alone lest the petitioners be offended, he shall look to the business of those who are practising austerities, as well as of those who are experts in witchcraft and Yoga.

Of a king, the religious vow is his readiness to action; satisfactory discharge of duties is his performance of sacrifice; equal attention to all is the offer of fees and ablution towards consecration.

In the happiness of his subjects lies his happiness; in their welfare his welfare; whatever pleases himself he shall not consider as good, but whatever pleases his subjects he shall consider as good.

Hence the king shall ever be active and discharge his duties; the root of wealth is activity, and of evil its reverse.

In the absence of activity acquisitions present and to come will perish; by activity he can achieve both his desired ends and abundance of wealth.

5.8 ARTHASHASTRA, BOOK 1, CHAPTER 21: PERSONAL SAFETY OF A KING

On getting up from the bed, the king shall be received by troops of women armed with bows. In the second compartment, he shall be received by the Kañcuki (presenter of the king's coat), the Uṣṇīṣi (presenter of king's head-dress), aged persons, and other harem attendants.

In the third compartment, he. shall be received by crooked and dwarfish persons; in the fourth, by prime ministers, kinsmen, and door-keepers with barbed missiles in their hand.

The king shall employ as his personal attendants those whose fathers and grandfathers had been royal servants, those who bear close relationship to the king, those who are well trained and loyal, and those who have rendered good service.

Neither foreigners, nor those who have earned neither rewards nor honour by rendering good service, nor even natives found engaged in inimical works shall form the bodyguard of the king or the troops of the officers in charge of the harem.

In a well-guarded locality, the head-cook shall supervise the preparation of varieties of relishing dishes. The king shall partake of such fresh dishes after making an oblation out of them first to the, fire and then to birds.

When the flame and the smoke turn blue and crackle, and when birds (that eat the oblation) die, presence of poison (in the dish) shall be inferred. When the vapour arising from cooked rice possesses the colour of the neck of a peacock, and appears chill as if suddenly cooled, when vegetables possess an unnatural colour, and are watery and hardened, and appear to have suddenly turned dry, being possessed of broken layers of blackish foam, and being devoid of smell, touch and taste natural to them; when utensils reflect light either more or less than usual, and are covered with a layer of foam at their edges; when any liquid preparation possesses streaks on its surface; when milk bears a bluish streak in the centre of its surface; when liquor and water possess reddish streaks; when curd is marked with black and dark streaks, and honey with white streaks; when watery things appear parched as if over-cooked and look blue and swollen; when dry things have shrunk and changed in their colour; when hard things appear soft, and soft things hard; when minute animalcule die in the vicinity of the dishes; when carpets and curtains possess blackish circular spots, with their threads and hair fallen off; when metallic vessels set with gems appear tarnished as though by roasting, and have lost their polish, colour, shine, and softness of touch, presence of poison shall be inferred.

As to the person who has administered poison, the marks are parched and dry mouth; hesitation in speaking; heavy perspiration; yawning; too much bodily tremor; frequent tumbling; evasion of speech; carelessness in work; and unwillingness to keep to the place assigned to him.

Hence physicians and experts capable of detecting poison shall ever attend upon the king.

Having taken out from the store-room of medicines that medicine the purity of which has been proved by experiment, and having himself together with the decoction and the purveyor tested it, the physician shall hand over the medicine to the king. The same rule shall apply to liquor and other beverages.

Having cleaned their person and hands by fresh bath and put on newly-washed garment, servants in charge of dresses and toilets shall serve the king with dresses and toilets received under seal from the officer in-charge of the harem.

Prostitutes shall do the duty of bath-room servants, shampooers, bedding-room servants, washermen, and flower garland-makers, while presenting to the king water, scents, fragrant powders, dress and garlands; servants along with the above prostitutes shall first touch these things by their eyes, arms and breast.

The same rule shall apply to whatever has been received from an outside person.

Musicians shall entertain the king with those kinds of amusements in which weapons, fire, and poison are not made use of. Musical instruments as well as the ornaments of horses, chariots, and elephants shall invariably be kept inside (the harem).

The king shall mount over chariots or beasts of burden only when they are first mounted over by his hereditary driver or rider.

He shall get into a boat only when it is piloted by a trustworthy sailor and is conjoined to a second boat. He shall never sail on any ship which had once been weather-beaten; and (while boating on a good ship) his army shall all the while stand on the bank or the shore.

He shall get into such water as is free from large fishes and crocodiles. He shall ramble only in such forests as are freed from snakes and crocodiles.

With a view of acquiring efficiency in the skill of shooting arrows at moving objects, he shall engage himself in sports only in such forests as are cleared by hunters and hound-keepers from the fear of highway-robbers, snakes, and enemies.

Attended by trustworthy bodyguard armed with weapons, he shall give interview to saints and ascetics. Surrounded by his assembly of ministers, he shall receive the envoys of foreign states.

Attired in military dress and having mounted a horse, a chariot or an elephant, he shall go to see his army equipped in military array.

On the occasion of going out of, and coming into (the capital), the king's road shall on both sides be well-guarded by staff-bearers and freed from the presence of armed persons and ascetics.

He shall go to witness festive trains, fairs, procession, or sacrificial performances only when they are policed by bands of "The Ten Communities".

Just as he attends to the personal safety of others through the agency of spies, so a wise king shall also take care to secure his person from external dangers.

CHAPTER 6

KAUTILYA'S ARTHASHASHASTRA, BOOK 2: DUTIES OF GOVERNMENT SUPERINTENDENTS

6.1 ARTHASHASTRA, BOOK 2, CHAPTER 2: DIVISION OF LAND

The king shall make provision for pasture grounds on uncultivable tracts.

Brāhmans shall be provided with forests for sema plantation, for religious learning, and for the performance of penance, such forests being granted with safety for animate or inanimate objects, and being named after the tribal name (gotra) of the Brāhmans resident therein.

A forest as extensive as the above, provided with only one entrance, rendered inaccessible by the construction of ditches all round, with plantations of delicious fruit trees, bushes, bowers, and thornless trees, with an expansive lake of water, full of harmless animals, and with tigers, beasts of prey, male and female elephants, young elephants, and bisons—all deprived of their claws and teeth—shall be formed for the king's sports.

On the extreme limit of the country or in any other suitable locality, another game forest with game beasts, open to all, shall also be made. In view of procuring all kinds of forest produce, one or several forests shall be specially reserved.

Manufactories to prepare commodities from forest produce and forests productive of commodities shall also be set up.

In the extreme limit of the country, elephant forests, separated from wild tracts, shall be formed.

The superintendent of elephant forests with his retinue of forest guards shall not only maintain the upkeep of the forests, but also acquaint himself with all passages for entrance into, or exit from, such of them as are mountainous or boggy or contain rivers or lakes.

Whoever kills an elephant shall be put to death.

Whoever brings in the pair of tusks of an elephant, dead from natural causes, shall receive a reward of four-and-a-half paṇas.

Guards of elephant forests, assisted by those who rear elephants, those who enchain the legs of elephants, those who guard the boundaries, those who live in forests, as well as by those who nurse elephants, shall, with the help of five or seven female elephants to help in tethering wild ones, trace the whereabouts of herds of elephants by following the course of urine and dungs left by elephants and along forest tracts covered over with branches of Bhallātakī, and by observing the spots where elephants slept or sat before or left dungs, or where they had just destroyed the banks of rivers or lakes. They shall also precisely ascertain whether any mark is due to the movements of elephants in herds, of an elephant roaming single, of a stray elephant, of a leader of herds, of a tusker, of a rogue elephant, of an elephant in rut, of a young elephant, or of an elephant that has escaped from the cage.

Experts in catching elephants shall follow the instructions given to them by the elephant doctor, and catch such elephants as are possessed of auspicious characteristics and good character.

The victory of kings (in battles) depends mainly upon elephants; for elephants, being of large bodily frame, are capable not only to destroy the arrayed army of an enemy, his fortifications and encampments, but also to undertake works that are dangerous to life.

Elephants bred in countries, such as Kaliṅga, Aṅga, Karūśa, and the East are the best; those of the Daśārṇa and western countries are of middle quality; and those of Saurāṣṭra and Pañcajana countries are of low quality. The might and energy of all can, however, be improved by suitable training.

6.2 ARTHASHASTRA, BOOK 2, CHAPTER 3, CONSTRUCTION OF FORTS

On all the four quarters of the boundaries of the kingdom, defensive fortifications against an enemy in war shall be constructed on grounds naturally best fitted for the purpose: a water-fortification, such as an island in the midst of a river, or a plain surrounded by low ground, a mountainous fortification, such as a rocky tract or a cave; a desert, such as a wild tract devoid of water and overgrown with thicket growing in barren soil; or a forest fortification, full of wagtail, water and thickets.

Of these, water and mountain fortifications are best suited to defend populous centres; and desert and forest fortifications are habitations in wilderness.

Or having no refuge in times of dangers, the king may have his fortified capital (sthāniya) as the seat of his treasury in the centre of his kingdom: in a locality naturally best fitted for the purpose, such as the bank of the confluence of rivers, a deep pool of perennial water, or of a lake or tank, a fort, circular, rectangular, or square in form, surrounded with an artificial canal of water, and connected with both land and water paths (may be constructed).

Round this fort, three ditches with an intermediate space of one daṇḍa (six feet) from each other, fourteen, twelve and ten daṇḍas respectively in width, with depth less by one-quarter or by one-half of their width, square at their bottom and one-third as wide as at their top, with sides built of stones or bricks, filled with perennial flowing water or with water drawn from some other source, and possessing crocodiles and lotus plants shall be constructed.

At a distance of four daṇḍas (24 feet) from the (innermost) ditch, a rampart, six daṇḍas high and twice as much broad, shall be erected by heaping mud upwards and by making it square at the bottom, oval at the centre, pressed by the trampling of elephants and bulls, and planted with thorny and poisonous plants in bushes. Gaps in the rampart shall be filled up with fresh earth.

Above the rampart, parapets in odd or even numbers and with an intermediate space of from 12 to 24 hastas from each other shall be built of bricks and raised to a height of twice their breadth.

The passage for chariots shall be made of trunks of palm trees or of broad and thick slabs of stones with spheres like the head of a monkey carved on their surface; but never of wood, as fire finds a happy abode in it.

Towers, square throughout and with moveable staircase or ladder equal to its height, shall also be constructed.

In the intermediate space, measuring thirty daṇḍas, between two towers, there shall be formed a broad street with two-storied buildings covered over with a roof, and two-and-half times as long as it is broad.

Between the tower and the broad street there shall be constructed an Indrakośa, which is made up of covering pieces of perforated wooden planks, affording seats for three archers.

There shall also be made a road for gods which shall measure two hastas inside the (Indrakośa), four times as much by the sides, and eight hastas along the parapet.

Paths to ascend the parapet) as broad as a daṇḍa (six feet) or two shall also be made.

In an unassailable part (of the rampart), a passage for flight, and a door for exit shall be made.

Outside the rampart, passages for movements shall be closed by forming obstructions such as a knee-breaker, a trident, mounds of earth, pits, wreaths of thorns, instruments made like the tail of a snake, palm leaf, triangle, and of dog's teeth, rods, ditches filled with thorns and covered with sand, frying pans and water pools.

Having made on both sides the rampart bulge out to the extent of a daṇḍa-and-a-half, an entrance gate (to the fort) one-sixth as broad as the width of the street shall be fixed.

A square is formed by successive addition of one daṇḍa up to eight daṇḍas commencing from five, or in the proportion, one-sixth of the length up to one-eighth.

The rise in level shall be made by successive addition of one hasta up to 18 hastas, commencing from 15 hastas.

In fixing a pillar, six parts are to form its height on the floor, twice as much (12 parts) to be entered into the ground, and one-fourth for its capital.

Of the first floor, five parts (are to be taken) for the formation of a hall, a well, and a boundary house; two-tenths of it for the formation of two platforms opposite to each other; an upper storey twice as high as its width; carvings of images; an uppermost storey, half or three-fourths as broad as the first floor; side walls built of bricks; on the left side, a staircase circumambulating from left to right; on the right, a secret staircase hidden in the wall; a top-support of ornamental arches projecting as far as two hastas; two door-panels, (each) occupying three-fourths of the space; two and two cross-bars to fasten the door; an iron bolt (indrakīla) as long as an aratni (24 aṅgulas); a boundary gate five hastas in width; four beams to shut the door against elephants; and turrets (outside the rampart) raised up to the height of the face of a man, removable or irremovable, or made of earth in places devoid of water.

A turret above the gate and starting from the top of the parapet shall be constructed, its front resembling an alligator up to three-fourths of its height.

In the centre of the parapets, there shall be constructed a deep lotus pool; a rectangular building of four compartments, one within the other; an abode of the Goddess Kumāri, having its external area one-and-a-half times as broad as that of its innermost room; a circular building with an archway; and in accordance with available space and materials, there shall also be constructed canals to hold weapons, and three times as long as broad.

In those canals, there shall be collected stones, spades, axes, varieties of staffs, cudgels, hammers, clubs, discus, machines (yantra), and such weapons as can destroy a hundred persons at once, together with spears, tridents, bamboo-sticks with pointed edges made of iron, camel-necks, explosives, and whatever else can be devised and formed from available materials.

6.3 ARTHASHASTRA, BOOK 2, CHAPTER 8: DETECTION OF EMBEZZLEMENT

All undertakings depend upon finance. Hence foremost attention shall be paid to the treasury.

Public prosperity, rewards for good conduct, capture of thieves, dispensing with (the service of too many) government servants, abundance of harvest, prosperity of commerce, absence of troubles and calamities, diminution of remission of taxes, and income in gold are all conducive to financial prosperity.

Obstruction, loan, trading, fabrication of accounts, causing the loss of revenue, self-enjoyment, barter, and defalcation, are the causes that tend to deplete the treasury.

Failure to start an undertaking or to realise its results, or to credit its profits (to the treasury) is known as obstruction. Herein a fine of ten times the amount in question shall be imposed.

Lending the money of the treasury on periodical interest is a loan.

Carrying on trade by making use of government money is trading.

These two acts shall be punished with a fine of twice the profit earned.

Whoever makes as unripe the ripe time or as ripe the unripe time (of revenue collection) is guilty of fabrication. Herein a fine of ten times the amount shall be imposed.

Whoever lessens a fixed amount of income or enhances the expenditure is guilty of causing the loss of revenue. Herein a fine of four times the loss shall be imposed.

Whoever enjoys himself or causes others to enjoy whatever belongs to the king is guilty of self-enjoyment. Herein death sentence shall be passed for enjoying gems, middlemost amercement for enjoying valuable articles, and restoration of the articles together with a fine equal to their value shall be the punishment for enjoying articles of inferior value.

The act of exchanging government articles for (similar) articles of others is barter. This offence is explained by self-enjoyment.

Whoever does not take into the treasury the fixed amount of revenue collected, or does not spend what is ordered to be spent, or misrepresents the net revenue collected, is guilty of defalcation of government money. Herein a fine of twelve times the amount shall be imposed.

There are about forty ways of embezzlement:

> ➢ what is realized earlier is entered later on;
> ➢ what is realized later is entered earlier;
> ➢ what ought to be realized is not realized;
> ➢ what is hard to realize is shown as realized;
> ➢ what is collected is shown as not collected;
> ➢ what has not been collected is shown as collected;
> ➢ what is collected in part is entered as collected in full;
> ➢ what is collected in full is entered as collected in part;

- what is collected is of one sort, while what is entered is of another sort;
- what is realized from one source is shown as realized from another;
- what is payable is not paid; what is not payable is paid; not paid in time; paid untimely;
- small gifts made large gifts;
- large gifts made small gifts;
- what is gifted is of one sort while what is entered is of another;
- the real donee is one while the person entered (in the register) as donee is another;
- what has been taken into (the treasury) is removed while what has not been credited to it is shown as credited;
- raw materials that are not paid for are entered, while those that are paid for are not entered;
- an aggregate is scattered in pieces;
- scattered items are converted into an aggregate;
- commodities of greater value are bartered for those of small value;
- what is of smaller value is bartered for one of greater value;
- price of commodities enhanced;
- price of commodities lowered;
- number of nights increased;
- number of nights decreased;
- the year not in harmony with its months;
- the month not in harmony with its days;
- inconsistency in the transactions carried on with personal supervision;
- misrepresentation of the source of income;
- inconsistency in giving charities;
- incongruity in representing the work turned out;

> ➤ inconsistency in dealing with fixed items;
> ➤ misrepresentation of test marks or the standard of fineness (of gold and silver);
> ➤ misrepresentation of prices of commodities;
> ➤ making use of false weights and measures;
> ➤ deception in counting articles;
> ➤ and making use of false cubic measures such as bhājana— these are the several ways of embezzlement.

Under the above circumstances, the persons concerned, such as the treasurer, the prescriber, the receiver, the payer, the person who caused the payment, the ministerial servants of the officer shall each be separately examined. If any one of these tells a lie, he shall receive the same punishment as the chief officer who committed the offence.

A proclamation in public shall be made to the effect "whoever has suffered at the hands of this offender may make their grievances known to the king."

Those who respond to the call shall receive such compensation as is equal to the loss they have sustained.

When there are a number of offences in which a single officer is involved, and when his being guilty of parokta in any one of those charges has been established, he shall be answerable for all those offences. Otherwise (i.e. when it is not established), he shall be tried for each of the charges.

When a government servant has been proved to be guilty of having misappropriated part of a large sum in question, he shall be answerable for the whole.

Any informant who supplies information about embezzlement just under perpetration shall, if he succeeds in proving it, get as reward one-sixth of the amount in question; if he happens to be a government servant, he shall get for the same act one-twelfth of the amount.

If an informant succeeds in proving only a part of a big embezzlement, he shall, nevertheless, get the prescribed share of the part of the embezzled amount proved.

An informant who fails to prove (his assertion) shall be liable to monetary or corporal punishment, and shall never be acquitted.

When the charge is proved, the informant may impute the tale bearing to someone else or clear himself in any other way from the blame. Any informant who withdraws his assertion prevailed upon by the insinuations of the accused shall be condemned to death.

6.4   ARTHASHASTRA, BOOK 2, CHAPTER 12: CONDUCTING MINING OPERATIONS AND MANUFACTURE

Possessed of the knowledge of the science dealing with copper and other minerals experienced in the art of distillation and condensation of mercury and of testing gems, aided by experts in mineralogy and equipped with mining laborers and necessary instruments, the superintendent of mines shall examine mines which, on account of their containing mineral excrement, crucibles, charcoal, and ashes, may appear to have been once exploited or which may be newly discovered on plains or mountain slopes possessing mineral ores, the richness of which can be ascertained by weight, depth of colour, piercing smell, and taste.

Liquids which ooze out from pits, caves, slopes, or deep excavations of well-known mountains; which have the colour of the fruit of rose-apple (jambu), of mango, and of fan palm; which are as yellow as ripe turmeric, sulphurate of arsenic, honeycomb, and vermilion; which are as resplendent as the petals of a lotus, or the feathers of a parrot or a peacock; which are adjacent to (any mass of) water or shrubs of similar colour; and which are greasy, transparent, and very heavy are ores of gold. Likewise liquids which, when dropped on water, spread like oil to which dirt and filth adhere, and which amalgamate themselves more than cent per cent with copper or silver.

Of similar appearance as the above, but of piercing smell and taste, is bitumen.

Those ores which are obtained from plains or slopes of mountains; which are either yellow or as red as copper or reddish yellow; which are disjoined and marked with blue lines; which have the colour of black beans, green beans, and sesamum; which are marked with spots like a drop of curd and resplendent as turmeric, yellow myrobalan, petals of a lotus, aquatic plant, the liver or the spleen; which possess a sandy layer within them and are marked with figures of a circle or a svastika; which contain globular masses and which, when roasted do not split, but emit much foam and smoke are the ores of gold, and are used to form amalgams with copper or silver.

Those ores which have the colour of a conch shell, camphor, alum, butter, a pigeon, turtle dove, Vimalaka (a kind of precious stone), or the neck of a peacock; which are as resplendent as opal, agate, cane-sugar, and granulated sugar; which has the colour of the flower of kovidāra, of lotus, of pātalī, of kalāya (a kind of Phraseolus), of kṣauma (flax), and of atasī; which may be in combination with lead or iron; which smell like raw meat, are disjoined grey or blackish white, and are marked with lines or spots; and which, when roasted, do not split, but emit much foam and smoke are silver ores.

The heavier the ores, the greater will be the quantity of metal in them.

The impurities of ores, whether superficial or inseparably combined with them, can be got rid of and the metal melted when the ores are (chemically) treated with Tīkṣṇa, urine (mūtra), and alkalis, and are mixed or smeared over with the mixture of (the powder of) Rājavṛkṣa, Vaṭa, and Pīlu, together with cow's bile and the urine and dung of a buffalo, an ass and an elephant.

(Metals) are rendered soft when they are treated with (the powder of) kandalī (mushroom), and vajrakanda (Antiquorum) together with the ashes of barley, black beans, palāśā, and pīlu, or with the milk of both the cow and the sheep. Whatever metal is split into a hundred thousand parts is rendered soft when it is thrice soaked in the mixture made up of honey (madhu), madhuka, sheep's milk, sesamum oil, clarified butter, jaggery, kiṇva (ferment) and mushroom.

Permanent softness is also attained when the metal is treated with the powder of cow's teeth and horn.

Those ores which are obtained from plains or slopes of mountains; and which are heavy, greasy, soft, tawny, green, dark bluish-yellow, pale red, or red are ores of copper.

Those ores which have the colour of kākamecaka, pigeon, or cow's bile, and which are marked with white lines and smell like raw meat are the ores of lead.

Those ores which are as variegated in colour as saline soil or which have the colour of a burnt lump of earth are the ores of tin.

Those ores which are of orange colour (kurumba), or pale red, or of the colour of the flower of sinduvāra are the ores of tīkṣṇa.

Those ores which are of the colour of the leaf of kāṇḍa or of the leaf of birch are the ores of vaikṛntaka.

Pure, smooth, effulgent, sounding (when struck), very hard (śītatīvra), and of little colour (tanurāga) are precious stones.

The yield of mines may be put to such uses as are in vogue.

Commerce in commodities manufactured from mineral products shall be centralized, and punishment for manufacturers, sellers, and purchasers of such commodities outside the prescribed locality shall also be laid down.

A mine laborer who steals mineral products except precious stones shall be punished with a fine of eight times their value.

Any person who steals mineral products or carries on. mining operations without license, shall be bound (with chains) and caused to work (as a prisoner).

Mines which yield such minerals as are made use of in preparing vessels as well as those mines which require large outlay to work out may be leased out for a fixed number of the shares of the output or for a fixed rent. Such mines as can be worked out without much outlay shall be directly exploited (by government agency).

The superintendent of metals shall carry on the manufacture of copper, lead, tin, brass, bronze or bell-metal), tāla (sulphurate of arsenic), and lodhra, and also of commodities from them.

The superintendent of mint shall carry on the manufacture of silver coins made up of four parts of copper and one-sixteenth part of any one of the metals, tīkṣna, trapu, sīsa, and añjana. These shall be a paṇa, half a paṇa, a quarter and one-eighth.

Copper coins made up of four parts of an alloy (pādajīva) shall be a māṣaka, half a māṣaka, kākaṇī, and half a kākaṇī.

The examiner of coins shall regulate currency both as a medium of exchange and as legal tender admissible into the treasury. The premia levied on coins paid (into the treasury shall be) eight per cent known as rūpika, five per cent known as vyājī, one-eighth paṇa per cent as parīkṣika (testing charge), besides a fine of 25 paṇas to be imposed on offenders other than the manufacturer, the seller, the purchaser and the examiner.

The superintendent of ocean mines shall attend to the collection of conch shells, diamonds, precious stones, pearls, corals, and salt and also regulate the commerce in the above commodities.

Soon after crystallization of salt is over, the superintendent of salt shall in time collect both the money rent and the quantity of the shares of salt due to the government; and by the sale of salt (thus collected as shares), he shall realise not only its value, but also the premium of five per cent, both in cash.

Imported salt shall pay one-sixth portion to the kings. The sale of this portion shall fetch the premia of five per cent, of eight per cent in cash. The purchasers shall pay not only the toll, but also the compensation equivalent to the loss entailed on the king's commerce. In default of the above payment, he shall be compelled to pay a fine of 600 paṇas.

Adulteration of salt shall be punished with the highest amercement; likewise persons other than hermits manufacturing salt without license.

Men learned in the Vedas, persons engaged in penance, as well as laborers may take with them salt for food; salt and alkalis for purposes other than this shall be subject to the payment of toll.

Thus, besides collecting from mines the ten kinds of revenue, such as

- value of the output,
- the share of the output,
- the premium of five per cent,
- the testing charge of coins,
- fine previously announced,
- toll,
- compensation for loss entailed on the king's commerce,
- fines to be determined in proportion to the gravity of crimes,
- coinage,
- and the premium of eight per cent, the government shall keep as a state monopoly both mining and commerce (in minerals).

Thus, taxes on all commodities intended for sale shall be prescribed once for all.

Mines are the source of treasury; from treasury comes the power of government; and the earth whose ornament is treasury is acquired by means of treasury and army.

6.5   ARTHASHASTRA, BOOK 2, CHAPTER 20: MEASUREMENT OF SPACE AND TIME

The superintendent of lineal and measure shall possess the knowledge of measuring space and time.

- ➢ 8 atoms are equal to 1 particle thrown off by the wheel of a chariot.
- ➢ 8 particles are equal to 1 likṣā.
- ➢ 8 likṣās are equal to the middle of a yūka (louse) or a yūka of medium size.
- ➢ 8 yūkas are equal to 1 yava (barley) of middle size.
- ➢ 8 yavas are equal to 1 aṅgula (three-fourths of an English inch). [Or the middlemost joint of the middle finger of a man of medium size may be taken to be equal to an aṅgula.]
- ➢ 4 aṅgulas are equal to 1 dhanurgraha.
- ➢ 8 aṅgulas are equal to 1 dhanurmuṣṭi.
- ➢ 12 aṅgulas are equal to 1 vitasti, or 1 chāyāpauruṣa.
- ➢ 14 aṅgulas are equal to 1 śama, śala, pariraya, or pada.
- ➢ 2 vitastis are equal to 1 aratni or 1 prājāpatya hasta.
- ➢ 2 vitastis plus 1 dhanurgraha are equal to = 1 hasta used in measuring balances and cubic measures, and pasture lands.
- ➢ 2 vitastis plus 1 dhanurmuṣṭi are equal to = 1 kiṣku or 1 kaṃsa.
- ➢ 42 aṅgulas are equal to 1 kiṣku according to sawyers and black smiths, and used in

measuring the grounds for the encampment of the army, for forts and palaces.

> 54 aṅgulas are equal to 1 hasta used in measuring timber forests.

> 84 aṅgulas are equal to 1 vyāma, used in measuring ropes and the depth of digging, in terms of a man's height.

> 4 aratnis are equal to 1 daṇḍa, 1 dhanus, 1 nālikā and 1 pauruṣa.

> 108 aṅgulas are equal to 1 gārhapatya dhanus (i.e. a measure used by carpenters called gṛhapati). This measure is used in measuring roads and fort walls.

> The same (108 aṅgulas) are equal to 1 pauruṣa, a measure used in building sacrificial altars.

> 6 kaṃsas or 192 aṅgulas are equal to 1 daṇḍa, used in measuring such lands as are gifted to Brāhmans.

> 10 daṇḍas are equal to 1 rajju.

> 2 rajjus are equal to 1 parideśa (square measure).

> 3 rajjus are equal to 1 nivartana (square measure).

> The same (3 rajjus) plus 2 daṇḍas on one side only [=] are equal to 1 bahu (arm).

> 1000 dhanus are equal to 1 goruta (sound of a cow).

> 4 gorutas are equal to 1 yojana.

Thus are the lineal and square measures dealt with.

6.5.1   With regard to the measures of time:

(The divisions of time are) a truṭi, lava, nimeṣa, kāṣṭhā, kalā, nālikā, muhūrta, forenoon, afternoon, day, night, pakṣa, month, ṛtu (season), ayana (solstice), saṃvatsara (year), and yuga.

> 2 truṭis are equal to 1 lava,

> 2 lavas are equal to 1 nimeṣa.

> 5 nimeṣas are equal to 1 kāṣṭhā.

> 30 kaṣṭhās are equal to 1 kalā.

> 40 kalās are equal to 1 nālikā, or the times during which one āḍhaka of water passes out of a pot through an aperture of

the same diameter as that of a wire of 4 aṅgulas in length and made of 4 māṣas of gold.

> ➤ 2 nālikās are equal to 1 muhūrta.

> ➤ 15 muhūrtas are equal to 1 day or 1 night.

Such a day and night happen in the months of Caitra and Āśvayuja. Then after the period of six months it increases or diminishes by three muhūrtas.

When the length of shadow is eight pauruṣas (96 aṅgulas), it is 1/15th part of the day.

When it is 6 pauruṣas (72 aṅgulas), it is 1/14th part of the day; when 4 pauruṣas, ⅛th part; when 2 pauruṣas, ⅙th part; when 1 pauruṣa, ¼th part; when it is 8 aṅgulas, 8/15th part (trayodaśabhāga); when 4 aṅgulas, ⅜th part; and when no shadow is cast, it is to be considered midday.

Likewise when the day declines, the same process at reverse order shall be observed.

It is in the month of Āṣāḍha that no shadow is cast at midday. After Āṣāḍha, during the six months from Śrāvana upwards, the length of shadow successively increases by two aṅgulas, and during the next six months, from Māgha upwards, it successively decreases by two aṅgulas.

Fifteen days and nights together make up one pakṣa. That pakṣa during which the moon waxes is white (śukla), and that pakṣa during which the moon wanes is bahula.

Two pakṣas make one month (māsa). Thirty days and nights together make one work-a-month (prakarmamāsa). The same (30 days and nights) with an additional half a day makes one solar month (saura).

The same (30) less by half a day makes one lunar month (candramāsa).

Twenty-seven (days and nights) make a sidereal month (nakṣatramāsa).

Once in thirty-two months there comes one malamāsa, profane month, i.e. an extra month, added to lunar year to harmonize it with the solar.

Once in thirty-five months there comes a malamāsa for aśvavāhas.

Once in forty months there comes a malamāsa for hastivāhas.

> Two months make one ṛtu (season).
> Śrāvaṇa and Proṣṭhapada make the rainy season (varṣā).
> Āśvayuja and Kārtika make the autumn (śarad).
> Mārgaśīrṣa and Pauṣamake the winter (hemanta).
> Māgha and Phālguṇa make the dewy season (śīśira).
> Caitra and Vaiśākha make the spring (vasanta).
> Jyeṣṭhāmūlīya and Āṣāḍha make the summer (grīṣma).

Seasons from śiśira and upwards are the summer solstice (uttarāyaṇa), and (those) from varṣā and upwards are the winter solstice (dakṣiṇāyana). Two solstices (ayanas) make one year (saṃvatsara). Five years make one yuga.

The sun carries off (harati) 1/60th of a whole day every day, and thus makes one complete day in every two months (ṛtau). Likewise the moon (falls behind by 1/65th of a whole day every day and falls behind one day in every two months). Thus in the middle of every third year, they (the sun and the moon) make one adhimāsa, additional month, first in the summer season and second at the end of five years.

6.6 ARTHASHASTRA, BOOK 2, CHAPTER 22: REGULATION OF TOLL-DUES

Merchandise, external, (i.e., arriving from country parts), internal, (i.e., manufactured inside forts), or foreign, (i.e., imported from foreign countries) shall all be liable to the payment of toll alike when exported and imported.

> Imported commodities shall pay ⅕th of their value as toll.

> Of flowers, fruits, vegetables, roots, bulbous roots (kanda), pallikya, seeds, dried fish, and dried meat, the superintendent shall receive ⅙th as toll.

> As regards conch shells, diamonds, precious stones, pearls, corals, and necklaces, experts acquainted with the time, cost, and finish of the production of such articles shall fix the amount of toll.

> Of fibrous garments, cotton cloths, silk, mail armor, sulphuret of arsenic, red arsenic, vermilion, metals, and coloring ingredients; of sandal, brown sandal, pungents, ferments, dress, and the like; of wine, ivory, skins, raw materials used in making fibrous or cotton garments, carpets, curtains, and products yielded by worms; and of wool and other products yielded by goats and sheep, he shall receive 1/12th or 1/15th, as toll.

> Of cloths, quadrupeds, bipeds, threads, cotton, scents, medicines, wood, bamboo, fibers, skins and clay pots; of grains, oils, sugar, salt, liquor, cooked rice and the like, he shall receive 1/20th or 1/25th, as toll.

> Gate dues shall be ⅕th of toll-dues; this tax may be remitted if circumstances necessitate such favour. Commodities shall never be sold where they are grown or manufactured.

> When minerals and other commodities are purchased from mines, a fine of 600 panas shall be imposed.

> When flowers or fruits are purchased from flower or fruit gardens, a fine of 54 panas shall be imposed.

> When vegetables, roots, bulbous roots are purchased from vegetable gardens, a fine of 51¾ panas shall be imposed.

> When any kind of grass or grain is purchased from field, a fine of 53 panas shall be imposed.

(Permanent) fines of 1 paṇa and 1½ paṇas shall be levied on agricultural produce (sītātyaya).

Hence, in accordance with the customs of countries or of communities, the rate of toll shall be fixed on commodities, either old or new; and fines shall be fixed in proportion to the gravity of offences.

6.7 ARTHASHASTRA, BOOK 2, CHAPTER 34: SUPERINTENDENT OF PASSPORTS AND PASTURE LANDS

The superintendent of passports shall issue passes at the rate of a māṣa per passport. Whoever is provided with a pass shall be at liberty to enter into or go out of, the country. Whoever, being a native of the country, enters into or goes out of the country without a pass, will be fined 12 paṇas. He shall be punished with the first amercement for producing a false pass. A foreigner guilty of the same offence shall be punished with the highest amercement.

The superintendent of pasture lands shall examine passes.

Pasture grounds shall be opened between any two dangerous places.

Valleys shall be cleared from the fear of thieves, elephants, and other beasts.

In barren tracts of the country, there shall be constructed not only tanks, buildings for shelter, and wells, but also flower gardens and fruit gardens.

Hunters with their hounds shall explore forests. At the approach of the thieves or enemies, they shall so hide themselves by ascending trees or mountains as to escape from the thieves, and blow conch shells or beat drums. As to the movements of enemies or wild tribes, they may send information by flying the pigeons of royal household with passes or causing fire and smoke at successive distances.

It shall be his (Superintendent) duty to protect timber and elephant forests, to keep roads in good repair, to arrest thieves, to secure the safety of mercantile traffic, to protect cows, and to conduct the transaction of the people.

6.8 ARTHASHASTRA, BOOK 2, CHAPTER 35: REVENUE-COLLECTORS AND SPIES

Having divided the kingdom into four districts, and having also sub-divided the villages as of first, middle, and lowest rank, he (the collector-general) shall bring them under one or another of the following heads: villages that are exempted from taxation; those that supply soldiers; those that pay their taxes in the form of grains, cattle, gold, or raw material; and those that supply free labor and dairy produce in lieu of taxes.

It is the duty of Gopa, village accountant, to attend to the accounts of five or ten villages, as ordered by the Collector-General.

By setting up boundaries to villages, by numbering plots of grounds as cultivated, uncultivated, plains, wet lands, gardens, vegetable gardens, fences, forests, altars, temples of gods, irrigation works, cremation grounds, feeding houses, places where water is freely supplied to travelers, places of. pilgrimage, pasture grounds and roads, and thereby fixing the boundaries of various villages, of fields, of forests, and of roads, he shall register gifts, sales, charities, and remission of taxes regarding fields.

Also having numbered the houses as tax-paying, or non-tax-paying, he shall not only register the total number of the inhabitants of all the four castes in each village, but also keep an account of the exact number of cultivators, cowherds, merchants, artisans, laborers, slaves, and biped and quadruped animals, fixing at the same time the amount of gold, free labor, toll, and fines that can be collected from it (each house).

He shall also keep an account of the number of young and old men that reside in each house, their history, occupation, income, and expenditure.

Likewise Sthānika (local) district officer, shall attend to the accounts of one-quarter of the kingdom.

In those places which are under the jurisdiction of gopa and sthānika, commissioners, specially deputed by the collector-general shall not only inspect the work done and means employed by the village and district officers, but also collect the special religious tax known as bali.

Spies, under the disguise of householders (cultivators), who shall be deputed by the collector-general for espionage, shall ascertain the validity of the accounts (of the village and district officers) regarding the fields, houses and families of each village—the area and output of produce regarding fields, right of ownership and remission of taxes with regard to houses, and the caste and profession regarding families.

They shall also ascertain the total number of men and beasts as well as the amount of income and expenditure of each family.

They shall also find out the causes of emigration and immigration of persons of migratory habit, the arrival and departure of men and women of condemnable character, as well as the movements of (foreign) spies.

Likewise spies under the guise of merchants shall ascertain the quantity and price of the royal merchandise, such as minerals, or products of gardens, forests, and fields, or manufactured articles.

As regards foreign merchandise of superior or inferior quality arriving thither by land or water, they shall ascertain the amount of toll, road cess, conveyance cess, military cess, ferry fare, and one-sixth portion (paid or payable by the merchants), the charges incurred by them for their own subsistence, and for the accommodation of their merchandise in warehouse.

Similarly spies under the guise of ascetics shall, as ordered by the collector-general, gather information as to the proceedings, honest or dishonest, of cultivators, cowherds, merchants, and heads of government departments.

In places where altars are situated or where four roads meet, in ancient ruins, in the vicinity of tanks, rivers, bathing places, in places of pilgrimage and hermitage, and in desert tracts, mountains, and thick grown forests, spies under the guise of old and notorious thieves with their student bands shall ascertain the causes of arrival and departure, and halt of thieves, enemies, and persons of undue bravery.

The collector-general shall thus energetically attend to the affairs of the kingdom. Also his subordinates, constituting his various establishment of espionage, shall, along with their colleagues and followers, attend to their duties likewise.

CHAPTER 7

KAUTILYA'S ARTHASHASTRA, BOOK 3: CONCERNING LAW

7.1 ARTHASHASTRA, BOOK 3, CHAPTER 2: CONCERNING MARRIAGE

Marriage is the basis of all disputes or dealings.

The giving-in marriage of a maiden well-adorned is called Brāhma-marriage. The joint-performance of sacred duties (by a man and a woman) is known as prājāpatya marriage.

(The giving in marriage of a maiden) for a couple of cows is called Ārsha. (The giving in marriage of a maiden) to an officiating priest in a sacrifice is called Daiva. The voluntary union of a maiden with her lover is called Gāndharva. Giving a maiden after receiving plenty of wealth, is. termed Āsura. The abduction of a maiden is called Rākṣasa. The abduction of a maiden while she is asleep and in intoxication is called Paiśāca marriage.

Of these, the first four are ancestral customs of old and are valid on their being approved of by the father. The rest are to be sanctioned by both the father and the mother; for it is they that receive the money paid by the bridegroom for their daughter. In case of the absence by death of either the father or the mother, the survivor will receive the śulka. If both of them are dead, the maiden herself shall receive it. Any kind of marriage is approvable, provided it pleases all those (that are concerned in it).

7.1.1 Property of Women

Means of subsistence or jewellery constitutes what is called the property of a woman. Means of subsistence valued at above two thousand shall be endowed (in her name). There is no limit to jewellery. It is no guilt for the wife to make use of this property in maintaining her son, her daughter-in-law, or herself, whenever her absent husband has made no provision for her maintenance. In calamities, disease and famine, in warding off dangers and in charitable acts, the husband, too, may make use of this property. Neither shall there be any complaint against the enjoyment of this property by mutual consent by a couple who have brought forth a twin. Nor shall there be any complaint if this property has been enjoyed for three years by those who are wedded in accordance with the customs of the first four kinds of marriage. But the enjoyment of this property in the case of Gāndharva and Āsura marriages shall be liable to be restored, together with interest on it. In the cases of such marriages as are called Rākṣasa and Paiśāca, the use of this property shall be dealt with as theft. Thus, the duty of marriage is dealt with.

On the death of her husband a woman, desirous to lead a pious life, shall at once receive not only her endowment and jewellery, but also the balance of śulka due to her. If after obtaining these two things she re-marries another, she shall be caused to pay them back together with interest (on their value). If she is desirous of a second marriage, she shall be given on the occasion of her re-marriage; whatever either her father-in-law or her husband or both had given to her. The time at which women can re-marry shall be explained in connection with the subject of long sojourn of husbands.

If a widow marries any man other than of her father-in-law's selection, she shall forfeit whatever had been given to her by her father-in-law and her deceased husband.

The kinsmen of a woman shall return to her old father-in-law whatever property of her own she had taken with her while re-marrying a kinsman. Whoever justly takes a woman under his protection shall equally protect her property. No woman shall succeed in her attempt to establish her title to the property of her deceased husband, after she re-marries.

If she lives a pious life, she may enjoy it. No woman with a son or sons shall (after re-marriage) be at liberty to make free use of her own property; for that property of hers, her sons shall receive.

If a woman after re-marriage attempts to take possession of her own property under the plea of maintaining her sons by her former husband, she shall be made to endow it in their name. If a woman has many male children by many husbands, then she shall conserve her property in the same condition as she had received from her husbands. Even that property which has been given her with full powers of enjoyment and disposal, a remarried woman shall endow in the name of her sons.

A barren widow who is faithful to the bed of her dead husband may, under the protection of her teacher, enjoy her property as long as she lives: for it is to ward off calamities that women are endowed with property. On her death, her property shall pass into the hands of her kinsman. If the husband is alive and the wife is dead, then her sons and daughters shall divide her property among themselves. If there are no sons, her daughters shall have it. In their absence her husband shall take that amount of money (śulka) which he had given her, and her relatives shall re-take whatever in the shape of gift or dowry they had presented her. Thus, the determination of the property of a woman is dealt with.

7.1.2 Re-marriage of Males

If a woman either brings forth no (live) children, or has no male issue, or is barren, her husband shall wait for eight years (before marrying another). If she bears only a dead child, he has to wait for ten years. If she brings forth only females, he has to wait for twelve years. Then if he is desirous to have sons, he may marry another. In case of violating this rule, he shall be made to pay her not only śulka, her property and an adequate monetary compensation, but also a fine of 24 paṇas to the government. Having given the necessary amount of śulka and property even to those women who have not received such things on the occasion of their marriage with him, and also having given his wives the proportionate compensation and on adequate subsistence (vṛtti), he may marry any number of women; for women are created for the sake of sons. If many or all of them are at the same time in menses, he shall lie with that woman among them whom he married earlier or who has a living son. In case of his concealing the fact of her being in menses or neglecting to lie with any of them after her menses, he shall pay a fine of 96 paṇas. Of women who either have sons or are pious or barren, or bring forth only a dead child or are beyond the age of menstruation, none shall be associated with against her liking. If a man has no inclination, he may not lie with his wife who is either afflicted with leprosy or is a lunatic. But if a woman is desirous of having sons, she may lie with men suffering from such disease.

* If a husband either is of bad character, or is long gone abroad, or has become a traitor to his king, or is likely to endanger the life of his wife, or has fallen from his caste, or has lost virility, he may be abandoned by his wife.

7.2 ARTHASHASTRA, BOOK 3, CHAPTER 3: DUTY OF A WIFE

Women, when twelve years old, attain their puberty and men when sixteen years old. If, after attaining their puberty, they prove disobedient to lawful authority, women shall be fined 15 paṇas, and men twice the amount.

7.2.1 Maintenance of a Woman

A woman who has a. right to claim maintenance for an unlimited period of time, shall be given as much food and clothing as is necessary for her, or more than is necessary in proportion to the income of the maintainer. If the period (for which such things are to be given to her with one-tenth of the amount in addition) is limited, then a certain amount of money, fixed in proportion to the income of the maintainer, shall be given to her: so also if she has not been given her śulka, property, and compensation (due to her for allowing her husband to re-marry). If she places herself under the protection of any one belonging to her father-in-law's family, or if she begins to live independently, then her husband shall not be sued (for her maintenance). Thus the determination of maintenance is dealt with.

7.2.2 Cruelty to Women

Women of refractive nature shall be taught manners by using not even such expressions as "Thou, half naked; thou, fully naked; thou, cripple; thou, fatherless; thou, motherless". Or three beats, either with a bamboo bark or with a rope or with the palm of the hand, may be given on her hips. Violation of the above rules shall be liable to half the punishment levied for defamation and criminal hurt. The same kind of punishments shall be meted out to a woman who, moved with jealousy or hatred, shows cruelty to her husband.

7.2.3 Enmity between Husband and Wife

A woman, who hates her husband, who has passed the period of seven turns of her menses, and who loves another, shall immediately return to her husband both the endowment and jewelry she has received from him, and allow him to lie down with another woman, A man, hating his wife, shall allow her to take shelter in the house of a mendicant woman, or of her lawful guardians or of her kinsmen. If a man falsely denies his intercourse with his wife, though it be proved by eye-witnesses—or through a spy, he shall pay a fine of 12 paṇas. A woman, hating her husband, cannot dissolve her marriage with him against his will. Nor can a man dissolve his marriage with his wife against her will. But from mutual enmity, divorce may be obtained. If a man, apprehending danger from his wife, desires divorce, he shall return to her whatever she was given (on the occasion of her marriage). If a woman, under the apprehension of danger from her husband, desires divorce, she shall forfeit her claim to her property; marriages contracted in accordance with the customs of the first four kinds of marriages cannot be dissolved.

7.2.4 Transgression

If a woman engages herself in amorous sports, or drinking in the face of an order to the contrary, she shall be fined 3 panas. She shall pay a fine of 6 panas for going out at daytime to sports or to see a woman or spectacles. She shall pay a fine of 12 panas if she goes out to see another man or for sports. For the same offences committed at night, the fines shall be doubled. If a woman goes out while the husband is asleep or under intoxication, or if she shuts the door of the house against her husband, she shall be fined 12 panas. If a woman keeps him out of the house at night, she shall pay double the above fine. If a man and a woman make signs to each other with a view to sensual enjoyment, or carry-on secret conversation (for the same purpose), the woman shall pay a fine of 24 panas, and the man double the amount. A woman, holding out her hair, the tie of her dress round her loins, her teeth or her nails, shall pay the first amercement, and a man, doing the same, twice the first amercement. For holding conversation in suspicious places, whips may be substituted for fines. In the centre of the village, an outcaste person (caṇḍāla) may whip such women five times on each of the sides of their body. She may get rid of being whipped by paying a pana for each whip. Thus transgression is dealt with.

7.2.5 Forbidden Transactions

With regard to a man and a woman who, though forbidden to carry on any mutual transaction, help each other, the woman shall be fined 12, 24 and 54 panas respectively, according as the help consists of (i) small things, of (ii) costly things, and (iii) of gold or gold coin; and the man, at double the above rates. With regard to similar transaction between a man and a woman who cannot mix with each other, half of the above punishment shall be levied. Similar punishment shall be meted out for any forbidden transaction with any men. Thus forbidden transactions are dealt with.

* Treason, transgression and wandering at will shall deprive a woman of her claim not only to (i) some-form of subsistence of above 2,000 paṇas and jewelry, (ii) and āhita, compensation she may have obtained for allowing her husband to marry another woman, but also (iii) to śulka, money which her parents may have received from her husband.

7.3 ARTHASHASTRA, BOOK 3, CHAPTER 5: DIVISION OF INHERITANCE

Sons whose fathers and mothers or ancestors are alive cannot be independent. After their time, division of ancestral property among descendants from the same ancestor shall take place, calculating (according to fathers).

Self-acquired property of any of the sons, with the exception of that kind of property which is earned by means of parental property is not divisible. Sons or grandsons till the fourth generation from the first parent shall also have prescribed shares in that property which is acquired by means of their undivided ancestral property; for the line as far as the fourth generation is uninterrupted. But those whose line or genealogy from the first ancestor is interrupted (i.e., those who are subsequent to the fourth generation), shall have equal divisions. Those who have been living together shall re-divide their property, whether they had already divided their ancestral property before or they had received no such property at all. Of sons, he who brings the ancestral property to a prosperous condition shall also have a share of the profit.

If a man has no male issue, his own brothers, or persons who have been living with him, shall take possession of his property; and in their absence his daughters (born of marriages other than the first four), shall have his property. If one has sons, they shall have the property; if one has (only) daughters born of such marriage as is contracted in accordance with the customs of any of the first four kinds of marriage, they shall have the property; if there are neither sons nor such daughters, the dead man's father, if living, shall have it; if he, too, is not alive, the dead man's father's brothers and the sons of his brothers shall have it; if there are many brothers of his father, all of them shall divide it; and each of the many sons of such brothers shall have one share due to his father; if the brothers are the sons of many fathers, they shall divide it, calculating from their fathers.

Among a dead man's father, brother, and brother's sons, the succeeding ones shall depend on the preceding ones if living (for their shares); likewise the youngest on the eldest for is half share.

A father, distributing his property while he his alive, shall make no distinction in dividing it among his sons. Nor shall a father deprive without sufficient reason any of the sons of his share. Father being dead leaving no property, the elder sons shall show favour to the younger ones, if the latter are not of bad character.

7.3.1   Time of Dividing Inheritance

Division of inheritance shall be made when all the inheritors have attained their majority. If it is made before, the minors shall have their shares, free of all debts. These shares of the minors shall be placed in the custody of the relatives of their mothers, or of aged gentlemen of the village, till they attain their adulthood. The same rule shall hold good in the case of those who have gone abroad. Unmarried brothers shall also be paid as much marriage cost as is equal to that incurred in the marriages of married brothers. Daughters, too (unmarried), shall be paid adequate dowry, payable to them on the occasion of their marriages.

Both assets and liabilities shall be equally divided.

The poor people shall equally distribute among themselves even the mud vessels.

In the opinion of Kauṭilya, it is unnecessary to say so; for as a rule, division is to be made of all that is in existence, but of nothing that is not in existence. Having declared before witnesses the amount of property common to all as well as the property constituting additional shares of the brothers (in priority of their birth), division of inheritance shall be carried on. Whatever is badly and unequally divided, or is involved in deception, concealment or secret acquisition, shall be re-divided.

Property for which no claimant is found shall go to the king, except the property of a woman, of a dead man for whom no funeral rites have been performed, or of a niggardly man with the exception of that of a Brāhman learned in the Vedas. That (the property of the learned) shall be made over to those who are well-versed in the three Vedas.

Persons fallen from caste, persons born of outcaste men, and eunuchs shall have no share; likewise idiots, lunatics, the blind and lepers. If the idiots, etc., have wives with property, their issues who are not equally idiots, etc., shall share inheritance. All these persons excepting those that are fallen from caste shall be entitled to only food and clothing.

* If these persons have been married (before they became fallen, etc.), and if their line is likely to become extinct, their relatives may beget sons for them and give proportional shares of inheritance to those sons.

7.4 ARTHASHASTRA, BOOK 3, CHAPTER 6: SPECIAL SHARES IN INHERITANCE

Goats shall be the special shares of the eldest of sons, born of the same mother, among Brāhmans; horses among Kṣatriyas; cows among Vaiśyas; and sheep among Śūdras. The blind of the same animals shall be given the special shares to the middlemost sons; species of variegated colour of the same animals shall be the special shares to the youngest of sons. In the absence of quadruped, the eldest shall take an additional share of one-tenth of the whole property excepting precious stones; for by this act alone, he will be bound in his duty to his ancestors.

The above method is in accordance with the rules observed among the followers of Uśanas.

The father being dead, his carriage and jewelry shall be the special share to the eldest; his bed, seat, and bronze plate in which he used to take his meals, to the middlemost; and black grains, iron, domestic utensils, cows and cart to the youngest. The rest of the property, or the above things, too, may be equally divided among themselves. Sisters shall have no claim to inheritance; they shall have the bronze plate and jewelry of their mother after her death. The eldest son having no manly qualities shall have only one-third of the special share usually given to the eldest; if the eldest son follows a condemnable occupation or if he has given up the observance of religious duties, he shall have only one-fourth of the special share; if he is unrestrained in his actions he shall have nothing.

The same rule shall hold good with the middlemost and youngest sons; of these two, one who is endowed with manliness (mānuṣopeta), shall have half the special share usually given to the eldest.

7.4.1   With regard to sons of many wives:

Of sons of two wives of whom only one woman has gone through all the necessary religious ceremonials, or one of whom has been married as a maiden, and the other not as a maiden, or one of whom has brought forth twins, it is by birth that primogenitureship is decided.

In the case of sons such as Sūta, Māgadha, Vrātya, and Rathakāra, inheritance will go to the capable; and the rest will depend upon him for subsistence. In the absence of the capable, all will have equal shares.

Of sons begotten by a Brāhman in the four castes, the son of a Brāhman woman shall take four shares; the son of a Kṣatriya woman three shares; the son of a Vaiśya woman two shares; and the son of a Śūdra woman one share.

The same rule shall hold good in the case of Kṣatriya and Vaiśya fathers begetting sons in three or two castes in order.

An Anantara son of a Brāhman, i.e, a son begotten by a Brāhman on a woman of next lower caste, shall, if endowed with manly or superior qualities, take an equal share (with other sons of inferior qualities); similarly Anantara sons of Kṣatriya or Vaiśya fathers shall, if endowed with manly or superior qualities, take half or equal shares (with others). An only son to two mothers of different castes shall take possession of the whole property and maintain the relatives of his father, A Pāraśava son begotten by a Brāhman on a Śudra woman, shall take one-third share; a sapiṇḍa (an agnate) or a kulya (the nearest cognate) of the Brāhman shall take the remaining two shares, being thereby obliged to offer funeral libation; in the absence of agnates or cognates, the deceased father's teacher or student shall take the two shares.

* Or on the wife of such a Brāhman shall a sagotra, relative bearing the same family name, or a mātṛbandhu, relative of his mother, beget a natural son (kṣetraja), and this son may take that wealth.

7.5 ARTHASHASTRA, BOOK 3, CHAPTER 11: RECOVERY OF DEBTS

An interest of a paṇa and a quarter per month per cent is just. Five paṇas per month per cent is commercial interest. Ten paṇas per month per cent prevails among forests. Twenty paṇas per month per cent prevails among sea traders. Persons exceeding, or causing to exceed, the above rate of interest shall be punished with the first amercement; and hearers of such transaction shall each pay half of the above fined.

The nature of the transactions between creditors and debtors on which the welfare of the kingdom depends, shall always be scrutinized. Interest in grains in seasons of good harvest shall not exceed more than half when valued in money. Interest on stocks shall be one-half of the profit, and be regularly paid as each year expires. If it is allowed to accumulate owing either to the intention or to the absence abroad (of the receiver or payer), the amount payable shall be equal to twice the share or principal. A person claiming interest when it is not due, or representing as principal the total amount of his original principal and the interest thereon shall pay a fine of four times the amount under dispute.

A creditor who sues for four times the amount, lent by him shall pay a fine of four times the unjust amount.

Of this fine, the creditor shall pay three-quarters and the debtor one-quarter. Interest on debts due from persons who are engaged in sacrifices taking a long time, or who are suffering from disease, or who are detained in the houses of their teachers (for learning), or who are either minors or too poor, shall not accumulate.

A creditor refusing to receive the payment of his debt shall pay a fine of 12 paṇas. If the refusal is due to some (reasonable) cause, then the amount free from interest (for subsequent time) shall be kept in the safe custody of others. Debts neglected for ten years, except in the case of minors, aged persons, diseased persons, persons involved in calamities, or persons who are sojourning abroad or have fled the country and except in the case of disturbances in the kingdom, shall not be received back.

Sons of a deceased debtor shall pay the principal with interest. (In the absence of sons) kinsmen claiming the share of the dead man or sureties, such as joint partners of the debt shall pay the same. No other kind of surety is valid; a minor, as surety.

A debt, the payment of which is not limited by time or place or both, shall be paid by the sons, grandsons or any other heirs of the dead debtor. Any debt, the payment of which is not limited by time or place or both and for which life, marriage, or land is pledged, shall be borne by sons or grandsons.

7.5.1   Regarding Many Debts Against One

Excepting the case of a debtor going abroad, no debtor shall simultaneously be sued for more than one debt by one or two creditors. Even in the case of a debtor going abroad, he shall pay his debts in the order in which he borrowed them or shall first pay his debts due to the king or a learned Brāhman.

Debts contracted (from each other) by either a husband or wife, either a son or a father, or any one among brothers of undivided interests shall be irrecoverable.

Cultivators or government servants shall not be caught hold of for debts while they are engaged in their duties (or at work).

A wife, who has (not) heard of the debt, shall not be caught hold of for the debt contracted by her husband, excepting in the case of herdsmen and joint-cultivators. But a husband may be caught for the debt contracted by his wife., if it is admitted that a man fled the country without providing for the debt contracted by his wife, the highest amercement shall be meted out; if not admitted, witnesses shall be depended upon.

7.5.2   Witnesses

It is obligatory to produce three witnesses who are reliable, honest and respected. At least two witnesses acceptable to the parties are necessary; never one witness in the case of debts.

Wife's brothers, co-partners, prisoners, creditors, debtors, enemies, maimed persons, or persons once punished by the government shall not be taken as witnesses. Likewise persons legally unfit to carry on transactions, the king, persons learned in the Vedas, persons depending for their maintenance on villages, lepers, persons, suffering from bodily eruptions, outcaste persons, Caṇḍālas, persons of mean avocation, the blind, the deaf, the dumb, egotistic persons, females, or government servants shall not be taken as witnesses excepting in case of transactions in one's own community. In dispute concerning assault, theft, or abduction, persons other than wife's brothers, enemies, and co-partners, can be witnesses. In secret dealings, a single woman or a single man who has stealthily heard or seen them can be a witness, with the exception of the king or an ascetic. On the side of prosecution masters against servants, priests or teachers against their disciples, and parents against their sons can be witnesses; persons other than these may also be witnesses in criminal cases. If the above persons (masters and servants, etc.) sue each other, they shall be punished with the highest amercement. Creditors guilty of parokta shall pay a fine of 10 times the amount; but if incapable to pay so much, they shall at least pay five times the amount sued for; thus the section on witnesses is dealt with.

7.5.3   Taking Oaths

Witness shall be taken before Brāhmans, vessels of water and fire. A Brāhman witness shall be told, "Tell the truth"; a Kṣatriya or a Vaiśya witness shall be told thus: "If thou utterest falsehood, thou do not attain the fruit of thy sacrificial and charitable deeds; but having broken the array of thy enemies in war, thou do go a beggar with a skull in thy hand."

7.6   ARTHASHASTRA, BOOK 3, CHAPTER 12: CONCERNING DEPOSITS

The rules concerning debts shall also apply to deposits. Whenever forts or country parts are destroyed by enemies or wild tribes; whenever villages, merchants, or herds of cattle are subjected to the inroads of invaders; whenever the kingdom itself is destroyed; whenever extensive fires or floods bring about entire destruction of villages, or partly destroy immovable properties, movable properties having been rescued before; whenever the spread of fire or rush of floods is so sudden that even movable properties could not be removed; or whenever a ship laden with commodities is either sunk or plundered (by pirates); deposits lost in many of the above ways shall not be reclaimed. The depository who has made use of the deposit for his own comfort shall not only pay a compensation to be fixed after considering the circumstances of the place and time, but also a fine of 12 panas. Not only shall any loss in the value of the deposit, due to its use, be made good, but a fine of 24 panas also be paid. Deposits damaged or lost, in any way shall also be made good. When the depository is either dead or involved in calamities, the deposit shall not be sued for. If the deposit is either mortgaged or sold or lost, the depository shall not only restore four times its value, but pay a fine of five times the stipulated value. If the deposit is exchanged for a similar one (by the depository), or lost in any other way, its value shall be paid.

7.6.1   Pledges

The same rule shall hold good in the case of pledges whenever they are lost, used up, sold, mortgaged, or misappropriated.

A pledge, if productive, shall never be lost to the debtor, nor shall any interest on the debt be charged; but if unproductive (i.e. hypothecation), it may be lost, and interest on the debt shall accumulate. The pledgee who does not re-convey the pledge when the debtor is ready for it shall be fined 12 panas.

In the absence of the creditor or mediator, the amount of the debt may be kept in the custody of the elders of the village and the debtor may have the pledged property redeemed; or with its value fixed at the time and with no interest chargeable for the future, the pledge may be left where it is. When there is any rise in the value of the pledge or when it is apprehended that it may be depreciated or lost in the near future, the pledgee may, with permission from the judges, or on the evidence furnished by the officer in charge of pledges, sell the pledge either in the presence of the debtor or under the presidency of experts who can. see whether such apprehension is justified.

An immovable property, pledged and enjoyable with or without labor, shall not be caused to deteriorate in value while yielding interest on the money lent, and profit on the expenses incurred in maintaining it.

The pledgee who enjoys the pledge without permission shall not only pay the net profit he derived from it, but also forfeit the debt. The rules regarding deposits shall hold good in other matters connected with pledges.

7.6.2 Property Entrusted to Another for Delivery to a Third Person

The same rules shall apply to order, and property entrusted for delivery to a third person.

If, through a merchant, a messenger is entrusted with a property for delivery to a third person and such messenger does not reach the destined place, or is robbed of the property by thieves, the merchant shall not be responsible for it; nor shall a kinsman of the messenger who dies on his way be responsible for the property.

For the rest, the rules regarding deposits shall also hold good here.

7.6.3 Borrowed or Hired Properties

Properties either borrowed or hired shall be returned as intact as they were when received. If, owing to distance in time or place, or owing to some inherent defects of the properties or to some unforeseen accidents, properties either borrowed or hired are lost or destroyed, they need not be made good. The rules regarding deposits shall also apply here.

7.6.4 Retail Sale

Retail dealers, selling the merchandise of others at prices prevailing at particular localities and times shall hand over to the wholesale dealers as much of the sale proceeds and profit as is realized by them. The rules regarding pledges shall also apply here. If, owing to distance in time or place, there occurs any fall in the value of the merchandise, the retail dealers shall pay the value and profit at that rate which obtained when they received the merchandise.

Servants selling commodities at prices prescribed by their masters shall realise no profit. They shall only return the actual sale proceeds. If prices fall, they shall pay only as much of the sale proceeds as is realized at the low rate.

But such merchants as belong to trade-guilds or are trustworthy and are not condemned by the king need not restore even the value of that merchandise which is lost or destroyed owing to its inherent defects or to some unforeseen accidents. But of such merchandise as is distanced by time or place, they shall restore as much value and profit as remains after making allowance for the wear and tear of the merchandise; and also proportional part of every commodity.

For the rest, the rules regarding deposits shall apply here. It explains retail sale.

7.6.5 Sealed Deposits

The rules laid down concerning unsealed deposits shall apply to sealed deposits also. A man handing over a sealed deposit to other than the real depositor shall be punished. In the case of a depository's denial of having received a deposit, the antecedent circumstances of the deposit and (the character and social position of) the depositor are the only evidences. Artisans are naturally of impure character. It is not an approved custom with them to deposit for some reliable reason.

When a depository denies having received a sealed deposit which was not, however, deposited for any reasonable cause, the depositor may obtain secret permission (from the judges) to produce such witnesses as he might have stationed under a wall while depositing.

In the midst of a forest or in the middle of a voyage an old or afflicted merchant might with confidence put in the custody of a depository some valuable article with certain secret mark, and go on his way. On his sending this information to his son or brother, the latter may ask for the sealed deposit. If the depository does not quietly return it, he shall not only forfeit his credit, but be liable to the punishment for theft besides being made to restore the deposit.

A reliable man, bent on leaving this world and becoming an ascetic, may place a certain sealed deposit with some secret mark in the custody of a man, and, returning after a number of years, ask for it. If the depository dishonestly denies it, he shall not only be made to restore it, but be liable to the punishment for theft.

A childish man with a sealed deposit with some secret mark may, while going through a street at night, feel frightened at his being captured by the police for untimely walking, and, placing the deposit in the custody of a man, go on his way. But subsequently put into the jail, he may ask for it. If the depository dishonestly denies, he shall not only be made to restore it, but be liable to the punishment for theft.

By recognizing the sealed deposit in the custody of a man, any one of the depositor's family may probably ask not only for the deposit, but also for information as to the whereabouts of the depositor. If the custodian denies either, he shall be treated as before.

In all these cases, it is of first importance to inquire how the property under dispute came in one's possession, what are the circumstances connected with the various transaction concerning the property, and what is the status of the plaintiff in society as to wealth.

The above rules shall also apply to all kinds of transaction between any two persons.

* Hence before witnesses and with no secrecy whatever, shall all kinds of agreements be entered into; either with one's own or different people, shall the circumstances of the time and place be minutely considered first.

7.7 ARTHASHASTRA, BOOK 3, CHAPTER 20: GAMBLING, BETTING AND MISCELLANEOUS OFFENCES

With a view to find out spies or thieves, the superintendent of gambling shall, under the penalty of a fine of 12 panas if played elsewhere, centralize gambling.

In complaints regarding gambling, the winner shall be punished with the first amercement and the vanquished with the middlemost amercement; for though not skillful enough to win, as ardently desired by him, the vanquished fellow does not tolerate his defeat.

But Kauṭilya objects to it: for if the punishment for the vanquished were to be doubled, none would complain to the king. Yet gamblers are naturally false players.

The superintendents of gambling shall, therefore, be honest and supply dice at the rate of a kākaṇi of hire per pair. Substitution by tricks of hand of dice other than thus supplied shall be punished with a fine of 12 panas. A false player shall not only be punished with the first amercement and fines leviable for theft and deceit, but also be made to forfeit the stakes he has won.

The superintendent shall take not only 5 per cent of the stakes won by every winner, and the hire payable for supplying dice and other accessories of dice play, but also the fee chargeable for supplying water and accommodation, besides the charge for license.

He can at the same time carry on the transactions of sale or mortgage of things. If he does not forbid tricks of hand and other deceitful practices, he shall be punished with twice the amount of the fine (levied from the deceitful gamblers).

The same rules shall apply to betting and challenging, except those in learning and art.

7.7.1 Miscellaneous Offences

As regards miscellaneous offences:

When a person does not return in required place or time the property he has borrowed or hired, or placed in his custody as a deposit, sits under the shade for more than one and a quarter of an hour as prescribed, evades under the excuse of being a Brāhman the payment due while passing military stations or crossing rivers, and bawls out or invites others to fight against his neighbors, he shall be punished with a fine of 12 paṇas.

When a person does not hand over the property entrusted to him for delivery to a third person, drags with his hand the wife of his brother, has connection with a public woman kept by another, sells merchandise that is under ill repute, breaks open the sealed door of a house, or causes hurt to any of the forty-house-holders or neighbors, a fine of 48 paṇas shall be imposed.

When a person misappropriates the revenue he collects as the agent of a household, violates by force the chastity of a widow of independent living, when an outcaste (Caṇḍāla) person touches an Ārya woman, when a person does not run to render help to another in danger, or runs without a cause, and when a person entertains, in dinner dedicated to gods or ancestors, Buddhists (śākya), Ājīvakas, Śūdras and exiled persons (pravrajita), a fine of 100 paṇas shall be imposed.

When an unauthorized person examines (an offender) on oath, executes government work though not a government servant, renders minor quadrupeds impotent, or causes abortion to a female slave by medicine, he shall be punished with the first amercement.

When between father and son, husband and wife, brother and sister, maternal uncle and nephew or teacher and student, one abandons the other while neither of them is an apostate; and when a person abandons in the centre of a village another person whom he brought there for his own help, the first amercement shall be levied.

When a person abandons his companion in the midst of a forest, he shall be punished with the middlemost amercement.

When a person threatens and abandons his companion in the midst of a forest, he shall be punished with the highest amercement.

Whenever persons who have started together on some journey abandon one another as above, half of the above fine shall be levied.

When a person keeps or causes to keep another person in illegal confinement, releases a prisoner from prison, keeps, or causes another to keep, a minor in confinement, he shall be punished with a fine of 1,000 paṇas.

The rates of fines shall vary in accordance with the rank of persons concerned and the gravity of the crimes.

Such persons as a pilgrim, an ascetic engaged in penance, a diseased person, any one suffering from hunger, thirst, or fatigue from journey, a villager from country parts, any one that has suffered much from punishment and a moneyless pauper shall be shown mercy.

Such transactions as pertain to gods, Brāhmans, ascetics, women, minors, aged persons, diseased persons and helpless creatures shall, though not be complained of, be settled by the judges themselves; and in such transactions as the above, excuses due to time, place, or possession shall not be pleaded.

Such persons as are noted for their learning, intelligence, bravery, high birth, or magnificent works shall be honoured.

* Judges shall thus settle disputes free from all kinds of circumvention, with mind unchanged in all moods or circumstances, pleasing and affable to all.

CHAPTER 8

KAUTILYA'S ARTHASHASTRA, BOOK 4: REMOVAL OF THORNS

8.1 ARTHASHASTRA, BOOK 4, CHAPTER 7: EXAMINATION OF SUDDEN DEATH

In cases of sudden death, the corpse shall be smeared over with oil and examined.

Any person whose corpse is tainted with mucus and urine, with organs inflated with wind, with hands and legs swollen, with eyes open, and with neck marked with ligatures, may be regarded as having been killed by suffocation and suppression of breathing.

Any person with contracted arms and thighs may be regarded as having been killed by hanging.

Any dead person with swollen hands, legs and belly, with sunken eyes and inflated navel, may be regarded as having been killed by hanging.

Any dead person with stiffened rectum and eyes, with tongue bitten between the teeth, and with belly swollen, may be considered as having been killed by drowning.

Any dead person, wetted with blood and with limbs wounded and broken, may be regarded as having been killed with sticks or ropes.

Any dead person with fractures and broken limbs, may be regarded as having been thrown down.

Any dead person with dark coloured hands, legs, teeth, and nails, with loose skin, hairs fallen, flesh reduced, and with face bedaubed with foam and saliva, may be regarded as having been poisoned.

Any dead person of similar description with marks of a bleeding bite, may be considered as having been bitten by serpents and other poisonous creatures.

Any dead person, with body spread and dress thrown out after excessive vomiting and purging, may be considered as having been killed by the administration of the juice of the madana plant.

Death due to any one of the above causes is, sometimes under the fear of punishment, made to appear as having been brought about by voluntary hanging, by causing marks of ligature round the neck.

In death due to poison, the undigested portion of meal may be examined in milk. Or the same extracted from the belly and thrown on fire may, if it makes "ciṭciṭa" sound and assumes the rainbow colour, be declared as poisoned.

Or when the belly remains unburnt, although the rest of the body is reduced to ashes, the dead man's servants may be examined as to any violent and cruel treatments they may have received at the hands of the dead. Similarly, such of the dead man's relatives as a person of miserable life, a woman with affections placed elsewhere, or a relative defending some woman that has been deprived of her inheritance by the dead man, may also be examined.

The same kind of examination shall be conducted concerning the hanging of the body of an already dead man.

Causes such as past evils or harm done to others by a dead man, shall be inquired into regarding any death due to voluntary hanging.

All kinds of sudden death centre round one or the other of the following causes:

> ➤ Offence to women or kinsmen, claiming inheritance, professional competition, hatred against rivals, commerce,

guilds and any one of the legal disputes, is the cause of anger: anger is the cause of death.

> When, owing to false resemblance, one's own hirelings, or thieves for money, or the enemies of a third person murder one, the relatives of the deceased shall be inquired as follows:

> Who called the deceased; who was with him; who accompanied him on his journey; and who took him to the scene of death?

Those who happened to be at the locality of murder shall be severally asked as follows:

> By whom was the deceased brought there; whether they (the witnesses) saw any armed person lurking in the place and showing-signs of troubled appearance?

> Any clue afforded by them shall be followed in further enquiry.

* After examining the personal property, such as travelling requisites, dress, jewels, or other things which the deceased had on his body while murdered, such persons as supplied or had something to do with those things shall be examined as to the associates, residence, cause of journey, profession, and other calls of the deceased.

* If a man or woman under the infatuation of love, anger or other sinful passions commits, or causes to commit, suicide by means of ropes, arms, or poison, he or she shall be dragged by means of a rope along the public road by the hands of a Caṇḍāla.

* For such murderers as the above, neither cremation rites nor any obsequies usually performed by relatives shall be observed.

* Any relative who performs funeral rites to such wretches, shall either himself be deprived of his own funeral or be abandoned by his kith and kin.

* Whoever associates himself with such persons as perform forbidden rites shall, with his other associates, if any, forfeit within a year the privileges of conducting or superintending a sacrifice, of teaching, and of giving or receiving gifts.

8.2   ARTHASHASTRA, BOOK 4, CHAPTER 12: SEXUAL INTERCOURSE WITH MINOR GIRLS

He who defiles a maiden of equal caste before she has reached her maturity shall have his hand cut off or pay a fine of 400 panas; if the maiden dies in consequence, the offender shall be put to death.

He who defiles a maiden who has attained maturity shall have his middle finger cut off or pay a fine of 200 panas, besides giving an adequate compensation to her father.

No man shall have sexual intercourse with any woman against her will.

He who defiles a willing maiden shall pay a fine of 54 panas, while the maiden herself shall pay a fine of half the amount.

When a man impersonates another man who has already paid the nuptial fee to a woman, he shall have his hand cut off or pay a fine of 400 panas, besides making good the nuptial fee.

No man who has connection with a maiden that has passed seven menses and has not yet succeeded in marrying her, though she has been betrothed to him, shall either be guilty or pay any compensation to her father; for her father has lost his authority over her in consequence of having deprived her so long of the result of her menses.

It is no offence for a man of equal caste and rank to have connection, with a maiden who has been unmarried three years after her first menses. Nor is it an offence for a man, even of different caste, to have connection with a maiden who has spent more than three years after her first menses and has no jewelry on her person; for taking possession of paternal property (under such circumstances) shall be regarded as theft.

Any person who, while pretending to secure a bride to a particular person, ultimately obtains her for a third person, shall be fined 200 panas.

If a person substitutes in marriage another maiden for the one he has before shown, he shall, if the substitute is of the same rank, be fined 100 panas; and 200 panas if she is of a lower rank. The substituted maiden shall be fined 54 panas, while the offender shall also be compelled to return both the nuptial fee and the amount of expenditure (incurred by the bridegroom). When a man refuses to give in marriage a particular maiden as agreed upon, he shall pay double the above fine. When a man substitutes in marriage a maiden of different blood or is found to have bestowed false praises (on her quality), he shall not only pay a fine of 200 panas and return the nuptial fee, but also make good the expenditure.

When a woman being desirous of intercourse, yields herself to a man of the same caste and rank, she shall be fined 12 panas, while any other woman who is an abettor in the case shall be fined twice as much. Any woman who abets a man in having intercourse with a maiden against her will shall not only pay a fine of 100 panas, but also please the maiden, providing her with an adequate nuptial fee.

A woman who, of her own accord, yields herself to a man, shall be a slave to the king.

For committing intercourse with a woman outside a village, or for spreading false report regarding such things, double the usual fines shall be imposed.

He who carries off a maiden by force shall be fined 200 panas; if the maiden thus carried off has golden ornaments on her person, the highest amercement shall be imposed. If a number of persons abduct a maiden, each of them shall be punished as above.

When a man has connection with a harlot's daughter, he shall not only pay a fine of 54 paṇas, but also give her mother sixteen times her daily income.

When a man defiles the daughter of his own male or female slave, he shall not only pay a fine of 24 paṇas, but also provide the maiden with an adequate nuptial fee (śulka) and jewelry.

When a man has connection with a woman who has been held in slavery on account of certain ransom due from her, he shall not only pay a fine of 12 paṇas, but also provide the woman with dress and maintenance.

Abettors in all the above cases shall each have the same punishment as the principal offender.

A relative, or a servant of an absentee husband may take the latter's wife of loose character under his own protection (may marry her). Being under such protection, she shall wait for the return of her husband. If her husband, on his return, entertains no objection, both the protector and the woman shall be acquitted. If he raises any objection, the woman shall have her ears and nose cut off, while her keeper shall be put to death as an adulterer.

When a man falsely accuses another of having committed theft while in reality the latter is guilty of adultery, the complainant shall be fined 500 paṇas.

He who lets off an adulterer by receiving gold shall pay a fine of eight times the value of the gold (he received).

(Adultery may be proved by circumstances, such as) hand to hand fight, abduction, any marks made on the body of the culprits, opinion of experts on consideration of the circumstances, or the statements of women involved in it.

When a man rescues a woman from enemies, forests, or floods, or saves the life of a woman who has been abandoned in forests, forsaken in famine, or thrown out as if dead, he may enjoy her as agreed upon during the rescue.

A woman of high caste, with children and having no desire for sexual enjoyment, may be let off after receiving an adequate amount of ransom,

* Those women who have been rescued from the hands of thieves, from floods, in famine, or in national calamities, or who, having been abandoned, missed, or thrown out as if dead in forests, have been taken home, may be enjoyed by the rescuer as agreed upon.

* But no such women as have been cast out under royal edict, or by their own kinsmen; nor such as belong to high caste, or do not like to be rescued, nor even those who have children, shall be rescued either for ransom or for their person.

8.3 ARTHASHASTRA, BOOK 4, CHAPTER 13: PUNISHMENT FOR VIOLATING JUSTICE

He who causes a Brahman to partake of whatever food or drink is prohibited shall be punished with the highest amercement. He who causes a Kṣatriya to do the same shall be punished with the middlemost amercement; a Vaiśya, with the first amercement; and a Śūdra, with a fine of 54 paṇas.

Those who voluntarily partake of whatever is condemned, either as food or drink, shall be outcasts.

He who forces his entrance into another's house during the day shall be punished with the first amercement; and during the night with the middlemost. Any person who, with weapon in hand, enters into another's house, either during the day or night, shall be punished with the highest amercement.

When beggars or pedlars and lunatics or mad persons attempt to enter into a house by force, or when neighbors force their entrance into a house in danger, they shall not be punished, provided no such entrance is specially prohibited.

He who mounts the roof of his own house after midnight shall be punished with the first amercement; and of another's house, with the middlemost amercement.

Those who break the fences of villages, gardens, or fields shall also be punished with the middlemost amercement.

Having made the value, etc., of their merchandise known (to the headman of the village), traders shall halt in some part of a village. When any part of their merchandise which has not been truly sent out of the village during the night has been stolen or lost, the headman of the village shall make good the loss.

Whatever of their merchandise is stolen or lost in the intervening places between any two villages shall the superintendent of pasture lands make good. If there are no pasture lands (in such places), the officer called corarajjuka, shall make good the loss. If the loss of merchandise occurs in such parts of the country as are not provided even with such security (a corarajjuka), the people in the boundaries of the place shall contribute to make up the loss. If there are no people in the boundaries, the people of five or ten villages of the neighbourhood shall make up the loss.

Harm due to the construction of unstable houses, carts with no support, or with a beam or weapon hung above, or with damaged support, or with no covering, and harm due to causing a cart to fall in pits, or a tank, or from a dam, shall be treated as assault.

Gutting of trees, stealing the rope with which a tamable animal is tied, employing untamed quadrupeds, throwing sticks, mud, stones, rods, or arrows on chariots, or elephants, raising or waving the arm against chariots or elephants, shall also be treated as assault.

(The charioteer) who cries out (to a passer-by), "Get out," shall not be punished for collision.

A man who is hurt to death by an elephant under provocation (caused by himself) shall supply not only a kumbha of liquor (less by a droṇa), garlands, and scents, but also as much cloth as is necessary to wash the tusks; for death caused by an elephant is as meritorious as the sacred bath taken at the end of a horse-sacrifice. Hence this offer (of liquor, etc.), is known as "washing the legs."

When an indifferent passer-by is killed by an elephant, the driver shall be punished with the highest amercement,

When the owner of a horned or tusked animal does not rescue a man from being destroyed by his animal, he shall be punished with the first amercement. If he heedlessly keeps quiet from rescuing though entreated, he shall be punished with twice the first amercement.

When a person causes or allows horned or tusked animals to destroy each other, he shall not only pay a fine equal to the value of the destroyed animal or animals, but also make good the loss (to the sufferer).

When a man rides over an animal which is left off in the name of gods, or over a bull, an ox, or over a female calf, he shall be fined 500 paṇas. He who drives away the above animals shall be punished with the highest amercement.

When a person carries off such inferior quadrupeds as are productive of wool or milk, or are useful for loading, or riding, he shall not only pay a fine equal to their value, but also restore them.

The same punishment shall be imposed in the case of driving away inferior quadrupeds for purposes other than ceremonials performed in honour of gods or ancestors.

When an animal, which has its nose-string cut off or which is not well tamed to yoke, causes hurt; or when an animal, either coming furiously against a man or receding backwards with the cart to which it is tied, causes hurt, or when an animal causes hurt in confusion brought about by the thronging of people and other animals; the owner of the animal shall not be punished; but for hurt caused to men under circumstances other than the above, fines shall be imposed as laid down before, while the loss of any animal life due to such causes shall be made good. If the driver of a cart or carriage causing hurt is a minor, the master inside the cart or carriage shall be punished. In the absence of the master, any person who is seated inside, or the driver himself if he has attained his majority, shall be punished. Carts or carriages occupied by a minor or with no person shall be taken possession of by the king.

Whatever a man attempts to do to others by witchcraft shall be (practically) applied to the doer himself. Witchcraft merely to arouse love in an indifferent wife, in a maiden by her lover, or in a wife by her husband is no offence. But when it is injurious to others, the doer shall be punished with the middlemost amercement.

When a man performs witchcraft to win the sister of his own father or mother, the wife of a maternal uncle or of a preceptor, his own daughter-in-law, daughter, or sister, he shall have his limb cut off and also be put to death, while any woman who yields herself to such an offender shall also receive similar punishment. Any woman who yields herself to a slave, a servant, or a hired laborer shall be similarly punished.

A Kṣatriya who commits adultery with an unguarded Brāhman woman shall be punished with the highest amercement; a Vaiśya doing the same shall be deprived of the whole of his property; and a Śūdra shall be burnt alive wound round in mats.

Whoever commits adultery with the queen of the land shall be burnt alive in a vessel.

A man who commits adultery with a woman of low caste shall be banished, with prescribed mark branded on his forehead, or shall be degraded to the same caste.

A Śūdra or a Śvapāka who commits adultery with a woman of low caste shall be put to death, while the woman shall have her ears and nose cut off.

Adultery with a nun shall be punishable with a fine of 24 paṇas, while the nun who submits herself shall also pay a similar fine.

A man who forces his connection with a harlot shall be fined 12 paṇas.

When many persons perform witchcraft towards a single woman, each of them shall be punished with a fine of 24 paṇas.

When a man has connection with a woman against the order of nature, he shall be punished with the first amercement.

A man having sexual intercourse with another man shall also pay the first amercement.

* When a senseless man has sexual intercourse with beasts, he shall be fined 12 paṇas; when he commits the same act with idols (representatives) of goddesses, he shall be fined twice as much.

*When the king punishes an innocent man, he shall throw into water dedicating to god Varuṇa a fine equal to thirty times the unjust imposition; and this amount shall afterwards be distributed among the Brāhmans.

* By this act, the king will be free from the sin of unjust imposition; for king Varuṇa is the ruler of sinners among men.

CHAPTER 9

KAUTILYA'S ARTHASHASTRA, BOOK 7: END OF THE SIX-FOLD POLICY

9.1 ARTHASHASTRA, BOOK 7, CHAPTER 1: SIX-FOLD POLICY

The peace (sandhi), war (vigraha), observance of neutrality (āsana), marching (yāna), alliance (saṃśraya), and making peace with one and waging war with another are the six forms of state policy.

Kauṭilya says that, as their respective conditions differ, the forms of policy are six.

Of these, agreement with pledges is peace; offensive operation is war; indifference is neutrality; making preparations is marching; seeking the protection of another is alliance; and making peace with one and waging war with another, is termed a double policy. These are the six forms.

Whoever is inferior to another shall make peace with him; whoever is superior in power shall wage war; whoever thinks, "No enemy can hurt me, nor am I strong enough to destroy my enemy," shall observe neutrality; whoever is possessed of necessary means shall march against his enemy; whoever is devoid of necessary strength to defend himself shall seek the protection of another; whoever thinks that help is necessary to work out an end shall make peace with one and wage war with another. Such is the aspect of the six forms of policy.

Of these, a wise king shall observe that form of policy which, in his opinion, enables him to build, forts, to construct buildings and commercial roads, to open new plantations and villages, to exploit mines and timber and elephant forests and at the same time to harass similar works of his enemy.

Whoever thinks himself to be growing in power more rapidly both in quality and quantity (than his enemy), and the reverse of his enemy, may neglect his enemy's progress for the time.

If any two kings, hostile to each other, find the time of achieving the results of their respective works to be equal, they shall make peace with each other.

No king shall keep that form of policy, which causes him the loss of profit from his own works, but which entails no such loss on the enemy; for it is deterioration.

Whoever thinks that in the course of time his loss will be less than his acquisition as contrasted with that of his enemy, may neglect his temporary deterioration.

If any two kings, hostile to each other, and deteriorating, except to acquire equal amount of wealth in equal time, they shall make peace with each other.

That position in which neither progress nor retrogression is seen is stagnation.

Whoever thinks his stagnancy to be of a shorter duration and his prosperity in the long run to be greater than his enemy's, may neglect his temporary stagnation.

If any two kings, who are hostile to each other, and are in a stationary condition, except to acquire equal amount of wealth and power in equal time, they shall make peace with each other.

"Of course," says Kauṭilya, "there is no other alternative."

Or if a king thinks:

"That keeping the agreement of peace, I can undertake productive works of considerable importance and destroy at the same time those of my enemy; or apart from enjoying the results of my own works, I shall also enjoy those of my enemy in virtue of the agreement of peace; or I can destroy the works of my enemy by employing spies and other secret means; or by holding out such inducements as a happy dwelling, rewards, remission of taxes, little work and large profits and wages, I can empty my enemy's country of its population, with which he has been able to carry his own works; or being allied with a king of considerable power, my enemy will have his own work destroyed; or I can prolong my enemy's hostility with another king whose threats have driven my enemy to seek my protection; or being allied with me, my enemy can harass the country of another king who hates me; or oppressed by another king, the subjects of my enemy will immigrate into my country, and I can, therefore, achieve the results of my own works very easily; or being in a precarious condition due to the destruction of his works, my enemy will not be so powerful as to attack me; or by exploiting my own resources in alliance with any two (friendly) kings, I can augment my resources; or if a 'Circle of States' is formed by my enemy as one of its members, I can divide them and combine with the others; or by threats or favour, I can catch hold of my enemy, and when he desires to be a member of my own Circle of States, I can make him incur the displeasure of the other members and fall a victim to their own fury"—if a king thinks thus, then he may increase his resources by keeping peace.

Or if a king thinks:

"That as my country is full of born soldiers and of corporations of fighting men, and as it possesses such natural defensive positions as mountains, forests, rivers, and forts with only one entrance, it can easily repel the attack of my enemy; or having taken my stand in my impregnable fortress at the border of my country, I can harass the works of my enemy; or owing to internal troubles and loss of energy, my enemy will suffer early from the destruction works; or when my enemy is attacked by another king, I can induce his subjects to immigrate into my country," then he may augment his own resources by keeping open hostility with such an enemy.

Or if a king thinks:

"That neither is my enemy strong enough to destroy my works, nor am I his; or if he comes to fight with me like a dog with a boar, I can increase his afflictions without incurring any loss in my own works," then he may observe neutrality and augment his own resources.

Or if a king thinks:

"That by marching my troops it is possible to destroy the works of my enemy; and as for myself, I have made proper arrangements to safeguard my own works," then he may increase his resources by marching.

Or if a king thinks:

"That I am strong enough neither to harass my enemy's works nor to defend my own against my enemy's attack," then he shall seek protection from a king of superior power, and endeavor to pass from the stage of deterioration to that of stagnancy and from the latter to that of progress.

Or if a king thinks:

"That by making peace with one, I can work out my own resources, and by waging war with another, I can destroy the works of my enemy," then he may adopt that double policy and improve his resources.

* Thus, a king in the circle of sovereign states shall, by adopting the six-fold policy, endeavor to pass from the state of deterioration to that of stagnation, and from the latter to that of progress.

9.2 ARTHASHASTRA, BOOK 7, CHAPTER 6: MARCH OF COMBINED POWERS

The conqueror should thus over-reach the second element (the enemy close to his territory): He should engage his neighbouring enemy to undertake a simultaneous march with him and tell the enemy: "Thou march in that direction, and I shall march in this direction; and the share in the spoils is equal."

If the booty is to be equally divided, it is an agreement of peace; if otherwise, it is overpowering the enemy.

An agreement of peace may be made with promise to carry out a definite work or with no such promise.

When the agreement is to the effect that, "Thou march to that place, and I shall march to this place," it is termed an agreement of peace to carry out a work in a definite locality.

When it is agreed upon that, "Thou be engaged so long, I shall be engaged thus long," it is an agreement to attain an object in a fixed time.

When it is agreed upon that, "Thou try to accomplish that work, and I shall try to finish this work," it is an agreement to achieve a definite end.

When the conqueror thinks that, "My enemy (now an ally) has to march through an unknown country, which is intersected with mountains, forests, rivers, forts and deserts, which is devoid of foodstuffs, people, pastural grounds, fodder, firewood and water, and which is far away, different from other countries, and not affording suitable grounds for the exercise of his army; and I have to traverse a country of quite the reverse description," then he should make an agreement to carry out a work in a definite locality.

When the conqueror thinks that, "My enemy has to work with foodstuffs falling short and with no comfort during the rainy, hot or cold season, giving rise to various kinds of diseases and obstructing the free exercise of his army during a shorter or longer period of time than necessary for the accomplishment of the work in hand; and I have to work during a time of quite the reverse nature," then he should make time a factor of the agreement.

When the conqueror thinks that, "My enemy has to accomplish a work which, not lasting but trifling in its nature, enrages his subjects, which requires much expenditure of time and money, and which is productive of evil consequences, unrighteous, repugnant to the Madhyama and neutral kings, and destructive of all friendship whereas, I have to do the reverse," then he should make an agreement to carry out a definite work.

Likewise with space and time, with time and work, with space: and work, and with space, time, and work, made as terms of an agreement, it resolves itself into seven forms.

Long before making such an agreement, the conqueror has to fix his own work and then attempt to over-reach his enemy.

When, in order to destroy an enemy who has fallen into troubles and who is hasty, indolent, and not foresighted, an agreement of peace with no terms of time, space, or work is made with an enemy merely for mutual peace, and when, under cover of such an agreement, the enemy is caught hold of at his weak points and is struck, it is termed peace with no definite terms. With regard to this there is a saying as follows:

* "Having kept a neighbouring enemy engaged with another neighbouring enemy, a wise king should proceed against a third king, and having conquered that enemy. of equal power, take possession of his territory."

Peace with no specific end, peace with binding terms, the breaking of peace, and restoration of peace broken, are other forms of peace.

Open battle, treacherous battle, and silent battle (i.e. killing an enemy by employing spies when there is no talk of battle at all) are the three forms of battle.

When, by making use of conciliation and other forms of stratagem and the like, a new agreement of peace is made and the rights of equal, inferior and superior powers concerned in the agreement are defined according to their respective positions, it is termed an agreement of peace with no specific end (other than self-preservation).

When, by the employment of friends (at the Courts of each other), the agreement of peace made is kept secure and the terms are invariably observed and strictly maintained so that no dissension may creep among the parties, it is termed peace with binding terms.

When, having proved through the agency of traitors and spies the treachery of a king, who has made an agreement of peace, the agreement is broken, it is termed the breaking of peace.

When reconciliation is made with a servant, or a friend, or any other renegade, it is termed the restoration of broken peace.

There are four persons who run away from, and return to, their master: one who had reason to run away and to return; one who had no reason either to run away or to return; one who had reason to run away, but none to return; and one who had no reason to run away, but had reason to come back.

He who runs away owing to his master's fault and returns in consideration of (his master's) good nature, or he who runs away attracted by the good nature of his master's enemy and returns finding fault with the enemy, is to be reconciled as he had reason to run away and to return.

Whoever runs away owing to his own fault and returns without minding the good nature either of his old or new master, is a fickle-minded person having no explanation to account for his conduct, and he should have no terms of reconciliation.

Whoever runs away owing to his master's fault and returns owing to his own defects, is a renegade who had reason to run away, but none to return: and his case is to be well considered (before he is taken back).

Whoever returns deputed by the enemy; or of his own accord, with the intention of hurting his old master, as is natural to persons of such bad character; or coming to know that his old master is attempting to put down the enemy, his new master, and apprehensive of danger to himself; or looking on the attempt of his new master to destroy his old master as cruelty—these should be examined; and if he is found to be actuated with good motives, he is to be taken back respectfully; otherwise, he should be kept at a distance.

Whoever runs away owing to his own fault and returns owing to his new master's wickedness is a renegade who had no reason to run away, but had reason to come back; such a person is to be examined.

When a king thinks that, "This renegade supplies me with full information about my enemy's weakness, and, therefore, he deserves to remain here; his own people with me are in friendship with my friends and at enmity with my enemies, and are easily excited at the sight of greedy and cruel persons or of a band of enemies," he may treat such a renegade as deserved.

Whoever has failed to achieve profit from his works, lost his strength, or made his learning a commercial article, or is very greedy, inquisitive to see different countries, dead to the feelings of friendship, or has strong enemies, deserves to be abandoned.

But Kauṭilya says that it is timidity, unprofessional business, and lack of forbearance (to do so). Whoever is injurious to the king's interests should be abandoned, while he who is injurious to the interests of the enemy should be reconciled; and whoever is injurious to the interests of both the king and his enemy should be carefully examined.

When it is necessary to make peace with a king with whom no peace ought to be made, defensive measures should be taken against that point where he can shew his power.

* In restoring broken peace, a renegade or a person inclined towards the enemy should be kept at such a distance that, till the close of his life, he may be useful to the state.

* Or, he may be set against the enemy or may be employed as a captain of an army to guard wild tracts against enemies, or thrown somewhere on the boundary.

* Or he may be employed to carry on a secret trade in new or old commodities in foreign countries, and may accordingly be accused of conspiracy with the enemy.

* Or, in the interests of future peace, a renegade who must be put to death may at once be destroyed.

* That kind of wicked character which has from the beginning grown upon a man owing to his association with enemies is, as ever, fraught with danger as constant living in company with a snake;

* and is ever-threatening with destruction just as a pigeon living on the seeds of plakṣa (holy fig-tree) is to the śālmali (silk-cotton) tree.

* When battle is fought in daylight and in some locality, it is termed an open battle; threatening in one direction, assault in another, destruction of an enemy captured while he was careless or in troubles;

* and bribing a portion of the army and destroying another portion, are forms of treacherous fight; an attempt to win over the chief officers of the enemy by intrigue, is the characteristic of silent battle.

9.3 ARTHASHASTRA, BOOK 7, CHAPTER 7:

Peace and War by Adopting the Double Policy

The conqueror may take in the aid of the second member (i.e. the immediate enemy) thus:

Having combined with a neighbouring king, the conqueror may march against another neighbouring king. Or if he thinks that "(my enemy) will neither capture my rear nor make an alliance with my assailable enemy against whom I am going to march; I shall have double the strength with him, i.e. the enemy suing peace; (my ally) will not only facilitate the collection of my revenue and supplies and put down the internal enemies who are causing me immense trouble, but also punish wild tribes and their followers entrenched in their strongholds, reduce my assailable enemy to a precarious condition or compel him to accept the proffered peace, and having received as much profit as he desires, he will endeavor to endear my other enemies to me," then the conqueror may proclaim war against one and make peace with another, and endeavor to get an army for money or money for the supply of an army from among his neighbouring kings.

When the kings of superior, equal or inferior power make peace with the conqueror and agree to pay a greater, or equal, or less amount of profit in proportion to the army supplied, it is termed even peace; that which is of the reverse character is styled uneven peace; and when the profit is proportionally very high, it is termed deception.

When a king of superior power is involved in troubles, or is come to grief or is afflicted with misfortune, his enemy, though of inferior power, may request of him the help of his army in return for a share in the profit proportional to the strength of the army supplied. If the king to whom peace is offered on such terms is powerful enough to retaliate, he may declare war; otherwise he may accept the terms.

In view of marching for the purpose of exacting some expected revenue to be utilized in recouping his own strength and resources, an inferior king may request of a superior the help of the latter's army for the purpose of guarding the base and the rear of his territory in return for the payment of a greater share in the profit than the strength of the army supplied deserves. The king to whom such a proposal is made may accept the proposal, if the proposer is of good intentions; otherwise he may declare war.

When a king of inferior power or one who is provided with the aid of forts and friends has to make a short march in order to capture an enemy without waging war or to receive some expected profit, he may request a third king of superior power, involved under various troubles and misfortunes, the help of the latter's army in return for the payment of a share in the profit less than the strength of the army supplied deserves. If the king to whom this proposal is made is powerful enough to, retaliate, he may declare war; otherwise he may accept the proposal.

When the king of superior power and free from all troubles Is desirous of causing to his enemy loss of men and money in the latter's ill-considered undertaking, or of sending his own treacherous army abroad, or bringing his enemy under the clutches of an mimical army, or of causing trouble to a reducible and tottering enemy by setting an inferior king against that enemy, or is desirous of having peace for the sake of itself and is possessed of good intentions, he may accept a less share in the profit (promised for the army supplied to another), and endeavor to make wealth by combining with an ally if the latter is equally of good intentions; otherwise he may declare war (against that ally).

A Icing may deceive or help his equal as follows:

When a king proposes peace to another king of equal power on the condition of receiving the help of the latter's army strong-enough to oppose an enemy's army, or to guard the front, centre, and rear of his territory, or to help his friend, or to protect any other wild tracts of his territory, in return for the payment of a share in the profit proportionally equal to the strength of the army supplied, the latter may accept the terms if the proposer is of good intentions; otherwise he may declare war.

When a king of equal power, capable of receiving the help of an army from another quarter requests of another king in troubles due to the diminished strength of the elements of sovereignty, and with many enemies, the help of the latter's army in return for the payment of a share in the profit less than the strength of the army supplied deserves, the latter, if powerful, may declare war; or accept the terms otherwise.

When a king who is under troubles, who has his works at the mercy of his neighbouring kings, and who has yet to make an army, requests of another king of equal power the help of the latter's army in return for the payment of a share in the profit greater than the strength of the army supplied deserves, the latter may accept the terms if the proposer is of good intentions; otherwise war may be declared.

When, with desire of putting down a king in troubles due to the diminished strength of the elements of sovereignty, or with the desire of destroying his well-begun work of immense and unfailing profit, or with the intention of striking him in his own place or on the occasion of marching, one, though frequently getting immense (subsidy) from an assailable enemy of equal, inferior, or superior power, sends demands to him again and again, then he may comply with the demands of the former if he is desirous of maintaining his own power by destroying with the army of the former an impregnable fortress of an enemy, or a friend of that enemy, or laying waste the wild tracts of that enemy, or if he is desirous of exposing the army of the ally to wear and tear even in good roads and good seasons, or if he is desirous of strengthening his own army with that of his ally, and thereby putting down the ally, or winning over the army of the ally.

When a king is desirous of keeping under his power another king of superior or inferior power as an assailable enemy and of destroying the latter after routing out another enemy with the help of the latter, or when he is desirous of getting back whatever he has paid (as subsidy), he may send a proposal of peace to another on the condition of paying more than the cost of the army supplied. If the king to whom this proposal is made is powerful enough to retaliate he may declare war; or if otherwise, he may accept the terms; or he may keep quiet allied with the assailable enemy; or he may supply the proposer of peace with his army full of traitors, enemies and wild tribes.

When a king of superior power falls into troubles owing to the weakness of the elements of his sovereignty, and requests of an inferior king the help of the latter's army in return for the payment of a share in the profit proportionally equal to the strength of the army supplied, the latter, if powerful enough to retaliate, may declare war; if otherwise, accept the terms.

A king of superior power may request of an inferior the help of the latter's army in return for the payment of a share in the profit less than the cost of the army supplied; and the latter, if powerful enough to retaliate, may declare war, or accept the terms otherwise.

* The king who is sued for peace and also the king who offers peace should both consider the motive with which the proposal of peace is made, and adopt that course of action which, on consideration seems to be productive of good results.

9.4 ARTHASHASTRA, BOOK 7, CHAPTER 15: MEASURES CONDUCIVE TO PEACE

When a weak king is attacked by a powerful enemy, the former should seek the protection of one who is superior to his enemy, and whom his enemy's power of deliberation cannot affect. Of kings who are equal in the power of deliberation, difference should be sought in unchangeable prosperity and in association with the aged.

In the absence of a superior king, he should combine with a number of his equals who are equal in power to his enemy and whom his enemy's power of purse, army, and intrigue cannot reach. Of kings who are equally possessed of the power of purse, army, and intrigue, difference should be sought in their capacity for making vast preparations.

In the absence of equals, he should combine with a number of inferior kings who are pure and enthusiastic, who can oppose the enemy, and whom his enemy's power of purse, army, and intrigue cannot reach. Of kings who are equally possessed of enthusiasm and capacity for action, difference should be sought in the opportunity of securing favorable battlefields. Of kings who are equally possessed of favorable battlefields, difference should be sought in their ever being ready for war. Of kings who are equally possessed of favorable battlefields and who are equally ready for war, difference should be sought in their possession of weapons and armor necessary for war.

In the absence of any such help, he should seek shelter inside a fort in which his enemy with a large army can offer no obstruction to the supply of foodstuff, grass, firewood and water, but would sustain a heavy loss of men and money. When there are many forts, difference should be sought in their affording facility for the collection of stores and supplies. Kautilya is of opinion that, one should entrench oneself in a fort inhabited by men and provided with stores and supplies. Also, for the following reasons, one should shelter oneself in such a fort:

"I shall oppose him (the enemy) with his rear-enemy's ally or a Madhyama king, or with a neutral king, I shall either capture or devastate his kingdom with the aid of a neighbouring king, a wild tribe, a scion of his family, or an imprisoned prince; by the help of my partisans with him, I shall create troubles in his fort, country or camp; when he is near, I shall murder him with weapons, fire, or poison, or any other secret means at my pleasure; I shall cause him to sustain a heavy loss of men and money in works undertaken by himself or made to be undertaken at the instance of my spies; I shall easily sow the seeds of dissension among his friends or his army when they have suffered from loss of men and money; I shall catch hold of his camp by cutting off supplies and stores going to it; or by surrendering myself (to him), I shall create some weak points in him and put him down with all my resources; or having curbed his spirit, I shall compel him to make peace with me on my own terms; when I obstruct his movements troubles arise to him from all sides; when he is helpless, I shall slay him with the help of my hereditary army or with his enemy's army, or with wild tribes; I shall maintain the safety and security of my vast country by entrenching myself within my fort; the army of myself and of my friends will be invincible when collected together in this fort; my army, which is trained to fight from valleys, pits, or at night, will bring him into difficulties on his way, when he is engaged in an immediate work; owing to loss of men and money, he will make himself powerless when he arrives here at a bad place and in a bad time; owing to the existence of forts and of wild tribes (on the way), he will find this country accessible only at considerable cost of men and money; being unable to find positions favorable for the exercise of the armies of himself and of his friends, suffering from disease, he will arrive here in distress; or having arrived here, he will not return."

In the absence of such circumstances, or when the enemy's army is very strong, one may run away abandoning one's fort.

My teacher says that one may rush against the enemy like a moth against a flame; success in one way or other (i.e. death or victory) is certain for one who is reckless of life.

No, says Kauṭilya, having observed the conditions conducive to peace between himself and his enemy, he may make peace; in the absence of such conditions, he may, by taking recourse to threats, secure peace or a friend; or he may send a messenger to one who is likely to accept peace; or having pleased with wealth and honour the messenger sent by his enemy, he may tell the latter: "This is the king's manufactory; this is the residence of the queen and the prince; myself and this kingdom are at your disposal, as approved of by the queen and the princes."

Having secured his enemy's protection, he should behave himself like a servant to his master by serving the protector's occasional needs. Forts and other defensive works, acquisition of things, celebration of marriages, installation of the heir-apparent, trade in horses, capture of elephants, construction of covert places for battle (sattra), marching against an enemy, and holding sports—all these he should undertake only at the permission of his protector. He should also obtain his protector's permission before making any agreement with people settled in his country or before punishing those who may run away from country. If the citizens and country people living in his kingdom prove disloyal or inimical to him, he may request of his protector another good country; or he may get rid of wicked people by making use of such secret means as are employed against traitors. He should not accept the offer of a good country even from a friend. Unknown to his protector, he may see the protector's minister, high priest, commander of the army or heir-apparent. He should also help his protector as much as he can. On all occasions of worshipping gods and making prayers, he should cause his people to pray for the long life of his protector; and he should always proclaim his readiness to place himself at the disposal of his protector.

* Serving him who is strong and combined with others, and being far away from the society of suspected persons, a conquered king should thus always behave himself towards his protector.

9.5   ARTHASHASTRA, BOOK 7, CHAPTER 18: CONDUCT OF A MADHYAMA KING, A NEUTRAL KING, AND OF A CIRCLE OF STATES

The third and the fifth states from a Madhyama[1] king are states friendly to him; while the second, the fourth, and the sixth are unfriendly. If the Madhyama king shows favour to both of these states, the conqueror should be friendly with him; if he does not favour them, the conqueror should be friendly with those states.

If the Madhyama king is desirous of securing the friendship of the conqueror's would-be friend, then having set his own and his friend's friends against the Madhyama and having separated the Madhyama from the latter's friends, the conqueror should preserve his own friend; or the conqueror may incite the Circle of States against the Madhyama by telling them: "This Madhyama king has grown haughty, and is aiming at our destruction; let us therefore combine and interrupt his march."

If the Circle of States is favorable to his cause, then he may aggrandize himself by putting down the Madhyama; if not favorable, then having helped his friend with men and money, he should, by means of conciliation and gifts, win over either the leader or a neighbouring king among the kings who hate the Madhyama, or who have been living with mutual support, or who will follow the one that is won over (by the conqueror), or who do not rise owing to mutual suspicion; thus by winning over a second (king), he should double his own power; by securing a third, he should treble his own power; thus gaining in strength, he should put down the Madhyama king.

When place and time are found unsuitable for success in the above attempt, he should, by peace, seek the friendship of one of the enemies of the Madhyama king, or cause some traitors to combine against the Madhyama; if the Madhyama king is desirous of reducing the conqueror's friend, the conqueror should prevent it, and tell the friend: "I shall protect you as long as you are weak," and should accordingly protect him when he is poor in resources; if the Madhyama king desires to rout out a friend of the conqueror, the latter should protect him in his difficulties; or having removed him from the fear of the Madhyama king, the conqueror should provide him with new lands and keep him under his (the conqueror's) protection, lest he might go elsewhere.

If, among the conqueror's friends who are either reducible or assailable enemies of the Madhyama king, some undertake to help the Madhyama, then the conqueror should make peace with a third king; and if among the Madhyama king's friends who are either reducible or assailable enemies of the conqueror, some are capable of offence and defence and become friendly to the conqueror, then he should make peace with them; thus the conqueror can not only attain his own ends, but also please the Madhyama king.

If the Madhyama king is desirous of securing a would-be friend or the conqueror as a friend, then the conqueror may make peace with another king, or prevent the friend from going to the Madhyama, telling him: "It is unworthy of you to forsake a friend who is desirous of your friendship," or the conqueror may keep quiet, if the conqueror thinks that the Circle of States would be enraged against the friend for deserting his own party. If the Madhyama king is desirous of securing the conqueror's enemy as his friend, then the conqueror should indirectly (i.e. without being known to the Madhyama) help the enemy with wealth and army.

If the Madhyama king desires to win the neutral king, the conqueror should sow the seeds of dissension between them.

Whoever of the Madhyama and the neutral kings is esteemed by the Circle of States, his protection should the conqueror seek.

The conduct of the Madhyama king explains that of the neutral king.

If the neutral king is desirous of combining with the Madhyama king, then the conqueror should so attempt as to frustrate the desire of the neutral king to over-reach an enemy or to help a friend or to secure the services of the army of another neutral king. Having thus strengthened himself, the conqueror should reduce his enemies and help his friends, though their position is inimical towards him.

Those who may be inimical to the conqueror are, a king who is of wicked character and who is therefore always harmful, a rear-enemy in combination with a frontal enemy, a reducible enemy under troubles, and one who is watching the troubles of the conqueror to invade him.

Those who may be friendly with the conqueror are, one who marches with him with the same end in view, one who marches with him with a different end in view, one who wants to combine with the conqueror to march (against a common enemy), one who marches under an agreement for peace, one who marches with a set purpose of his own, one who rises along with others, one who is ready to purchase or to sell either the army or the treasury, and one who adopts the double policy (i.e. making peace with one and waging war with another).

Those neighbouring kings who can be servants to the conqueror are, a neighbouring king under the apprehension of an attack from a powerful king, one who is situated between the conqueror and his enemy, the rear-enemy of a powerful king, one who has voluntarily surrendered oneself to the conqueror, one who has surrendered oneself under fear, and one who has been subdued. The same is the case with those kings who are next to the territory of the immediate enemies of the conqueror.

* Of these kings, the conqueror should, as far as possible, help that friend who has the same end in view as the conqueror in his conflict with the enemy, and thus hold the enemy at bay.

* When, after having put down the enemy, and after having grown in power, a friend becomes un-submissive, the conqueror should cause the friend to incur the displeasure of a neighbor and of the king who is next to the neighbor.

* Or the conqueror may employ a scion of the friend's family or an imprisoned prince to seize his lands; or the conqueror may so act that his friend, desirous of further help, may continue to be obedient.

* The conqueror should never help his friend when the latter is more and more deteriorating; a politician should so keep his friend that the latter neither deteriorates nor grows in power.

* When, with the desire of getting wealth, a wandering friend (i.e. a nomadic king) makes an agreement with the conqueror, the latter should so remove the cause of the friend's flight that he never flies again.

* When a friend is as accessible to the conqueror as to the latter's enemy, the conqueror should first separate that obstinate friend from the enemy, and then destroy him, and afterwards the enemy also.

* When a friend remains neutral, the conqueror should cause him to incur the displeasure of his immediate enemies; and when he is worried in his wars with them, the conqueror should oblige him with help,

* When, owing to his own weakness, a friend seeks protection both from the conqueror and the latter's enemy, the conqueror should help him with the army, so that he never turns his attention elsewhere.

* Or having removed him from his own lands, the conqueror may keep him in another tract of land, having made some previous arrangements to punish or favour the friend.

* Or the conqueror may harm him when he has grown powerful, or destroy him when he does not help the conqueror in danger and when he lies on the conqueror's lap in good faith.

* When an enemy furiously rises against his own enemy (i.e. the conqueror's friend) under troubles, the former should be put down by the latter himself with troubles concealed.

* When a friend keeps quiet after rising against an enemy under troubles, that friend will be subdued by the enemy himself after getting rid of his troubles.

* Whoever is acquainted with the sense of polity should clearly observe the conditions of progress, deterioration, stagnation, reduction, and destruction, as well as the use of all kinds of strategic means.

* Whoever thus knows the inter-dependence of the six kinds of policy plays at his pleasure with kings, bound round, as it were, in chains skillfully devised by himself.

CHAPTER 10

KAUTILYA'S ARTHASHASTRA, BOOK 9: WORK OF AN INVADER

10.1   ARTHASHASTRA, BOOK 9, CHAPTER 1: KNOWLEDGE AND THE TIME OF INVASION

The conqueror should know the comparative strength and weakness of himself and of his enemy; and having ascertained the power, place, time, the time of marching and of recruiting the army, the consequences, the loss of men and money, and profits and danger, he should march with his full force; otherwise, he should keep quiet.

Of enthusiasm and power, enthusiasm is better: a king, himself energetic, brave, strong, free from disease, skillful in wielding weapons, is able with his army as a secondary power to subdue a powerful king; his army, though small, will, when led by him, be capable of turning out any work. But a king who has no enthusiasm in himself will perish, though he is powerful and possessed of a strong army.

No, says Kauṭilya, he who is possessed of power over-reaches, by the sheer force of his power, another who is merely enthusiastic. Having acquired, captured, or brought another enthusiastic king as well as brave soldiers, he can make his enthusiastic army of horses, elephants, chariots, and others to move anywhere without obstruction. Powerful kings, whether women, young men, lame, or blind, conquered the earth by winning over or purchasing the aid of enthusiastic persons.

Of power (money and army) and skill in intrigue, power is better; for a king, though possessed of skill for intrigue becomes a man of barren mind if he has no power; for the work of intrigue is well defined. He who has no power loses his kingdom as sprouts of seeds in drought vomit their sap.

No, says Kauṭilya, skill for intrigue is better; he who has the eye of knowledge, and is acquainted with the science of polity, can, with little effort, make use of his skill for intrigue, and can succeed by means of conciliation, and other strategic means and by spies and chemical appliances in over-reaching even those kings who are possessed of enthusiasm and power. Thus of the three acquirements, viz. enthusiasm, power and skill for intrigue, he who possesses more of the quality mentioned later than the one mentioned first in the order of enumeration will be successful in over-reaching others.

Country (space) means the earth; in it the thousand yojanas of the northern portion of the country that stretches between the Himalayas and the ocean from the dominion of no insignificant emperor; in it there are such varieties of land, as forests, villages, mountains, level plains, and uneven grounds. In such lands he should undertake such work as he considers to be conducive to his power and prosperity. That part of the country in which his army finds a convenient place for its maneuver, and which proves unfavorable to his enemy, is the best; that part of the country which is of the reverse nature is the worst; and that which partakes of both the characteristics is a country of middling quality.

Time consists of cold, hot, and rainy periods. The divisions of time are: the night, the day, the fortnight, the month, the season, solstices, the year, and the yuga (cycle of five years). In these divisions of time he should undertake such works as are conducive to the growth of his power and prosperity. That time which is congenial for the maneuver of his army, but which is of the reverse nature for his enemy, is the best; that which is of the reverse nature is the worst; and that which possesses both the characteristics is of middling quality.

Of strength, place, and time, strength is the best; for a man who is possessed of strength can overcome the difficulties due either to the unevenness of the ground or to the cold, hot, or rainy periods of time. Some say that place is the best, for the reason that a dog, seated in a convenient place, can drag a crocodile, and that a crocodile in low ground can drag a dog.

Others say that time is the best, for the reason that during the day-time the crow kills the owl and that at night the owl the crow.

No, says Kauṭilya, of strength, place, and time, each is helpful to the other; whoever is possessed of these three things should, after having placed one-third or one-fourth of his army to protect his base of operations against his rear-enemy and wild tribes in his vicinity, and after having taken with him as much army and treasure as is sufficient to accomplish his work, march during the month of Mārgaśīrṣa (December) against his enemy whose collection of foodstuffs is old and insipid, and who has not only not gathered fresh foodstuffs, but also not repaired his fortifications, in order to destroy the enemy's rainy crops and autumnal handfuls. He should march during the month of Caitra (March), if he means to destroy the enemy's autumnal crops, and vernal handfuls. He should march during the month of Jyeshta (May-June) against one whose storage of fodder, firewood and water has diminished and who has not repaired his fortifications, if he means to destroy the enemy's vernal crops and handfuls of the rainy season. Or he may march during the dewy season against a country which is of hot climate and in which fodder and water are obtained in little quantities. Or he may march during the summer against a country in which the sun is enshrouded by mist and which is full of deep valleys and thickets of trees and grass, or he may march during the rains against a country which is suitable for the maneuver of his own army and which is of the reverse nature for his enemy's army. He has to undertake a long march between the month of Mārgaśīrṣa (December) and Taiṣa (January), a march of mean length between March and April, and a short march between May and June; and in order to be near, a fourth variety of march may be made against one in trouble.

Marching against an enemy under troubles has been explained in connection with "March after Declaring War."

One should almost invariably march against an enemy in troubles.

But Kauṭilya says: that when one's resources are sufficient, one should march, since the troubles of an enemy cannot be properly recognized; or whenever one finds it possible to reduce or destroy an enemy by marching against him, then one may undertake a march.

When the weather is free from heat, one should march with an army mostly composed of elephants. Elephants with profuse sweat in hot weather are attacked by leprosy; and when they have no water for bathing and drinking, they lose their quickness and become obstinate. Hence, against a country containing plenty of water and during the rainy season, one should march with an army mostly composed of elephants. Against a country of the reverse description, i.e. which has little rain and muddy water, one should march with an army mostly composed of asses, camels, and horses.

Against a desert, one should march during the rainy season with all the four constituents of the army (elephants, horses? chariots and men). One should prepare a Programme of short and long distance to be marched in accordance with the nature of the ground to be traversed, viz. even ground, uneven ground, valleys and plains.

* When the work to be accomplished is small, march against all kinds of enemies should be of a short duration; and when it is great, it should also be of long duration; during the rains, encampment should be made abroad.

10.2 ARTHASHASTRA, BOOK 9, CHAPTER 5: EXTERNAL AND INTERNAL DANGERS

The various kinds of dangers are: that which is of external origin and of internal abetment; that which is of internal origin and of external abetment; that which is of external origin and of external abetment; and that which is of internal origin and of internal abetment.

Where foreigners carry on an intrigue with local men or local men with foreigners, there the consequence of the intrigue carried on by the combination of local and foreign persons will be very serious. Abettors of an intrigue have a better chance of success than its originators; for when the originators of an intrigue are put down, others will hardly succeed in undertaking any other intrigue. Foreigners can hardly win over local persons by intrigue; nor can local men seduce foreigners. Foreigners will find their vast efforts after all unavailing, and only conducive to the prosperity of the king (against whom they want to conspire).

When local persons are abetting (with foreigners), the means to be employed to suppress them are conciliation and gifts.

The act of pleasing a man with a high rank and honour is conciliation; favour and remission of taxes or employment to conduct state works is what is termed gifts.

When foreigners are abetting, the king should employ the policy of dissension and coercion. Spies under the guise of friends may inform foreigners: "Mind, this man is desirous of deceiving you with the help of his own spies, who are disguised as traitors." Spies under the garb of traitors may mix with traitors and separate them from foreigners, or foreigners from local traitors. Fiery spies may make friendship with traitors and kill them with weapons or poison; or having invited the plotting foreigners, they may murder the latter.

Where foreigners carry on an intrigue with foreigners, or local men with local men, there the consequences of the intrigue, unanimously carried on with a set purpose, will be very serious. When guilt is got rid of, there will be no guilty persons; but when a guilty person is got rid of, the guilt will contaminate others. Hence, when foreigners carry on an intrigue, the king should employ the policy of dissension and coercion. Spies under the guise of friends may inform foreign conspirators: "Mind, this your king, with the desire of enriching himself, is naturally provoked against you all." Then fiery spies may mix with the servants and soldiers of the abettor (of foreign conspirators) and kill them with weapons, poison, and other means. Other spies may then expose or betray the abettor.

When local men carry on an intrigue with local men, the king should employ necessary strategic means to put it down. He may employ the policy of conciliation with regard to those who keep the appearance of contentment, or who are naturally discontented or otherwise. Gifts may be given under the pretext of having been satisfied with a favoured man's steadfastness in maintaining the purity of his character, or under the plea of anxious care about his weal or woe. A spy under the garb of a friend may tell the local persons: "Your king is attempting to find your heart; you should tell him the truth." Or local men may be separated from each other, by telling them: "This man carries such a tale to the king against you." And coercive measure may be employed as described in the chapter on "Awards of Punishments."

Of these four kinds of danger, internal danger should first be got rid of; for it has been already stated that internal troubles, like the fear from a lurking snake, are more serious than external troubles.

* One must consider that of these four kinds of danger, that which is mentioned first is less grave than the one subsequently mentioned, whether or not it is caused by powerful persons; otherwise (i.e. when the danger is caused by insignificant persons), simple means may be used to get rid of it.

10.3 ARTHASHASTRA, BOOK 9, CHAPTER 6: PERSONS ASSOCIATED WITH TRAITORS AND ENEMIES

There are two kinds of innocent persons, those who have disassociated themselves from traitors, and those who have kept themselves away from enemies.

In order to separate citizens and country-people from traitors, the king should employ all the strategic means, except coercion. It is very difficult to inflict punishment on an assembly of influential men; and if inflicted at all, it may not produce the desired effect, but may give rise to undesirable consequences. He may, however, take steps against the leaders of the seditious, as show in in the chapter on "Awards of Punishments."

In order to separate his people from an enemy, he should employ conciliation and other strategic means to frustrate the attempt of those who are the enemy's principal agents or by whom the enemy's work is to be carried out.

Success in securing the services of capable agents depends upon the king; success of efforts depends upon ministers; and success to be achieved through capable agents is, therefore, dependent both upon the king and his ministers.

When, in spite of the combination of traitors and loyal persons, success is achieved, it is mixed success; when people are thus mixed, success is to be achieved through the agency of loyal persons; for in the absence of a support, nothing that requires a support for its existence can exist. When success is involved in the union of friends and enemies, it is termed a success contaminated by an enemy; when success is contaminated by an enemy, it is to be achieved through the agency of a friend; for it is easy to attain success through a friend, but not through an enemy.

When a friend does not come to terms, intrigue should be frequently resorted to. Through the agency of spies, the friend should be won over after separating him from the enemy. Or attempts may be made to win him over who is the last among combined friends; for when he who is the last among combined friends is secured, those who occupy the middle rank will be separated from each other; or attempts may be made to win over a friend who occupies middle rank; for when a friend occupying middle rank among combined kings is secured, friends occupying the extreme ranks cannot keep the union. (In brief) all those measures which tend to break their combination should be employed.

A virtuous king may be conciliated by praising his birth, family, learning and character, and by pointing out the relationship which his ancestors had (with the proposer of peace), or by describing the benefits and absence of enmity shown to him.

Or a king who is of good intentions, or who has lost his enthusiastic spirits, or whose strategic means are all exhausted and thwarted in a number of wars, or who has lost his men and wealth, or who has suffered from sojourning abroad, or who is desirous of gaining a friend in good faith, or who is apprehensive of danger from another, or who cares more for friendship than anything else, may be won over by conciliation.

Or a king who is greedy or who has lost his men may be won over by giving gifts through the medium of ascetics and chiefs who have been previously kept with him for the purpose.

Gifts are of five kinds: abandonment of what is to be paid; continuance of what is being given; repayment of what is received; payment of one's own wealth; and help for a voluntary raid on the property of others.

When any two kings are apprehensive of enmity and seizure of land from each other, seeds of dissension may be sown between them. The timider of the two may be threatened with destruction and may be told: "Having made peace with (someone), this king works against you; his friend is entrusted with the work of making peace, of which you are no party."

When from one's own country or from another's country merchandise or commodities for manufacture in a manufactory are going to an enemy's country, spies may spread the information that those commodities are obtained from one whom the enemy wanted to march against. When commodities are thus gathered in abundance (the owner of the articles) may send a message to the enemy: "These commodities and merchandise are sent by me to you; please declare war against the combined kings or desert them; you will then get the rest of the tribute." Then spies may inform the other kings of the combination: "These articles are given to him by your enemy."

The conqueror may gather some merchandise peculiar to his enemy's country and unknown elsewhere. Spies, under the garb of merchants, may sell that merchandise to other important enemies and tell them that that merchandise was given (to the conqueror) by the enemy (whose country's product it is).

Or having pleased with wealth and honour those who are highly treacherous (among an enemy's people), the conqueror may cause them to live with the enemy, armed with weapons, poison and fire. One of the ministers of the king may be expelled. His sons and wife may be concealed and declared that they were killed at night. Then the minister may introduce other ministers (to the enemy). If they do (kill the enemy) as they are told, they may be caused to be set free; if they are unable to do so, they may be caused to be caught hold of. Whoever has gained the confidence of the enemy may tell the enemy that he (the enemy) has to guard his own person from such and such a chief. Then the recipient of salaries from the two states (the conqueror's and the enemy's state) may send instructions to destroy the chief.

Or such a king as is possessed of enthusiasm and power may be told: "Seize the country of this king, our treaty of peace standing as before." Then spies should inform the particular king of the attempt of these kings, and cause the destruction of the commissariat and of the followers of one of these kings. Other spies, pretending to be friends, should inform him that the other kings are aiming at his life.

When an enemy's brave soldier, elephant, or horse dies, or is killed, carried off by spies, other spies may tell the enemy that the death is due to mutual conflict among his followers. The man who is employed to commit such murders may be asked to repeat his work again on the condition of his receiving the balance due to him. He should receive the amount from the recipient of salaries from two states; when the king's party is thus divided, some may be won over (to the side of the conqueror).

This explains the case of the commander-in-chief, the prince, and the officers of the army (of the enemy).

Likewise seeds of dissension may be sown among combined-states. Thus the work of sowing the seeds of dissension.

Spies under concealment may, without the help of a fiery spy, murder by means of weapons, poison or other things a fortified enemy who is of mean character or who is under troubles; any one of the hidden spies may do the work when it is found easy: or a fiery spy alone may do the work by means of weapons, poison or fire; for a fiery spy can do what others require all the necessary aids to do.

Thus, the four forms of strategic means.

Of these means, that which comes first in the order of enumeration is, as stated in connection with "Invaders," easier than the rest. Conciliation is of single quality; gift is twofold, since conciliation precedes it; dissension is threefold, since conciliation and gift precede it; and conciliatory coercion is fourfold, since conciliation, gift, and dissension precede it.

The same means are employed in the case of local enemies, too; the difference is this: the chief messengers known to the manufactories may be sent to any one of the local enemies in order to employ him, for the purpose of making a treaty or for the purpose of destroying another person. When he agrees to the proposal, the messengers should inform (their master) of their success. Then recipients of salaries from two states should inform the people or enemies concerned in the local enemy's work: "This person (the local enemy) is your wicked king." When a person has reason to fear or hate another, spies may augment dissension between them by telling one of them: "This man is making an agreement with your enemy, and will soon deceive you; hence make peace (with the king) soon and attempt to put down this man." Or by bringing about friendship or marriage connection between persons who have not been hitherto connected, spies may separate them from others; or through the aid of a neighbouring king, a wild chief, a scion of an enemy's family, or an imprisoned prince, local enemies may be destroyed outside the kingdom; or through the agency of a caravan or wild tribes, a local enemy may be killed along with his army; or persons, pretending to be the supporters of a local enemy and who are of the same caste, may under favorable opportunities kill him; or spies under concealment may kill local enemies with fire, poison, and weapons.

* When the country is full of local enemies, they may be got rid of by making them drink poisonous (liquids); an obstinate (clever) enemy may be destroyed by spies or by means of (poisoned) flesh given to him in good faith.

CHAPTER 11

KAUTILYA'S ARTHASHASTRA, BOOK 10: RELATING TO WAR

11.1 ARTHASHASTRA, BOOK 10, CHAPTER 1: ENCAMPMENT

On a site declared to be the best according to the science of buildings, the leader, the carpenter, and the astrologer should measure a circular, rectangular, or square spot for the camp, which should, in accordance with the available space, consist of four gates, six roads, and nine divisions.

Provided with ditches, parapets, walls, doors, and watch towers for defence against fear, the quarters of the king, 1,000 bows long and half as broad, should be situated in one of the nine divisions to the north from the centre, while to the west of it his harem, and at its extremity, the army of the harem are to be situated. In his front, the place for worshipping gods; to his right the departments of finance and accounts; and to his left the quarters of elephants and horses mounted by the king himself. Outside this, and at a distance of 100 bows from each other, there should be four divisions made by carts, thorny trees, pillars and walls. In the first (of these four divisions), the prime minister and the priest (should have their quarters); to its right the store-house and the kitchen; to its left the store of raw products and weapons; in the second division the quarters of the hereditary army and of. horses and chariots; and of the commander; in the third, elephants, the śreni, and the praśāstri; in the fourth, free laborers, the leader, the army of the friend and the enemy with its own commander; traders, and prostitutes along the high road; outside this, hunters and keepers of dogs with their trumpets and with fire; also spies and sentinels; also to prevent the attack of enemies, wells, mounds and thorns should be arranged. The eighteen divisions of sentinels employed for the purposes of securing the safety of the king should be changing their watches in turn. In order to ascertain the movements of spies, a time-table of business should also be prepared during the day. Disputes, drinking, social gatherings, and gambling should also be prohibited. The system of passports should also be observed. The officer in charge of the boundary (of the camp) should supervise the conduct of the commander-in-chief and the observance of the instructions given to the army.

* The instructor, with his retinue and with carpenters and free laborers, should carefully march in front on the road, and should take protective measures and dig wells of water.

11.2   ARTHASHASTRA, BOOK 10, CHAPTER 2: MARCH OF THE CAMP

Having prepared a list of the villages and forests situated on the road with reference to their capacity to supply grass, firewood and water, march of the army should be regulated according to the Programme of short and long halts. Foodstuffs and provisions should be carried in double the quantity that may be required in any emergency. In the absence of separate means to carry foodstuffs, the army itself should be entrusted with the business of carrying them; or they may be stored in a central place.

In front the leader; in the centre the harem and the master (the king); on the sides horses and bodyguards; at the extremity of the (marching) circular array, elephants and the surplus army; on all sides the army habituated to forest-life; and other troops following the camp, the commissariat, the army of an ally, and his followers should select their own road: for armies who have secured suitable positions will prove superior in fight to those who are in bad positions.

The army of the lowest quality can march a yojana (55/44 miles a day); that of the middle quality a yojana and a half; and the best army two yojanas. Hence, it is easy to ascertain the rate of march. The commander should march behind and put up his camp in the front.

In case of any obstruction, the army should march in crocodile array in the front, in cart-like array behind, and on the sides in diamond-like array (i.e. in four or five rows, each having its front, rear and sides) and in a compact array on all sides. When the army is marching on a path passable by a single man, it should march in pin-like array. When peace is made with one, and war is to be waged with another, steps should be taken to protect the friends who are bringing help against enemies, such as an enemy in the rear, his ally, a Madhyama king, or a neutral king. Roads with obstructions should be examined and cleared. Finance, the army, the strength of the armies of friends, enemies, and wild tribes, the prospect of rains, and the seasons should be thoroughly examined.

When the protective power of fortifications and stores (of the enemies) is on its decay, when it is thought that distress of the hired army or of a friend's army (of the enemy) is impending; when intriguers are not for a quick march; or when the enemy is likely to come to terms (with the invader), slow march should be made; otherwise quick march should be made.

Waters may be crossed by means of elephants, planks spread over pillars erected, bridges, boats, timber and mass of bamboos, as well as by means of dry sour gourds, big baskets covered with skins, and rafts, etc.

When the crossing of a river is obstructed by the enemy, the invader may cross it elsewhere together with his elephants and horses, and entangle the enemy in an ambuscade.

He should protect his army when it has to pass a long desert without water; when it is without grass, firewood and water; when it has to traverse a difficult road; when it is harassed by enemy's attacks;

when it is suffering from hunger and thirst after a journey; when it is ascending or descending a mountainous country full of mire, water-pools, rivers and cataracts; when it finds itself crowded in a narrow and difficult path; when it is halting, starting or eating; when it is tired from a long march; when it is sleepy; when it is suffering from a disease, pestilence or famine; when a great portion of its infantry, cavalry and elephants is diseased; when it is not sufficiently strong; or when it is under troubles. He should destroy the enemy's army under such circumstances.

When the enemy's army is marching through a path traversable by a single man, the commander (of the invader's army) should ascertain its strength by estimating the quantity of foodstuffs, grass, bedding, and other requisites, fire pots, flags and weapons. He should also conceal those of his own army. Keeping a mountainous or river fortress with all its resources at his back in his own country, he should fight or put up his camp.

11.3   ARTHASHASTRA, BOOK 10, CHAPTER 3: FORMS OF TREACHEROUS FIGHTS

He who is possessed of a strong army, who has succeeded in his intrigues, and who has applied remedies against dangers may undertake an open fight, if he has secured a position favorable to himself; otherwise a treacherous fight.

He should strike the enemy when the latter's army is under troubles or is furiously attacked; or he who has secured a favorable position may strike the enemy entangled in an unfavorable position. Or he who possesses control over the elements of his own state may, through the aid of the enemy's traitors, enemies and inimical wild tribes, make a false impression of his own defeat on the mind of the enemy who is entrenched in a favorable position, and having thus dragged the enemy into an unfavorable position, he may strike the latter. When the enemy's army is in a compact body, he should break it by means of his elephants; when the enemy has come down from its favorable position, following the false impression of the invader's defeat, the invader may turn back and strike the enemy's army, broken or unbroken. Having struck the front of the enemy's army, he may strike it again by means of his elephants and horses when it has shown its back and is running away. When frontal attack is unfavorable, he should strike it from behind; when attack on the rear is unfavorable, he should strike it in front; when attack on one side is unfavorable, he should strike it on the other.

Or having caused the enemy to fight with his own army of traitors, enemies and wild tribes, the invader should with his fresh army strike the enemy when tired. Or having through the aid of the army of traitors given to the enemy the impression of defeat, the invader with full confidence in his own strength may allure and strike the over-confident enemy. Or the invader, if he is vigilant, may strike the careless enemy when the latter is deluded with the thought that the invader's merchants, camp and carriers have been destroyed. Or having made his strong force look like a weak force, he may strike the enemy's brave men when falling against him. Or having captured the enemy's cattle or having destroyed the enemy's dogs, he may induce the enemy's brave men to come out and may slay them. Or having made the enemy's men sleepless by harassing them at night, he may strike them during the day, when they are weary from want of sleep and are parched by heat, himself being under the shade. Or with his army of elephants enshrouded with cotton and leather dress, he may offer a night-battle to his enemy. Or he may strike the enemy's men during the afternoon when they are tired by making preparations during the forenoon; or he may strike the whole of the enemy's army when it is facing the sun and the wind.

A desert, a dangerous spot, marshy places, mountains, valleys, uneven boats, cows, cart-like array of the army, mist, and night are ambush.

The beginning of an attack is the time for treacherous fights.

As to an open or fair fight, a virtuous king should call his army together, and, specifying the place and time of battle, address them thus: "I am a paid servant like yourselves; this country is to be enjoyed (by me) together with you; you have to strike the enemy specified by me."

His minister and priest should encourage the army by saying thus:

"It is declared in the Vedas that the goal which is reached by sacrifices, after performing the final ablutions, in sacrifices in which the priests have been duly paid for, is the very goal which brave men are destined to attain." About this there are the two verses:

brāhmaṇebhyaścātmānamatisṛjet

* Beyond those places which Brāhmans, desirous of getting into heaven, attain together with their sacrificial instruments by performing a number of sacrifices, or by practicing penance, are the places which brave men, losing life in good battles, are destined to attain immediately.

navaṃ śarāvaṃ salilasya pūrṇaṃ susaṃskṛtaṃ darbhakṛtottarīyam

* Let not a new vessel filled with water, consecrated and covered over with darbha grass, be the acquisition of that man who does not fight in return for the subsistence received by him from his master, and who is therefore destined to go to hell.

Astrologers and other followers of the king should infuse spirit into his army by pointing out the impregnable nature of the array of his army, his power to associate with gods and his omniscient; and they should at the same time frighten the enemy. The day before the battle, the king should fast and lie down on his chariot with weapons. He should also make oblations into the fire, pronouncing the mantras of the Atharvaveda, and cause prayers to be offered for the good of the victors as well as of those who attain to heaven by dying in the battlefield. He should also submit his person to Brāhmans; he should make the central portion of his army consist of such men as are noted for their bravery, skill, high birth, and loyalty, and as are not displeased with the rewards and honors bestowed on them. The place that is to be occupied by the king is that portion of the army which is composed of his father, sons, brothers, and other men skilled in using weapons, and having no flags and head-dress. He should mount an elephant or a chariot, if the army consists mostly of horses; or he may mount that kind of animal of which the army is mostly composed or which is the most skillfully trained. One who is disguised like the king should attend to the work of arraying the army.

Soothsayers and court bards should describe heaven as the goal for the brave, and hell for the timid; and also extol the caste, corporation, family, deeds, and character of his men. The followers of the priest should proclaim the auspicious aspects of the witchcraft performed. Spies, carpenters and astrologers should also declare the success of their own operations and the failure of those of the enemy.

After having pleased the army with rewards and honors, the commander-in-chief should address it and say:

A hundred thousand for slaying the king (the enemy); fifty thousand for slaying the commander-in-chief, and the heir-apparent; ten thousand for slaying the chief of the brave; five thousand for destroying an elephant or a chariot; a thousand for killing a horse; a hundred (paṇas) for slaying the chief of the infantry; twenty for bringing a head; and twice the pay in addition to whatever is seized. This information should be made known to the leaders of every group of ten (men).

Physicians with surgical instruments, machines, remedial oils, and cloth in their lands; and women with prepared food and beverage should stand behind, uttering encouraging words to fighting men.

The army should be arrayed on a favorable position, facing other than the south quarter, with its back turned to the sun, and capable to rush as it stands. If the array is made on an unfavorable spot, horses should be run. If the army arrayed on an unfavorable position is confined or is made to run away from it (by the enemy), it will be subjugated either as standing or running away; otherwise it will conquer the enemy when standing or running away. The even, uneven, and complex nature of the ground in the front or on the sides or in the rear should be examined. On an even site, staff-like or circular array should be made; and on an uneven ground, arrays of compact movement or of detached bodies should be made.

Having broken the whole army (of the enemy), (the invader) should seek for peace; if the armies are of equal strength, he should make peace when requested for it; and if the enemy's army is inferior, he should attempt to destroy it, but not that which has secured a favorable position and is reckless of life.

* When a broken army, reckless of life, resumes its attack, its fury becomes irresistible; hence he should not harass a broken army (of the enemy).

11.4   ARTHASHASTRA, BOOK 10, CHAPTER 4: BATTLEFIELDS AND THE WORK OF INFANTRY, CAVALRY, CHARIOTS AND ELEPHANTS

For men who are trained to fight in desert tracts, forests, valleys, or plains, and for those who are trained to fight from ditches or heights, during the day or night, and for elephants which are bred in countries with rivers, mountains, marshy lands, or lakes; as well as for horses, such battlefields as they would find suitable (are to be secured).

That which is even, splendidly firm, free from mounds and pits made by wheels and footprints of beasts, not offering obstructions to the axle, free from trees, plants, creepers and trunks of trees, not wet, and free from pits, ant-hills, sand, and thorns, is the ground for chariots.

For elephants, horses and men, even or uneven grounds are good, either for war or for camp.

That which contains small stones, trees and pits that can be jumped over, and which is almost free from thorns, is the ground for horses.

That which contains big stone, dry or green trees and ant-hills, is the ground for the infantry.

That which is uneven with assailable hills and valleys, which has trees that can be pulled down and plants that can be torn, and which is full of muddy soil free from thorns, is the ground for elephants.

That which is free from thorns, not very uneven, but very expansive, is an excellent ground for the infantry.

That which is doubly expansive, free from mud, water and roots of trees, and which is devoid of piercing gravel, is an excellent ground for horses.

That which possesses dust, muddy soil, water, grass and weeds, and which is free from thorns (known as dog's teeth) and obstructions from the branches of big trees, is an excellent ground for elephants.

That which contains lakes, which is free from mounds and wet lands, and which affords space for turning, is an excellent ground for chariots.

Positions suitable for all the constituents of the army have been treated off. This explains the nature of the ground which is fit for the camp or battle of all kinds of the army.

Exploration on occupied positions, camps and forests; holding strategic positions, water, fording places, and positions agreeable with the direction of the wind and the sun; destruction or protection of the commissariat and of troops arriving afresh; supervision of the discipline of the army; lengthening the line of the army; protecting the sides of the army; first attack; dispersion (of the enemy's army); trampling it down; defence; seizing; letting it out; causing the army to take a different direction; carrying the treasury and the princes; falling against the rear of the enemy; chasing the timid; pursuit; and concentration—these constitute the work of horses.

Marching in the front; preparing the roads, camping grounds and path for bringing water; protecting the sides; firm standing, fording and entering into water while crossing pools of water and ascending from them; forced entrance into impregnable places; setting or quenching the fire; the subjugation of one of the four constituents of the army; gathering the dispersed army; breaking a compact army; protection against dangers; trampling down (the enemy's army); frightening and driving it; magnificence; seizing; abandoning; destruction of walls, gates and towers; and carrying the treasury—these constitute the work of elephants.

Protection of the army; repelling the attack made by all the four constituents of the enemy's army; seizing and abandoning (positions) during the time of battle; gathering a dispersed army; breaking the compact array of the enemy's army; frightening it; magnificence; and fearful noise—these constitute the work of chariots.

Always carrying the weapons to all places; and fighting—these constitute the work of the infantry.

The examination of camps, roads, bridges, wells and rivers; carrying the machines, weapons, armors, instruments and provisions; carrying away the men that are knocked down, along with their weapons and armors—these constitute the work of free laborers.

* The king who has a small number of horses may combine bulls with horses; likewise when he is deficient in elephants he may fill up the centre of his army with mules, camels and carts.

11.5   ARTHASHASTRA, BOOK 10, CHAPTER 5: DISTINCTIVE ARRAY OF TROOPS

Having fortified a camp at the distance of five hundred bows, he should begin to fight. Having detached the flower of the army and kept it on a favourable position not visible (to the enemy), the commander-in-chief and the leader should array the rest of the army. The infantry should be arrayed such that the space between any two men is a śama (14 aṅgulas); cavalry with three śamas;

chariots with four śamas; and elephants with twice or thrice as much space (as between any two chariots). With such an array free to move and having no confusion, one should fight. A bow means five aratnis (5 x 24 = 120 aṅgulas). Archers should be stationed at the distance of five bows (from one line to another); the cavalry at the distance of three bows; and chariots or elephants at the distance of five bows.

The intervening space between wings, flanks and front of the army should be five bows. There must be three men to oppose a horse; fifteen men or five horses to oppose a chariot or an elephant; and as many as (fifteen) servants for a horse, a chariot and an elephant should be maintained.

Three groups of three chariots each should be stationed in front; the same number on the two flanks and the two wings. Thus, in an array of chariots, the number of chariots amounts to forty-five; two hundred and twenty-five horses, six hundred and seventy-five men, and as many servants to attend upon the horses, chariots and elephants—this is called an even array of troops. The number of chariots in this array (of three groups of three chariots each) may be increased by two and two till the increased number amounts to twenty-one. Thus, this array of odd numbers of chariots gives rise to ten odd varieties. Thus, the surplus of the army may therefore be distributed in the above manner. Two-thirds of the (surplus) chariots may be added to the flanks and the wings, the rest being put in front. Thus, the added surplus of chariots should be one-third less (than the number added to the flanks and wings). This explains the distribution of surplus elephants and horses. As many horses, chariots and elephants may be added as occasion no confusion in fighting.

Excess of the army is called surplus; deficiency in infantry is called absence of surplus; excess of any one of the four constituents of the army is akin to surplus; excess of traitors is far from surplus; in accordance with one's own resources, one should increase one's army from four to eight times the excess of the enemy's army or the deficiency in the enemy's infantry.

The array of elephants is explained by the array of chariots. An array of elephants, chariots, and horses mixed together may also be made: at the extremities of the circle (array), elephants; and on the flanks, horses, and principal chariots. The array in which the front is occupied by elephants, the flanks by chariots and the wings by horses, is an array which can break the centre of the enemy's army; the reverse of this can harass the extremities of the enemy's army. An array of elephants may also be made: the front by such elephants as are trained for war; the flanks by such as are trained for riding; and the wings by rogue elephants. In an array of horses, the front by horses with mail armour; and the flanks and wings by horses without armour. In an array of infantry, men dressed in mail armour in front, archers in the rear, and men without armour on the wings; or horses on the wings, elephants on the flanks, and chariots in front; other changes may also be made so as to oppose the enemy's army successfully.

The best army is that which consists of strong infantry and of such elephants and horses as are noted for their breed, birth, strength, youth, vitality, capacity to run even in old age, fury, skill, firmness, magnanimity, obedience, and good habits.

One-third of the best of infantry, cavalry and elephants should be kept in front; two-thirds on both the flanks and wings; the array of the army according to the strength of its constituents is in the direct order; that which is arrayed mixing one-third of strong and weak troops is in the reverse order. Thus, one should know all the varieties of arraying the army.

Having stationed the weak troops at the extremities, one would be liable to the force of the enemy's onslaught. Having stationed the flower of the army in front, one should make the wings equally strong. One-third of the best in the rear, and weak troops in the centre—this array is able to resist the enemy; having made an array, he should strike the enemy with one or two of the divisions on the wings, flanks and front, and capture the enemy by means of the rest of the troops.

When the enemy's force is weak, with few horses and elephants, and is contaminated with the intrigue of treacherous ministers, the conqueror should strike it with most of his best troops. He should increase the numerical strength of that constituent of the army which is physically weak. He should array his troops on that side on which the enemy is weak or from which danger is apprehended.

Running against; running round; running beyond; running back; disturbing the enemy's halt; gathering the troops; curving, circling, miscellaneous operations; removal of the rear; pursuit of the line from the front, flanks and rear; protection of the broken army; and falling upon the broken army—these are the forms of waging war with horses.

The same varieties with the exception of (what is called) miscellaneous operations; the destruction of the four constituents of the army, either single or combined; the dispersion of the flanks, wings and front trampling down; and attacking the army when it is asleep—these are the varieties of waging war with elephants.

The same varieties, with the exception of disturbing the enemy's halt; running against; running back; and fighting from where it stands on its own ground—these are the varieties of waging war with chariots.

Striking in all places and at all times, and striking by surprise, are varieties of waging war with infantry.

* In this way, he should make odd or even arrays, keeping the strength of the four constituents of the army equal.

* Having gone to a distance of 200 bows, the king should take his position together with the reserve of his army; and without a reserve he should never attempt to fight, for it is by the reserved force that dispersed troops are collected together.

11.6 ARTHASHASTRA, BOOK 10, CHAPTER 6: ARRAY OF THE ARMY

Wings and front, capable to turn (against an enemy is what is called) a snake-like array; the two wings, the two flanks, the front and the reserve (form an array) according to the school of Bṛhaspati. The principal forms of the array of the army, such as that like a staff, like a snake, like a circle, and in detached order, are varieties of the above two forms of the array consisting of wings, flanks and front.

Stationing the army so as to stand abreast, is called a staff-like array (daṇḍa).

Stationing the army in a line so that one may follow the other, is called a snake-like array.

Stationing the army so as to face all the directions, is called a circle-like array (maṇḍala).

Detached arrangement of the army into small bodies so as to enable each to act for itself) is termed an array in detached order.

That which is of equal strength on its wings, flanks and front, is a staff-like array.

The same array is called pradara (breaking the enemy's array) when its flanks are made to project in front.

The same is called dṛḍhaka (firm) when its wings and flanks are stretched back.

The same is called asahya (irresistible) when its wings are lengthened.

When, having formed the wings, the front is made to bulge out, it is called an eagle-like array.

The same four varieties are called "a bow," "the centre of a bow," "a hold," and "a stronghold," when they are arranged in a reverse form.

That of which the wings are arrayed like a bow, is called victory.

The same with projected front is called vijaya (conqueror); that which has its flanks and wings formed like a staff, is called big ear; the same with its front made twice as strong as the conqueror, is called vast victory); that which has its wings stretched forward is called face of the army; and the same is called face of the fish, when it is arrayed in the reverse form.

The staff-like array in which one (constituent of the army) is made to stand behind the other, is called a pin-like array.

When this array consists of two such lines, it is called an aggregate; and when of four lines, it is called an invincible array—these are the varieties of the staff-like array.

The snake-like array, in which the wings, flanks and front are of unequal depth, is called sarpasārī (serpentine movement), or gomūtrikā (the course of a cow's urine).

When it consists of two lines in front and has its wings arranged as in the staff-like array, it is called a cart-like array; the reverse of this is called a crocodile-like array; the cart-like array, which consists of elephants, horses and chariots is called vāripatantaka—these are the varieties of the snake-like array.

The circle-like array, in which the distinction of wings, flanks and front is lost, is called facing all directions), or sarvatobhadra (all auspicious), aṣṭānika (one of eight divisions), or vijaya (victory)— these are the varieties of the circle-like array.

That of which the wings, flanks and front are stationed apart, is called an array in detached order; when five divisions of the army are arranged in detached order, it is called vajra (diamond), or godha (alligator); when four divisions, it is called udyānaka (park), or kākapadi (crow's foot); when three divisions, it is called ardhacandrikā (half-moon), —these are the varieties of the array in detached order.

The array in which chariots form the front, elephants the wings, and horses the rear, is called auspicious.

The array in which infantry, cavalry, chariots and elephants stand one behind the other is called immovable.

The array in which elephants, horses, chariots and infantry stand in order one behind the other is called invincible.

Of these, the conqueror should assail the pradara by means of the dṛḍhaka; dṛḍhaka by means of the asahya; śyena (eagle-like array) by means of cāpa (an array like a bow); a hold by means of a stronghold; sañjaya by means of vijaya; sthūlakarṇa by means of viśālavijaya; vāripatantaka by means of sarvatobhadra. He may assail all kinds of arrays by means of the durjaya.

Of infantry, cavalry, chariots and elephants, he should strike the first-mentioned with that which is subsequently mentioned; and a small constituent of the army with a big one.

For every ten members of each of the constituents of the army, there must be one commander, called padika; ten padikas under a senāpati; ten senāpatis under a nāyaka (leader).

The constituents of the array of the army should be called after the names of trumpet sounds, flags and ensigns. Achievement of success in arranging the constituents of the army in gathering the forces, in camping, in marching, in turning back, in making onslaughts, and in the array of equal strength depends upon the place and time of action.

* By the display of the army, by secret contrivances, by fiery spies employed to strike the enemy engaged otherwise, by witchcraft, by proclaiming the conqueror's association with gods, by carts, by the ornaments of elephants;

* by inciting traitors, by herds of cattle, by setting fire to the camp, by destroying the wings and the rear of the enemy's army, by sowing the seeds of dissension through the agency of men under the guise of servants;

* or by telling the enemy that his fort was burnt, stormed, or that some one of his family, or an enemy or a wild chief rose in rebellion—by these and other means the conqueror should cause excitement to the enemy.

* The arrow shot by an archer may or may not kill a single man; but skillful intrigue devised by wise men can kill even those who are in the womb.

CHAPTER 12

KAUTILYA'S ARTHASHASTRA, BOOK 12: CONCERNING A POWERFUL ENEMY

12.1 ARTHASHASTRA, BOOK 12, CHAPTER 1: DUTIES OF A MESSENGER

When a king of poor resources is attacked by a powerful enemy, he should surrender himself together with his sons to the enemy and live like a reed (in the midst of a current of water).

Bhāradvāja says that he who surrenders himself to the strong, bows down before Indra (the god of rain).

But Viśālākṣa says that a weak king should rather fight with all his resources, for bravery destroys all troubles; this (fighting) is the natural duty of a Kṣatriya, no matter whether he achieves victory or sustains defeat in battle.

No, says Kauṭilya, he who bows down to all like a crab on the banks (of a river) lives in despair; whoever goes with his small army to fight perishes like a man attempting to cross the sea without a boat. Hence, a weak king should either seek the protection of a powerful king or maintain himself in an impregnable fort.

Invaders are of three kinds: a just conqueror, a demon-like conqueror, and a greedy conqueror.

Of these, the just conqueror is satisfied with mere obeisance. Hence, a weak king should seek his protection.

Fearing his own enemies, the greedy conqueror is satisfied with what he can safely gain in land or money. Hence, a weak king should satisfy such a conqueror with wealth.

The demon-like conqueror satisfies himself not merely by seizing the land, treasure, sons and wives of the conquered, but by taking the life of the latter. Hence, a weak king should keep such a conqueror at a distance by offering him land and wealth.

When any one of these is on the point of rising against a weak king, the latter should avert the invasion by making a treaty of peace, or by taking recourse to the battle of intrigue, or by a treacherous fight in the battlefield. He may seduce the enemy's men either by conciliation or by giving gifts, and should prevent the treacherous proceedings of his own men either by sowing the seeds of dissension among them or by punishing them. Spies, under concealment, may capture the enemy's fort, country, or camp with the aid of weapons, poison, or fire. He may harass the enemy's rear on all sides; and he may devastate the enemy's country through the help of wild tribes. Or he may set up a scion of the enemy's family or an imprisoned prince to seize the enemy's territory. When all his mischief has been perpetrated, a messenger may be sent to the enemy (to sue for peace); or he may make peace with the enemy without offending the latter. If the enemy still continues the march, the weak king-may sue for peace by offering more than one-fourth of his wealth and army, the payment being made after the lapse of a day and night.

If the enemy desires to make peace on condition of the weak king surrendering a portion of his army, he may give the enemy such of his elephants and cavalry as are uncontrollable or as are provided with poison; if the enemy desires to make peace on condition of his surrendering his chief men, he may send over to the enemy such portion of his army as is full of traitors, enemies and wild tribes under the command of a trusted officer, so that both his enemy and his own undesirable army may perish; or he may provide the enemy with an army composed of fiery spies, taking care to satisfy his own disappointed men (before sending them over to the enemy); or he may transfer to the enemy his own faithful and hereditary army that is capable to hurt the enemy on occasions of trouble; if the enemy desires to make peace on condition of his paying a certain amount of wealth, he may give the enemy such precious articles as do not find a purchaser or such raw products as are of no use in war; if the enemy desires to make peace on condition of his ceding a part of his land, he should provide the enemy with that kind of land which he can recover, which is always at the mercy of another enemy, which possesses no protective defences, or which can be colonised at considerable cost of men and money; or he may make peace, surrendering his whole state except his capital.

* He should so contrive as to make the enemy accept that which another enemy is likely to carry off by force; and he should take care more of his person than of his wealth, for of what interest is perishing wealth?

12.2 ARTHASHASTRA, BOOK 12, CHAPTER 2: BATTLE OF INTRIGUE

If the enemy does not keep peace, he should be told:

"These kings perished by surrendering themselves to the aggregate of the six enemies; it is not worthy of you to follow the lead of these unwise kings; be mindful of virtue and wealth; those who advise you to brave danger, sin and violation of wealth, are enemies under the guise of friends; it is dangerous to fight with men who are reckless of their own lives; it is sin to cause the loss of life on both sides; it is violation of wealth to abandon the wealth at hand and the friend of no mean character (meaning the addresser himself); that king has many friends whom he will set against you with the same wealth (that is acquired with your help at my expense), and who will fall upon you from all sides; that king has not lost his influence over the Circle of the Madhyama and neutral states; but you have lost that power over them who are, therefore, waiting for an opportunity to fall upon you; patiently bear the loss of men and money again; break peace with that friend; then we shall be able to remove him from that stronghold over which he has lost his influence. Hence, it is not worthy of you to lend your ear to those enemies with the face of friends, to expose your real friends to trouble, to help your enemies to attain success, and to involve yourself in dangers costing life and wealth."

If without caring for the advice, the enemy proceeds on his own way, the weak king should create disaffection among the enemy's people by adopting such measures as are explained earlier. He should also make use of fiery spies and poison. Against what is described as deserving protection in the chapter, "Safety of His Own Person", fiery spies and poisoners should be employed (in the enemy's court). Keepers of harlots should excite love in the minds of the leaders of the enemy's army by exhibiting women endowed with youth and beauty. Fiery spies should bring about quarrels among them when one or two of them have fallen in love. In the affray that ensues they should prevail upon the defeated party to migrate elsewhere or to proceed to help the master (of the spies) in the invasion undertaken by the latter.

Or to those who have fallen in love, spies, under the guise of ascetics, may administer poison under the plea that the medical drugs given to them are capable of securing the object of love.

A spy, under the guise of a merchant, may, under the plea of winning the love of an immediate maid-servant of the beautiful queen (of the enemy), shower wealth upon her and then give her up. A spy in the service of the merchant may give to another spy, employed as a servant of the maid-servant, some medical drug, telling the latter that (in order to regain the love of the merchant) the drug may be applied to the person of the merchant (by the maid-servant). On her attaining success (the maid-servant) may inform the queen that the same drug may be applied to the person of the king (to secure his love), and then change the drug for poison.

A spy, under the guise of an astrologer, may gradually delude the enemy's prime minister with the belief that he is possessed of all the physiological characteristics of a king; a mendicant woman may tell the minister's wife that she has the characteristics of a queen and that she will bring forth a prince; or a woman, disguised as the minister's wife, may tell him that, "The king is troubling me; and an ascetic woman has brought to me this letter and jewelry."

Spies, under the guise of cooks, may, under the pretense of the king's (the enemy's) order, take some covetable wealth (to the minister) meant for use in an immediate expedition. A spy, under the guise of a merchant, may, by some contrivance or other, take possession of that wealth and inform the minister of the readiness of all the preparations (for the expedition). Thus by the employment of one, two, or three of the strategic means, the ministers of each of the combined enemies may be induced to set out on the expedition, and thus to be away from the inimical kings.

Spies, under the service of the officer in charge of the enemy's waste lands, may inform the citizens and country people residing in the enemy's fortified towns of the condition of the officer's friendship with the people, and say: "The officer in charge of the waste lands tells the warriors and departmental officers thus: 'The king has hardly escaped from danger and scarcely returns with life. Do not hoard up your wealth and thereby create enemies; if so, you will all be put to death.'" When all the people are collected together, fiery spies may take the citizens out of the town and kill their leaders, saying: "Thus will be treated those who do not hear the officer in charge of the waste lands." On the waste lands under the charge of the officer, the spies may throw down weapons, money and ropes bespattered with blood. Then other spies may spread the news that the officer in charge of the waste lands destroys the people and plunders them. Similarly, spies may cause disagreement between the enemy's collector-general and the people. Addressing the servants of the collector-general in the centre of the village at night, fiery spies may say: "Thus will be treated those who subject the people to unjust oppression." When the fault of the collector-general or of the officer in charge of the waste lands is widely known, the spies may cause the people to slay either of them, and employ in his place one of his family or one who is imprisoned.

* Spreading the false news of the danger of the enemy, they (spies) may set fire to the harem, the gates of the town and the store-house of grains and other things, and slay the sentinels who are kept to guard them.

12.3 ARTHASHASTRA, BOOK 12, CHAPTER 3: SLAYING THE COMMANDER-IN-CHIEF AND INCITING A CIRCLE OF STATES

Spies in the service of the king (the enemy) or of his courtiers may, under the pretence of friendship, say in the presence of other friends that the king is angry with the chiefs of infantry, cavalry, chariots and elephants. When their men are collected together, fiery spies having guarded themselves against night watches, may, under the pretence of the king's (the enemy's) order, invite the chiefs to a certain house and slay the chiefs when returning from the house. Other spies in the vicinity may say that it has been the king's (the enemy's) order to slay them. Spies may also tell those who have been banished from the country: "This is just what we foretold; for personal safety, you may go elsewhere."

Spies may also tell those who have not received what they requested of the king (the enemy) that the officer in charge of waste lands has been told by the king: "Such and such a person has begged of me what he should not demand; I refused to grant his request; he is in conspiracy with my enemy. So, make attempts to put him down." Then the spies may proceed in their usual way.

Spies may also tell those who have been granted their request by the king (the enemy) that the officer in charge of waste lands has been told by the king: "Such and such persons have demanded their due from me; I have granted them all their requests in order to gain their confidence. But they are conspiring with my enemy. So, make attempts to put them down." Then the spies may proceed in their usual way.

Spies may also tell those who do not demand their due from the king that the officer in charge of waste lands has been told: "Such and such persons do not demand their due from me. What else can be the reason than their suspicion about my knowledge of their guilt? So, make attempts to put them down." Then the spies may proceed in their usual way.

This explains the treatment of partisans.

A spy employed as the personal servant of the king (the enemy) may inform him that such and such ministers of his are being interviewed by the enemy's servants. When he comes to believe this, some treacherous persons may be represented as the messengers of the enemy, specifying as "this is that."

The chief officers of the army, the ministers and other officers may be induced by offering land and gold to fall against their own men and secede from the enemy (their king). If one of the sons of the commander-in-chief is living near or inside the fort, a spy may tell him: "You are the most-worthy son; still you are neglected; why are you indifferent? Seize your position by force; otherwise, the heir-apparent will destroy you."

Or some one of the family (of the commander-in-chief of the king), or one who is imprisoned may be bribed in gold and told: "Destroy the internal strength of the enemy, or a portion of his force in the border of his country or any other army."

Or having seduced wild tribes with rewards of wealth and honour, they may be incited to devastate the enemy's country. Or the enemy's rear-enemy may be told: "I am, as it were, a bridge to you all; if I am broken like a rafter, this king will down you all; let us, therefore, combine and thwart the enemy in his march." Accordingly, a message may be sent to individual or combined states to the effect: "After having done with me, this king will do his work of you; beware of it. I am the best man to be relied upon."

* In order to escape from the danger from an immediate enemy, a king should frequently send to a Madhyama or a neutral king (whatever would please him); or one may put one's whole property at the enemy's disposal.

12.4   ARTHASHASTRA, BOOK 12, CHAPTER 4: SPIES WITH WEAPONS, FIRE AND POISON

The conqueror's spies who are residing as traders in the enemy's forts, and those who are living as cultivators in the enemy's villages, as well as those who are living as cowherds or ascetics in the district borders of the enemy's country, may send through merchants information to another neighbouring enemy, or a wild chief, or a scion of the enemy's family, or an imprisoned prince, that the enemy's country is to be captured. When their secret emissaries come as invited, they are to be pleased with rewards of wealth and honour and shown the enemy's weak points; and with the help of the emissaries, the spies should strike the enemy at his weak points.

Or having put a banished prince in the enemy's camp, a spy, disguised as a vintner, in the service of the enemy, may distribute as a toast hundreds of vessels of liquor mixed with the juice of the madana plant; or, for the first day, he may distribute a mild or intoxicating variety of liquor, and on the following days such liquor as is mixed with poison; or having given pure liquor to the officers of the enemy's army, he may give them poisoned liquor when they are in intoxication.

A spy, employed as a chief officer of the enemy's army, may adopt the same measures as those employed by the vintner.

Spies, disguised as experts in trading in cooked flesh, cooked rice, liquor, and cakes, may vie with each other in proclaiming in public the sale of a fresh supply of their special articles at cheap price, and may sell the articles mixed with poison to the attracted customers of the enemy.

Women and children may receive, in their poisoned vessels, liquor, milk, curd, ghee, or oil from traders in those articles, and pour those fluids back into the vessels of the traders, saying that at a specified rate the whole may be sold to them. Spies, disguised as merchants, may purchase the above articles, and may so contrive that servants, attending upon the elephants and horses of the enemy, may make use of the same articles in giving rations and grass to those animals. Spies, under the garb of servants, may sell poisoned grass and water. Spies, let off as traders in cattle for a long time, may leave herds of cattle, sheep, or goats in tempting places, so as to divert the attention of the enemy from the attack which they (the enemy) intend to make; spies, as cowherds, may let off such animals as are ferocious among horses, mules, camels, buffaloes and other beasts, having smeared the eyes of those animals with the blood of a musk-rat; spies, as hunters, may let off cruel beasts from traps; spies, as snake charmers, may let off highly poisonous snakes; those who keep elephants may let off elephants (near the enemy's camp); those who live by making use of fire may set fire (to the camp, etc.). Secret spies may slay from behind the chiefs of infantry, cavalry, chariots and elephants, or they may set fire to the chief residences of the enemy. Traitors, enemies and wild tribes, employed for the purpose, may destroy the enemy's rear or obstruct his reinforcement; or spies, concealed in forests, may enter into the border of the enemy's country, and devastate it; or they may destroy the enemy's supply, stores, and other things, when those things are being conveyed on a narrow path passable by a single man.

Or in accordance with a pre-concerted plan, they may, on the occasion of a night-battle, go to the enemy's capital, and blowing a large number of trumpets, cry aloud: "We have entered into the capital, and the country has been conquered." After entering into the king's (the enemy's) palace, they may kill the king in the tumult; when the king begins to run from one direction to another, Mlecchas, wild tribes, or chiefs of the army, lying in ambush, or concealed near a pillar or a fence, may slay him; or spies, under the guise of hunters, may slay the king when he is directing his attack, or in the tumult of attack following the plan of treacherous fights. Or, occupying an advantageous position, they may slay the enemy when he is marching in a narrow path passable by a single man, or on a mountain, or near the trunk of a tree, or under the branches of a banyan tree, or in water; or they may cause him to be carried off by the force of a current of water let off by the destruction of a dam across a river, or of a lake or pond; or they may destroy him by means of an explosive fire or poisonous snake when he has entrenched himself in a fort, in a desert, in a forest, or in a valley. He should be destroyed with fire when he is under a thicket; with smoke when he is in a desert; with poison when he is in a comfortable place; with crocodile and other cruel beasts when he is in water; or they may slay him when he is going out of his burning house.

* By means of such measures as are narrated in the chapter, "Enticement of the Enemy by Secret Means," or by any other measures, the enemy should be caught hold of in places to which he is confined or from which he is attempting to escape.

12.5   ARTHASHASTRA, BOOK 12, CHAPTER 5: CAPTURE OF THE ENEMY

Contrivances to kill the enemy may be formed in those places of worship and visit, which the enemy, under the influence of faith, frequents on occasions of worshipping gods and of pilgrimage.

A wall or stone, kept by mechanical contrivance, may, by loosening the fastenings, be let to fall on the head of the enemy when he has entered into a temple; stones and weapons may be showered over his head from the topmost story; or a door-panel may be let to fall; or a huge rod kept over a wall or partly attached to a wall may be made to fall over him; or weapons kept inside the body of an idol may be thrown over his head; or the floor of those places where he usually stands, sits, or walks may be besprinkled with poison mixed with cow-dung or with pure water; or, under the plea of giving him flowers, scented powders, or of causing scented smoke, he may be poisoned; or by removing the fastenings made under a cot or a seat, he may be made to fall into a pit containing pointed spears; or when he is eager to escape from impending imprisonment in his own country, he may be led away to fall into the hands of a wild tribe or an enemy waiting for him not far from his country, or when he is eager to get out of his castle, he may be likewise misled or made to enter an enemy's country which is to be restored (to the conqueror); the enemy's people should also be kept under the protection of sons and brothers (of the conqueror) in some forts on a mountain, or in a forest, or in the midst of a river separated from the enemy's country by wild tracts of land.

Grass and firewood should be set on fire as far as a yojana (55/44 miles); water should be vitiated and caused to flow away; mounds, wells, pits and thorns (outside the fort wall) should be destroyed; having widened the mouth of the underground tunnel of the enemy's fort, his stores and leaders may be removed; the enemy may also be likewise carried off when the underground tunnel has been made by the enemy for his own use, the water in the ditch outside the fort may be made to flow into it; in suspicious places along the parapet (of the enemy's fort) and in the house containing a well outside the fort, empty pots or bronze vessels may be placed in order to find out the direction of the wind (blowing from the underground tunnel); when the direction of the tunnel is found out, a counter tunnel may be formed; or having opened the tunnel, it may be filled with smoke or water.

Having arranged for the defence of the fort by a scion of his family, the enemy may run in an opposite direction where it is possible for him to meet with friends, relatives, or wild tribes, or with his enemy's treacherous friends of vast resources, or where he may separate his enemy from the latter's friends, or where he may capture the enemy's rear, or country, or where he may prevent the transport of supplies to his enemy, or whence he may strike his enemy by throwing down trees at hand, or where he can find means to defend his own country or to gather reinforcements for his hereditary army; or he may go to any other country whence he can obtain peace on his own terms.

His enemy's (the conqueror's) allies may send a mission to him, saying: "This man, your enemy, has fallen into our hands; under the plea of merchandise or some presentation, send gold and a strong force; we shall either hand over to you your enemy bound in chains, or banish him." If he approves of it, the gold and the army he may send may be received (by the conqueror).

Having access to the enemy's castle, the officer in charge of the boundaries (of the enemy's country) may lead a part of his force and slay the enemy in good faith; under the plea of destroying a people in some place, he may take the enemy to an inimical army; and having led the enemy to the surrounded place, he may slay the enemy in good faith.

A pretending friend may send information to an outsider: "Grains, oil and jaggery and salt stored in the fort (of the enemy) have been exhausted; a fresh supply of them is expected to reach the fort at such and such a place and time; seize it by force." Then traitors, enemies, or wild tribes, or some other persons specially appointed for the purpose, may send a supply of poisoned grains, oil, jaggery, and salt to the fort. This explains the seizure of all kinds of supply.

Having made peace with the conqueror, he may give the conqueror part of the gold promised and the rest gradually. Thus he may cause the conqueror's defensive forces to be slackened and then strike them down with fire, poison or sword; or he may win the confidence of the conqueror's courtiers deputed to take the tribute.

Or if his resources are exhausted, he may run away, abandoning his fort; he may escape through a tunnel or through a hole newly made, or by breaking the parapet.

Or having challenged the conqueror at night, he may successfully confront the attack; if he cannot do this, he may run away by a side path; or, disguised as a heretic, he may escape with a small retinue; or he may be carried off by spies as a corpse; or disguised as a woman, he may follow a corpse (as it were, of her husband to the cremation ground); or on the occasion of feeding the people in honour of gods or of ancestors or in some festival, he may make use of poisoned rice and water, and having conspired with his enemy's traitors, he may strike the enemy with his concealed army; or, when he is surrounded in his fort, he may lie concealed in a hole bored into the body of an idol after eating sacramental food and setting up an altar; or he may lie in a secret hole in a wall, or in a hole made in the body of an idol in an underground chamber; and when he is forgotten, he may get out of his concealment through a tunnel, and, entering into the palace, slay his enemy while sleeping, or loosening the fastenings of a machine (yantra), he may let it fall on his enemy; or when his enemy is lying in a chamber which is besmeared with poisonous and explosive substances, or which is made of lac, he may set fire to it. Fiery spies, hidden in an underground chamber, or in a tunnel, or inside a secret wall, may slay the enemy when the latter is carelessly amusing himself in a pleasure park or any other place of recreation; or spies under concealment may poison him; or women under concealment may throw a snake, or poison, or fire or poisonous smoke over his person when he is asleep in a confined place; or spies, having access to the enemy's harem, may, when opportunities occur, due to the enemy whatever is found possible on the occasion, and then get out unknown. On such occasions, they should make use of the signs indicative of the purpose of their society.

* Having by means of trumpet sounds called together the sentinels at the gate, as well as aged men and other spies stationed by others, the enemy may completely carry out the rest of his work.

CHAPTER 13

KAUTILYA'S ARTHASHASTRA, BOOK 13: STRATEGIC MEANS TO CAPTURE A FORTRESS

13.1 ARTHASHASTRA, BOOK 13, CHAPTER 1: SOWING THE SEEDS OF DISSENSION

When the conqueror is desirous of seizing an enemy's village, he should infuse enthusiastic spirit among his own men and frighten his enemy's people by giving publicity to his power of omniscience and close association with gods.

Proclamation of his omniscience is as follows: rejection of his chief officers when their secret domestic and other private affairs are known; revealing the names of traitors after receiving information from spies specially employed to find out such men; pointing out the impolitic aspect of any course of action suggested to him; and pretensions to the knowledge of foreign affairs by means of his power to read omens and signs invisible to others when information about foreign affairs is just received through a domestic pigeon which has brought a sealed letter.

Proclamation of his association with gods is as follows: holding conversation with, and worshipping, the spies who pretend to be the gods of fire or altar when through a tunnel they come to stand in the midst of fire, altar, or in the interior of a hollow image; holding conversation with, and worshipping, the spies who rise up from water and pretend to be the gods and goddesses of Nāgas (snakes); placing under water at night a mass of sea-foam mixed with burning oil, and exhibiting it as the spontaneous outbreak of fire, when it is burning in a line; sitting on a raft in water, which is secretly fastened by a rope to a rock; such magical performance in water as is usually done at night by bands of magicians, using the sack of abdomen or womb of water animals to hide the head and the nose, and applying to the nose the oil, prepared from the entrails of red spotted deer and the serum of the flesh of the crab, crocodile, porpoise and otter; holding conversation, as though with women of Varuṇa (the god of water), or of Naga (the snake-god), when they are performing magical tricks in water; and sending out volumes of smoke from the mouth on occasions of anger.

Astrologers, soothsayers, horologists, story-tellers, as well as those who read the forebodings of every moment, together with spies and their disciples, inclusive of those who have witnessed the wonderful performance of the conqueror, should give wide publicity to the power of the king to associate with gods throughout his territory. Likewise in foreign countries, they should spread the news of gods appearing before the conqueror and of his having received from heaven weapons and treasure. Those who are well versed in horary and astrology and the science of omens should proclaim abroad that the conqueror is a successful expert in explaining the indications of dreams and in understanding the language of beasts and birds. They should not only attribute the contrary to his enemy, but also show to the enemy's people, the shower of firebrand with the noise of drums (from the sky) on the day of the birth-star of the enemy.

The conqueror's chief messengers, pretending to be friendly towards the enemy, should highly speak of the conqueror's respectful treatment of visitors, of the strength of his army, and of the likelihood of impending destruction of his enemy's men. They should also make it known to the enemy that, under their master, both ministers and soldiers are equally safe and happy, and that their master treats his servants with parental care in their weal or woe. By these and other means they should win over the enemy's men as pointed out above, and as we are going to treat of them again at length:

They should characterise the enemy as an ordinary donkey towards skilful persons; as the branch of lakuca (Artocarpus lacucha) broken to the officers of his army; as a goat on the shore to anxious persons; as a downpour of lightnings to those who are treated with contempt; as a reed, a barren tree, or an iron ball, or as false clouds to those who are disappointed; as the ornaments of an ugly woman to those who are disappointed in spite of their worshipful service; as a tiger's skin, or as a trap of death to his favourite's; and as eating a piece of the wood of pīlu (Careya-arborea), or as churning the milk of a she-camel or a she-donkey (for butter) to those who are rendering to him valuable help.

When the people of the enemy are convinced of this, they may be sent to the conqueror to receive wealth and honour. Those of the enemy who are in need of money and food should be supplied with an abundance of those things. Those who do not like to receive such things may be presented with ornaments for their wives and children.

When the people of the enemy are suffering from famine and the oppression of thieves and wild tribes, the conqueror's spies should sow the seeds of dissension among them, saying: "Let us request to die king for favour, and go elsewhere if not favoured."

* When they agree to such proposals, they should be supplied with money, grains, and other necessary help: thus, much can be done by sowing the seeds of dissension.

13.2   ARTHASHASTRA, BOOK 13, CHAPTER 2: ENTICEMENT OF KINGS BY SECRET CONTRIVANCES

An ascetic, with shaved head or braided hair and living in the cave of a mountain, may pretend to be four hundred years old, and, followed by a number of disciples with braided hair, halt in the vicinity of the capital city of the enemy. The disciples of the ascetic may make presentations of roots and fruits to the king and his ministers and invite them to pay a visit to the venerable ascetic. On the arrival of the king on the spot, the ascetic may acquaint him with the history of ancient kings and their states, and tell him: "Every time when I complete the course of a hundred years, I enter into the fire and come out of it as a fresh youth. Now, here in your presence, I am going to enter into the fire for the fourth time. It is highly necessary that you may be pleased to honour me with your presence at the time. Please request three boons." When the king agrees to do so, he may be requested to come and remain at the spot with his wives and children for seven nights to witness the sacrificial performance. When he does so, he may be caught hold of.

An ascetic, with shaved head or braided hair, and followed by a number of disciples with shaved heads or braided hair, and pretending to be aware of whatever is contained in the interior of the earth, may put in the interior of an ant-hill either a bamboo stick wound round with a piece of cloth drenched in blood and painted with gold dust, or a hollow golden tube into which a snake can enter and remain. One of the disciples may tell the king: "This ascetic can discover blooming treasure trove." When he asks the ascetic (as to the veracity of the statement), the latter should acknowledge it, and produce a confirmatory evidence (by pulling out the bamboo stick); or having kept some more gold in the interior of the ant-hill, the ascetic may tell the king: "This treasure trove is guarded by a snake and can possibly be taken out by performing necessary sacrifice." When the king agrees to do so, he may be requested to come and remain........(as before).

When an ascetic, pretending to be able to find out hidden treasure trove, is seated with his body burning with magical fire at night in a lonely place, disciples may bring the king to see him and inform the king that the ascetic can find out treasure trove. While engaged in performing some work at the request of the king, the latter may be requested to come and remain at the spot for seven nights...... (as before).

An accomplished ascetic may beguile a king by his knowledge of the science of magic known as jambhaka, and request him to come and remain........ (as before).

An accomplished ascetic, pretending to have secured the favour of the powerful guardian deity of the country, may often beguile the king's chief ministers with his wonderful performance and gradually impose upon the king.

Any person, disguised as an ascetic and living under water or in the interior of an idol entered into through a tunnel or an underground chamber, may be said by his disciples to be Varuṇa, the god of water, or of the king of snakes, and shown to the king. While going to accomplish whatever the king may desire, the latter may be requested to come and remain…….. (as before).

An accomplished ascetic, halting in the vicinity of the capital city, may invite the king to witness the person (of his enemy).

When he comes to witness the invocation of his enemy's life in the image to be destroyed, he may be murdered in an unguarded place.

Spies, who under the guise of merchants come to sell horses, may invite the king to examine and purchase any of the animals. While attentively examining the horses, he may be murdered in the tumult, or trampled down by horses.

Getting into an altar at night in the vicinity of the capital city of the enemy and blowing through tubes or hollow reeds the fire contained in a few pots, some fiery spies may shout aloud: "We are going to eat the flesh of the king or of his ministers; let the worship of the gods go on." Spies, under the guise of soothsayers and horologists, may spread the news abroad.

Spies, disguised as Nagas (snake-gods) and with their body besmeared with burning oil, may stand in the centre of a sacred pool of water or of a lake at night, and sharpening their iron swords or spikes, may shout aloud as before.

Spies, wearing coats formed of the skins of bears and sending out volumes of smoke from their mouth, may pretend to be demons, and after circumambulating the city thrice from right to left, may shout aloud as before at a place full of the horrid noise of antelopes and jackals; or spies may set fire to an altar or an image of a god covered with a layer of mica besmeared with burning oil[1] at night, and shout aloud as before. Others may spread this news abroad; or they may cause (by some contrivance or other) blood to flow out in floods from revered images of gods. Others may point to the flow of blood and say that it is an indication of defeat to the enemy. On the night of full or new moon days or in the vicinity of a cremation ground they may point to a Caitya tree with a human corpse, the upper part of which is eaten away. One, disguised as a demon, may call from the tree for the offering of a human victim. If a man boldly comes out to witness this, others may beat him to death with iron rods and make the people believe that he was killed by demons. Spies and other witnesses may inform the king of this wonder. Then spies, disguised as soothsayers and astrologers, may prescribe auspicious and expiatory rites to avert the evil consequences which would otherwise overtake the king and his country. When the king agrees to the proposal, he may be asked to perform in person special sacrifices and offerings with special mantras every night for seven days. Then (while doing this, he may be slain) as before.

In order to delude other kings, the conqueror may himself undertake the performance of expiatory rites to avert such evil consequences as the above and thus set an example to others.

In view of averting the evil consequences of unnatural occurrences, he (the conqueror) may collect money (from his subjects).

When the enemy is fond of elephants, spies may delude him with the sight of a beautiful elephant reared by the officer in charge of elephant forests. When he desires to capture the elephant, he may be taken to a remote desolate part of the forest, and killed or carried off as a prisoner. This explains the fate of kings addicted to hunting.

When the enemy is fond of wealth or women, he may be beguiled at the sight of rich and beautiful widows brought before him with a plaint for the recovery of a deposit kept by them in the custody of one of their kinsmen; and when he comes to meet with a woman at night as arranged, hidden spies may kill him with weapons or poison.

When the enemy is in the habit of paying frequent visits to ascetics, altars, sacred pillars, and images of gods, spies hidden in underground chambers or in subterranean passages, or inside the walls, may strike him down.

* Whatever may be the sights or spectacles which the king goes in person to witness: wherever he may engage himself in sports or in swimming in water;

* Wherever he may be careless in uttering such words of rebuke as "Tut," or on the occasions of sacrificial performance, or during the accouchement of women, or at the time of death or disease (of some person in the palace), or at the time of love, sorrow, or fear;

* Whatever may be the festivities of his own men, which the king goes to attend, wherever he is unguarded, or during a cloudy day, or in the tumultuous concourse of people;

* Or in an assembly of Brāhmans, or whenever he may go in person to see the outbreak of fire, or when he is in a lonely place, or when he is putting on dress or ornaments, or garlands of flower, or when he is lying in his bed or sitting on a seat;

* Or when he is eating or drinking, on these and other occasions, spies, together with other persons previously hidden at those places, may strike him down at the sound of trumpets.

* And they may get out as secretly as they came there with the pretence of witnessing the sights; thus, it is that kings and other persons are enticed to come out and be captured.

13.3 ARTHASHASTRA, BOOK 13, CHAPTER 3: WORK OF SPIES IN A SIEGE

The conqueror may dismiss a confidential chief of a corporation. The chief may go over to the enemy as a friend and offer to supply him with recruits and other help collected from the conqueror's territory; or, followed by a bond of spies, the chief may please the enemy by destroying a disloyal village or a regiment or an ally of the conqueror, and by sending as a present the elephants, horses, and disaffected persons of the conqueror's army or of the latter's ally; or a confidential chief officer of the conqueror may solicit help from a portion of the territory (of the enemy), or from a corporation of people (śreṇi) or from wild tribes; and when he has gained their confidence, he may send them down to the conqueror to be routed down on the occasion of a farcical attempt to capture elephants or wild tribes.

This explains the work of ministers and wild chiefs under the mission of the conqueror.

After making peace with the enemy, the conqueror may dismiss his own confidential ministers. They may request the enemy to reconcile them to their master. When the enemy sends a messenger for this purpose, the conqueror may rebuke him and say: "Thy master attempts to sow the seeds of dissension between myself and my ministers; so, thou should not come here again." Then one of the dismissed ministers may go over to the enemy, taking with him a band of spies, disaffected people, traitors, brave thieves, and wild tribes who make no distinction between a friend and a foe. Having secured the good graces of the enemy, the minister may propose to him the destruction of his officers, such as the boundary-guard, wild chief, and commander of his army, telling him: "These and other persons are in concert with your enemy." Then these persons may be put to death under the unequivocal orders of the enemy.

The conqueror may tell his enemy: "A chief with a powerful army means to offend us, so let us combine and put him down; you may take possession of his treasury or territory." When the enemy agrees to the proposal and comes out honoured by the conqueror, he may be slain in a tumult or in an open battle with the chief (in concert with the conqueror). Or having invited the enemy to be present as a thick friend on the occasion of a pretended gift of territory, or the installation of the heir-apparent, or the performance of some expiatory rites, the conqueror may capture the enemy. Whoever withstands such inducement may be slain by secret means. If the enemy refuses to meet any man in person, then also attempts may be made to kill him by employing his enemy. If the enemy likes to march alone with his army, but not in company with the conqueror, then he may be hemmed in between two forces and destroyed. If, trusting to none, he wants to march alone in order to capture a portion of the territory of an assailable enemy, then he may be slain by employing one of his enemies or any other person provided with all necessary help. When he goes to his subdued enemy for the purpose of collecting an army, his capital may be captured. Or he may be asked to take possession of the territory of another enemy or a friend of the conqueror; and when he goes to seize the territory, the conqueror may ask his (the conqueror's) friend to offend him (the conqueror), and then enable the friend to catch hold of the enemy. These and other contrivances lead to the same end.

When the enemy is desirous of taking possession of the territory of the conqueror's friend, then the conqueror may, under the pretence of compliance, supply the enemy with army. Then, having entered into a secret concert with the friend, the conqueror may pretend to be under troubles and allow himself to be attacked by the enemy combined with the neglected friend. Then, hemmed from two sides, the enemy may be killed or captured alive to distribute his territory among the conqueror and his friend.

If the enemy, helped by his friend, shuts himself in an impregnable fort, then his neighbouring enemies may be employed to lay waste his territory. If he attempts to defend his territory by his army, that army may be annihilated. If the enemy and his ally cannot be separated, then each of these may be openly asked to come to an agreement with the conqueror to seize the territory of the other. Then they will, of course, send such of their messengers as are termed friends and recipients of salaries from two states to each other with information: "This king (the conqueror), allied with my army, desires to seize thy territory." Then one of them may, with enragement and suspicion, act as before (i.e. fall upon the conqueror or the friend).

The conqueror may dismiss his chief officers in charge of his forests, country parts, and army, under the pretence of their intrigue with the enemy. Then going over to the enemy, they may catch hold of him on occasions of war, siege, or any other troubles; or they may sow the seeds of dissension between the enemy and his party, corroborating the causes of dissension by producing witnesses specially tutored.

Spies, disguised as hunters, may take a stand near the gate of the enemy's fort to sell flesh, and make friendship with the sentinels at the gate. Having informed the enemy of the arrival of thieves on two or three occasions, they may prove themselves to be of reliable character and cause him to split his army into two divisions and to station them in two different parts of his territory. When his villages are being plundered or besieged, they may tell him that thieves are come very near, that the tumult is very great, and that a large army is required. They may take the army supplied, and surrendering it to the commander laying waste the villages, return at night with a part of the commander's army, and cry aloud at the gate of the fort that the thieves are slain, that the army has returned victorious, and that the gate may be opened. When the gate is opened by the watchmen under the enemy's order or by others in confidence, they may strike the enemy with the help of the army.

Painters, carpenters, heretics, actors, merchants, and other disguised spies belonging to the conqueror's army may also reside inside the fort of the enemy. Spies, disguised as agriculturists, may supply them with weapons taken in carts loaded with firewood, grass, grains, and other commodities of commerce, or disguised as images and flags of gods. Then spies, disguised as priests, may announce to the enemy, blowing their conch-shells and beating their drums, that a besieging army, eager to destroy all, and armed with weapons, is coming closely behind them. Then in the ensuing tumult, they may surrender the fort gate and the towers of the fort to the army of the conqueror or disperse the enemy's army and bring about his fall.

Or taking advantage of peace and friendship with the enemy, army and weapons may be collected inside the enemy's fort by spies disguised as merchants, caravans, processions leading a bride, merchants selling horses, pedlars trading in miscellaneous articles, purchasers or sellers of grains, and as ascetics. These and others are the spies aiming at the life of a king.

The same spies, together with those described in "Removal of Thorns,"[1] may, by employing thieves, destroy the flock of the enemy's cattle or merchandise in the vicinity of wild tracts. They may poison, with the juice of the Madana plant, the foodstuffs and beverage kept, as previously arranged, in a definite place for the enemy's cowherds, and go out unknown. When the cowherds show signs of intoxication in consequence of their eating the above foodstuffs, spies, disguised as cowherds, merchants and thieves, may fail upon the enemy's cowherds, and carry off the cattle.

Spies, disguised as ascetics with shaved head or braided hair, and pretending to be the worshippers of God Shankarṣaṇa, may mix their sacrificial beverage with the juice of the Madana plant (and give it to the cowherds), and carry off the cattle.

A spy, under the guise of a vintner, may, on the occasion of procession of gods, funeral rites, festivals, and other congregations of people, go to sell liquor and present the cowherds with some liquor mixed with the juice of the Madana plant. Then others may fall upon the intoxicated cowherds (and carry off the cattle).

* Those spies, who enter into the wild tracts of the enemy with the intention of plundering his villages, and who, leaving that work, set themselves to destroy the enemy, are termed spies under the garb of thieves.

13.4 ARTHASHASTRA, BOOK 13, CHAPTER 4: OPERATION OF A SIEGE

Reduction (of the enemy) must precede a siege. The territory that has been conquered should be kept so peacefully that it might sleep without any fear. When it is in rebellion, it is to be pacified by bestowing rewards and remitting taxes, unless the conqueror means to quit it. Or he may select his battlefields in a remote part of the enemy's territory, far from the populous centres; for, in the opinion of Kauṭilya, no territory deserves the name of a kingdom or country unless it is full of people. When a people resist the attempt of the conqueror, then he may destroy their stores, crops, and granaries, and trade.

* By the destruction of trade, agricultural produce, and standing crops, by causing the people to run away, and by slaying their leaders in secret, the country will be denuded of its people.

When the conqueror thinks: "My army is provided with abundance of staple corn, raw materials, machines, weapons, dress, Labourers, ropes and the like, and has a favorable season to act, whereas my enemy has an unfavorable season and is suffering from disease, famine and loss of stores and defensive force, while his hired troops as well as the army of his friend are in a miserable condition"—then he may begin the siege.

Having well-guarded his camp, transports, supplies and also the roads of communication, and having dug up a ditch and raised a rampart round his camp, he may vitiate the water in the ditches round the enemy's fort, or empty the ditches of their water, or fill them with water if empty, and then he may assail the rampart and the parapets by making use of underground tunnels and iron rods. If the ditch is very deep, he may fill it up with soil. If it is defended by a number of men, he may destroy it by means of machines. Horse soldiers may force their passage through the gate into the fort and smite the enemy. Now and then, in the midst of tumult, he may offer terms to the enemy by taking recourse to one, two, three, or all of the strategic means.

Having captured the birds, such as the vulture, crow, naptṛ, bhāsa, parrot, maina, and pigeon, which have their nests in the fort walls, and having tied to their tails inflammable powder, he may let them fly to the forts. If the camp is situated at a distance from the fort and is provided with an elevated post for archers and their flags, then the enemy's fort may be set on Are. Spies, living as watchmen of the fort, may tie inflammable powder to the tails of mongooses, monkeys, cats and dogs, and let them go over the thatched roofs of the houses. A splinter of fire kept in the body of a dried fish may be caused to be carried off by a monkey, or a crow, or any other bird (to the thatched roofs of the houses).

Small balls prepared from the mixture of sarala (Pinus longifolia), deodar, stinking grass, guggulu (Bdellium), śrīveṣṭaka (turpentine), the juice of sajja (Vatica robusta), and lākṣa (lac) combined with dungs of an ass, camel, sheep, and goat are inflammable.

The mixture of the powder of priyāla (Ghiroñjia sapida), the charcoal of avalguja (oanyza, serratula, anthelmintica), madhūcchiṣṭa (wax), and the dung of a horse, ass, camel, and cow is an inflammable powder to be hurled against the enemy.

The powder of all the metals (sarvaloha) as red as fire, or the mixture of the powder of kumbhī (gmelia arberea), sīsa (lead) trapu (zinc), mixed with the charcoal powder of the flowers of pāribhadraka (deodar), palāśa (butea frondosa), and hair, and with oil wax, and turpentine, is also an inflammable powder.

A stick of vishvsaghati painted with the above mixture and wound round with a bark made of hemp, zinc, and lead, is a fire-arrow (to be hurled against the enemy).

When a fort can be captured by other means, no attempt should be made to set fire to it; for fire cannot be trusted; it not only offends gods, but also destroys the people, grains, cattle, gold, raw materials and the like. Also the acquisition of a fort with its property all destroyed is a source of further loss. Such is the aspect of a siege.

When the conqueror thinks: "I am well provided with all-necessary means and with workmen, whereas my enemy is diseased, with officers proved to be impure under temptations, with unfinished forts and deficient stores, allied with no friends, or with friends inimical at heart," then he should consider it as an opportune moment to take up arms and storm the fort.

When fire, accidental or intentionally kindled, breaks out; when the enemy's people are engaged in a sacrificial performance, or in witnessing spectacles or the troops, or in quarrel due to the drinking of liquor; or when the enemy's army is too much tired by daily engagements in battles and is reduced in strength in consequence of the slaughter of a number of its men in a number of battles; when the enemy's people wearied from sleeplessness have fallen asleep; or on the occasion of a cloudy day of floods, or of a thick fog or snow, general assault should be made.

Or having concealed himself in a forest after abandoning the camp, the conqueror may strike the enemy when the latter comes out.

A king, pretending to be the enemy's chief friend or ally, may make the friendship closer with the besieged, and send a messenger to say: "This is thy weak point; these are thy internal enemies; that is the weak point of the besieger; and this person (who, deserting the conqueror, is now coming to thee) is thy partisan." When this partisan is returning with another messenger from the enemy, the conqueror should catch hold of him, and having published the partisan's guilt, should banish him, and retire from the siege operations. Then the pretending friend may tell the besieged: "Gome out to help me, or let us combine and strike the besieger." Accordingly, when the enemy comes out, he may be hemmed between the two forces (the conqueror's force and the pretending friend's force) and killed or captured alive to distribute his territory (between the conqueror and the friend). His capital city may be razed to the ground; and the flower of his army be made to come out and be destroyed.

This explains the treatment of a conquered enemy or wild chief.

Either a conquered enemy or the chief of a wild tribe (in conspiracy with the conqueror) may inform the besieged: "With the intention of escaping from a disease, or from the attack in his weak point by his enemy in the rear, or from a rebellion in his army, the conqueror seems to be thinking of going elsewhere, abandoning the siege." When the enemy is made to believe this, the conqueror may set fire to his camp and retire. Then the enemy coming out may be hemmed... as before.

Or having collected merchandise mixed with poison, the conqueror may deceive the enemy by sending that merchandise to the latter.

Or a pretending ally of the enemy may send a messenger to the enemy, asking him: "Gome out to smite the conqueror already struck by me." When he does so, he may be hemmed... as before.

Spies, disguised as friends or relatives and with passports and orders in their hands, may enter the enemy's fort and help to its capture.

Or a pretending ally of the enemy may send information to the besieged: "I am going to strike the besieging camp at such a time and place; then you should also fight along with me." When the enemy does so, or when he comes out of his fort after witnessing the tumult and uproar of the besieging army in danger, he may be slain as before.

Or a friend or a wild chief in friendship with the enemy may be induced and encouraged to seize the land of the enemy when the latter is besieged by the conqueror. When accordingly any one of them attempts to seize the enemy's territory, the enemy's people or the leaders of the enemy's traitors may be employed to murder him (the friend or the wild chief); or the conqueror himself may administer poison to him. Then another pretending friend may inform the enemy that the murdered person was a fratricide (as he attempted to seize the territory of his friend in troubles). After strengthening his intimacy with the enemy, the pretending friend may sow the seeds of dissension between the enemy and his officers and have the latter hanged. Causing the peaceful people of the enemy to rebel, he may put them down, unknown to the enemy. Then having taken with him a portion of his army composed of furious wild tribes, he may enter the enemy's fort and allow it to be captured by the conqueror. Or traitors, enemies, wild tribes and other persons who have deserted the enemy, may, under the plea of having been reconciled, honoured and rewarded, go back to the enemy and allow the fort to be captured by the conqueror.

Having captured the fort or having returned to the camp after its capture, he should give quarter to those of the enemy's army who, whether as lying prostrate in the field, or as standing with their back turned to the conqueror, or with their hair disheveled, with their weapons thrown down or with their body disfigured and shivering under fear, surrender themselves. After the captured fort is cleared of the enemy's partisans and is well guarded by the conqueror's men, both within and without, he should make his victorious entry into it.

Having thus seized the territory of the enemy close to his country, the conqueror should direct his attention to that of the Madhyama king; this being taken, he should catch hold of that of the neutral king. This is the first way to conquer the world. In the absence of the Madhyama and neutral kings, he should, in virtue of his own excellent qualities, win the hearts of his enemy's subjects, and then direct his attention to other remote enemies. This is the second way. In the absence of a Circle of States (to be conquered), he should conquer his friend or his enemy by hemming each between his own force and that of his enemy or that of his friend respectively. This is the third way.

Or he may first put down an almost invincible immediate enemy. Having doubled his power by this victory, he may go against a second enemy: having trebled his power by this victory, he may attack a third. This is the fourth way to conquer the world.

Having conquered the earth with its people of distinct castes and divisions of religious life, he should enjoy it by governing it in accordance with the duties prescribed to kings.

* Intrigue, spies, winning over the enemy's people, siege, and assault are the five means to capture a fort.

13.5 ARTHASHASTRA, BOOK 13, CHAPTER 5: RESTORATION OF PEACE IN A CONQUERED COUNTRY

The expedition which the conqueror has to undertake may be of two kinds: in wild tracts or in single villages and the like.

The territory which he acquires may be of three kinds: that which is newly acquired, that which is recovered (from usurper), and that which is inherited.

Having acquired a new territory, he should cover the enemy's vices with his own virtues, and the enemy's virtues by doubling his own virtues, by strict observance of his own duties, by attending to his works, by bestowing rewards, by remitting taxes, by giving gifts, and by bestowing honours. He should follow the friends and leaders of the people. He should give rewards, as promised, to those who deserted the enemy for his cause; he should also offer rewards to them as often as they render help to him; for whoever fails to fulfil his promises becomes untrustworthy both to his own and his enemy's people. Whoever acts against the will of the people will also become unreliable. He should adopt the same mode of life, the same dress, language, and customs as those of the people. He should follow the people in their faith with which they celebrate their national, religious and congregational festivals or amusements. His spies should often bring home to the mind of the leaders of provinces, villages, castes, and corporations the hurt inflicted on the enemies in contrast with the high esteem and favour with which they are treated by the conqueror, who finds his own prosperity in theirs. He should please them by giving gifts, remitting taxes, and providing for their security. He should always hold religious life in high esteem. Learned men, orators, charitable and brave persons should be favoured with gifts of land and money and with remission of taxes. He should release all the prisoners, and afford help to miserable, helpless, and diseased persons. He should prohibit the slaughter of animals for half a month during the period of Cāturmāsya (from July to September), for four nights during the full moon, and for a night on the day of the birth star of the conqueror or of the national star. He should also prohibit the slaughter of females and young ones as well as castration. Having abolished those customs or transactions which he might consider either as injurious to the growth of his revenue and army or as unrighteous, he should establish righteous transactions. He should compel born thieves as well as the Mlecchas to change their habitations often and reside in many places. Such of his chief officers in charge of the forts, country parts, and the army, and ministers and priests, as are found to have been in conspiracy with the enemy should also be compelled to have their habitations in different places on the borders of the enemy's country. Such of his men as are capable to hurt him, but are convinced of their own fall with that of their master, should be pacified by secret remonstrance. Such renegades of his own country as are captured along with the enemy should be made to reside in remote corners. Whoever of the enemy's family is capable to wrest the conquered territory and is taking shelter in a wild tract on the border, often harassing the conqueror, should be provided with a sterile portion of territory or with a fourth part of a fertile tract on the condition of supplying to the conqueror a fixed amount of money and a fixed number of troops, in raising which he may incur the displeasure of the people and may be destroyed by them. Whoever has caused excitement to the people or incurred their displeasure should be removed and placed in a dangerous locality.

Having recovered a lost territory, he should hide those vices of his, owing to which he lost it, and increase those virtues by which he recovered it.

With regard to the inherited territory, he should cover the vices of his father, and display his own virtues.

* He should initiate the observance of all those customs, which, though righteous and practiced by others, are not observed in his own country, and give no room for the practice of whatever is unrighteous, though observed by others.

CHAPTER 14

KAUTILYA'S ARTHASHASTRA, BOOK 14: SECRET MEANS

14.1 ARTHASHASTRA, BOOK 14, CHAPTER 1: MEANS TO INJURE AN ENEMY

In order to protect the institution of the four castes, such measures as are treated of in secret science shall be applied against the wicked. Through the instrumentality of such men or women of Mleccha class as can put on disguises appropriate to different countries, arts, or professions, or as can put on the appearance of a hump-backed, dwarfish, or short-sized person, or of a dumb, deaf, idiot, or blind person, kālakūta and other manifold poisons should be administered in the diet and other physical enjoyments of the wicked. Spies lying in wait or living as inmates (in the same house) may make use of weapons on occasions of royal sports or musical and other entertainments. Spies, under the disguise of night-walkers or of fire-keepers may set fire (to the houses of the wicked).

The powder (prepared from the carcass) of animals such as citra, bheka (frog), kauṇḍinyaka, kṛkaṇa (perdix sylvatika), pañcakuṣṭha, and śatapadi (centipede); or of animals such as uccidiṅga (crab), kambali, kṛkalāsa (lizard), with the powder of the bark of śatakanda (Phyalis flexuosa); or of animals such as gṛhagaulika (a small house-lizard), andhāhika (a blind snake), krakaṇṭhaka (a kind of partridge), pūtikīṭa (a stinking insect), and gomārika, combined with the juice of bhallātaka (Semecarpus anacardium), and valgaka—the smoke caused by burning the above powders causes instantaneous death.

* Any of the (above) insects may be heated with a black snake and priyaṅgu (panic seed) and reduced to powder. This mixture, when burnt, causes instantaneous death.

The powder prepared from the roots of dhāmārgava (luffa foetida) and yātudhāna mixed with the powder of the flower of bhaliātaka (Semecarpus anacardium) causes, when administered, death in the course of half a month. The root of vyāghāta (casia fistula) reduced to powder with-the flower of bhallātaka (Semecarpus anacardium) mixed with the essence of an insect causes, when administered, death in the course of a month.

As much as a kalā (16th of a tola) to men; twice as much to mules and horses; and four times as much to elephants and camels.

The smoke caused by burning the powder of śatakardama, uccidiṅga (crab), karavīra (nerium odorum), kaṭutumbi (a kind of bitter gourd), and fish, together with the chaff of the grains of madana and kodrava (paspalam scrobiculatum), or with the chaff of the seeds of hastikarṇa (caster-oil tree) and palāśa (butea frondosa) destroys animal life as for as it is carried off by the wind.

The smoke caused by burning the powder of pūtikiṭa (a stinking insect), fish, kaṭutumbi (a kind of bitter gourd), the bark of śatakardama, and indragopa (the insect cochineal), or the powder of pūtikīṭa, kṣudrārāla (the resin of the plant, shorea robusta), and hemavidāri, mixed with the powder of the hoof and horn of a goat, causes blindness.

The smoke caused by burning the leaves of pūtikarañja (guilandina bonducella), yellow arsenic realgar, the seeds of guñja (abrus precatorius), the chaff of the seeds of red cotton, āsphota (a plant, careya arborea), khāca (salt), and the dung and urine of a cow, causes blindness.

The smoke caused by burning the skin of a snake, the dung of the cow and the horse, and the head of a blind snake causes blindness.

The smoke caused by burning the powder made of the mixture of the dung and urine of pigeons, frogs, flesh-eating animals, elephants, men, and boars, the chaff and powder of barley mixed with kāsisa (green sulphate of iron), rice, the seeds of cotton, kuṭaja (nerium antidysentericum), and kośātaki (luffa pentandra), cow's urine, the root of bhāṇḍi (hydroeotyle asiatica), the powder of nimba (nimba meria), śigru (hyperanthera morunga), phaṇirjaka (a kind of tulasi plant), kṣībapīluka (ripe coreya arborea), and bhāṅga (as common intoxicating drug), the skin of a snake and fish, and the powder of the nails and tusk of an elephant, all mixed with the chaff of madana and kodrava (paspalam scrobiculatum), or with the chaff of the seeds of hastikarṇa (castor-oil tree) and palāśa (butea frondosa) causes instantaneous death wherever the smoke is carried off by the wind.

When a man who has kept his eyes secure with the application of ointment and medicinal water burns, on the occasion of the commencement of a battle and the assailing of forts, the roots of kālī (tragia involucrata), kuṣṭha (costus), naḍa (a kind of reed), and śatāvarī (asperagus racemosus), or the powder of (the skin of) a snake, the tail of a peacock, kṛkaṇa (a kind of partridge), and pañcakuṣṭha, together with the chaff as previously described or with wet or dry chaff, the smoke caused thereby destroys the eye of all animals.

The ointment prepared by mixing the excretion of śārikā (maina), kapota (pigeon), baka (crane), and balākā (a kind of small crane), with the milk of maṅkāṣī (hyperanthera morunga), pīluka (a species of careya arborea) and snuhi (euphorbia), causes blindness and poisons water.

The mixture of yavaka (a kind of barley), the root of śālā (achyrantes triandria), the fruit of madana (dattūra plant?), the leaves of jāti, and the urine of a man mixed with the powder of the root of plakṣa (fig tree), and vidāri (liquorice), as well as the essence of the decoction of musta (a kind of poison), udumbara (glomerous fig tree), and kodrava (paspalam scrobiculatum), or with decoction of hastikarṇa (castor oil tree), and palāśa (butea frondosa), is termed the juice of madana (madanayoga).

The mixture of the powders of śṛṅgi (atis betula), gaumevṛkṣa, kaṇṭakāra (solanum xanthocarpum), and mayūrapadi, the powder of guñja seeds, lāṅgulī (jusseina repens), viṣamūlika, and iṅgudi (heart-pea), and the powder of karavīra (oleander), akṣipīluka (careya arborea), arka plant, and mṛgamāriṇī, combined with the decoction of madana and kodrava or with that of hastikarṇa and palāśa, is termed madana mixture (madanayoga).

The combination of (the above two) mixtures poisons grass and water when applied to them.

The smoke caused by burning the mixture of the powders of kṛkaṇa (a kind of partridge), kṛkalāsa (lizard), gṛhagaulika (a small house-lizard), and andhāhika (a blind snake), destroys the eyes and causes madness.

The (smoke caused by burning the) mixture of kṛkalāsa and gṛhagaulika causes leprosy.

The smoke caused by burning the same mixture together with the entrails of citrabheka (a kind of frog of variegated colour), and madhu (celtis orientalis), causes gonorrhoea.

The same mixture mixed with human blood causes consumption.

The powder of dūṣīviṣa, madana (dattūra plant), and kodrava (paspalam scrobiculatum), destroys the tongue.

The mixture of the powder of mātṛvāhaka, jalūkā (leech), the tail of a peacock, the eyes of a frog, and pilukā (careya arborea), causes the disease known as viṣūcika.

The mixture of pañcakuṣṭha, kauṇḍinyaka, rājavṛkṣa (cassia fistula), and madhupuṣpa (bassia latifolia), and madhu (honey), causes fever.

The mixture prepared from the powder of the knot of the tongue of bhāsa (a bird), and nakula (mongoose), reduced to a paste with the milk of a she-donkey, causes both dumbness and deafness.

The proportion of a dose to bring on the desired deformities in men and animals in the course of a fortnight or a month is as laid down before.

Mixtures become very powerful when, in the case of drugs, they are prepared by the process of decoction; and in the case of animals, by the process of making powders; or in all cases by the process of decoction.

Whoever is pierced by the arrow prepared from the grains of śālmali (bombax heptaphyllum) and vidāri (liquorice) reduced to powder and mixed with the powder of mūlavatsanābha (a kind of poison) and smeared over with the blood of cucundari (musk rat) bites some ten other persons, who in their turn bite others.

The mixture prepared from the flowers of bhallātaka (semecarpus anacardium), yātudhāna, dhāmārgava (achyranthes-aspera), and bāṇa (sal tree), mixed with the powder of elā (large cardamom), kākṣi (red aluminous earth), guggulu (bdellium), and hālāhala (a kind of poison), together with the blood of a goat and a man, causes biting madness.

When half a dharaṇa of this mixture, together with flour and oil-cakes, is thrown into water of a reservoir measuring a hundred bows in length, it vitiates the whole mass of water; all the fish swallowing or touching this mixture become poisonous; and whoever drinks or touches this water will be poisoned.

No sooner does a person condemned to death pull out from the earth an alligator or iguana (godhā) which, with three or five handfuls of both red and white mustard seeds, is entered into the earthy than he dies at its sight.

When, on the days of the stars of kṛttikā or bharaṇī and following the method of performing fearful rites, an oblation with a black cobra emitting forth at the shock of lightning or caught hold of by means of the sticks of a tree struck by lightning and perfumed is made into the fire, that fire continues to bum unquenchably.

* An oblation of honey shall be made into the fire fetched from the house of a blacksmith; of spirituous liquor into the fire brought from the house of a vintner; of clarified butter into the fire of a sacrificer.

* Of a garland into the fire kept by a sacrificer with one wife; of mustard seeds into the fire kept by an adulterous woman; of curds into the fire kept during the birth of a child; of rice-grain into the fire of a sacrificer;

* Of flesh into the fire kept by a Caṇḍāla; of human flesh into the fire burning in cremation grounds; an oblation of the serum of the flesh of a goat and a man shall be made by means of a sacrificial ladle into the fire which is made of all the above fires;

* Repeating the mantras addressed to the fire, an oblation of the wooden pieces of rājavṛkṣa (cassia fistula) into the same fire. This fire will unquenchably burn, deluding the eyes of the enemies.

CONTRIBUTIONS OF CHANAKYA

CHAPTER 15

RELEVANCE OF CHANAKYA IN THE BATTLES OF DAILY LIFE

Chanakya was a great man who lived nearly 2400 years ago, but his teachings resonate even today. He was a philosopher and teacher in the true sense of the terms. But Indian philosophy has an advantage—it is time-tested and will be tested every time. In every generation, people will debate and discuss whether a philosophy is still relevant and gives the same benefit that it provided generations ago. Nevertheless, history has shown that Indian thinkers and philosophers did not like to rest on their laurels, glorifying the past. They wanted to debate and discuss.

While millions used to die in wars, today millions die due to 'inner enemies'. These numbers are growing every year across the globe. From children and teenagers to mature adults, people are giving up so easily on the challenges of life. How can this generation, which has the benefit of technology, communication, access to information and easy travel, value life so little? That's when we wonder if the enemy has been internalized? It appears that we are not equipped to handle stress. We cannot deal with the simple problems of life. We are a lonely generation. We have probably solved and understood how to avoid external wars, but what about the inner wars and conflicts we go through on a daily basis? Who will teach us how to kill the inner enemy, the negative mind, the mind that gets stuck in a situation and does not find any solution? And the easy escape route seems to be to end one's life. Suicide is not a solution to problems. Chanakya did not appreciate people who committed suicide.

In the Arthashastra, there is a mention of punishing those who committed suicide by not allowing them funerals, as suicide means that a person has given up on the challenges that life has thrown at him. In Indian culture, it is believed that one who commits suicide is only delaying life's problems as these problems will reappear in the next life. So why not face the challenges in this lifetime itself? And that is exactly where Chanakya helps us. While he has taught us the art of war for an external enemy, we can use the same principles to defeat the inner enemy—our weak mind. Rhetoric such as 'be positive', 'think positive', only help to a certain extent, providing only temporary relief for the pain experienced by a person. Most of the time, rhetoric offers only surface-level medication. Therefore, it is imperative to look at some practical solutions that work.

The following ten tips given by Chanakya can be used anytime and anywhere. They can be used individually, or in combinations. We must bear in mind that they may seem superficial at first, but constant practice will bear fruits. If one can make one's mind strong and strategic in nature, one can win any battle in the world.

15.1   NEVER FIGHT A BATTLE ALONE, TAKE ALONG A FRIEND

Life is full of battles and it often seems like a struggle. From the moment we wake up until the time we go to bed, there are myriad problems that we come across. If we do not know how to handle situations when we are awake, nights can become sleepless too. Stress is a primary problem plaguing this generation. Stress to some extent is natural, but if we do not handle it, it can become a problem that consumes us. Today, mental health is one of the biggest challenges facing us. If not handled in the right manner, it can lead to depression and bring on suicidal tendencies. Chanakya's solution for stress is as simple as talking to a friend. When we have a friend with whom we can share and express our problems, it makes a significant difference. As human beings, we require fellow beings to share our feelings with, to discuss and debate and ultimately feel good. Technology cannot replace human interaction. It is important to understand the importance of having a group of friends who will be with us through thick and thin. The same advice is given by Chanakya while building a kingdom. In the Saptanga model of a kingdom, one of the most important pillars is a friend ('mitra'). Even the king requires a mitra, or a friend, to run his kingdom effectively. Imagine the kind of stress that a leader of a kingdom faces. She or he would have to bear full responsibility for keeping all the people of the land happy. Administration is a stressful activity. Yet, how does the leader keep cool and calm in the midst of all these challenges? If the king is not able to find a solution to a problem, he can go to another friendly king and discuss the problem. It is possible that a solution will emerge following the discussion. Friends act as more than mere listeners. They are people whom one can lean on and get advice from.

15.2 LISTEN TO THE WISE

Senior citizens are an extremely neglected lot in society today. Traditionally, India has had a joint family culture, which includes the elderly in the family. Nowadays, people are moving away from this and resorting to nuclear families. This has led to a lot of stress in working couples and single parents. It is generally believed that senior citizens are liabilities to a family. Children are growing impatient as they have to take care of the elderly, and when parents are sick and have outlived their utility, they become liabilities. Rising medical and living costs aren't helping either. Can these so-called liabilities become solutions to our current problems? Chanakya says, yes, they can. Senior citizens are assets to every generation. We should know how to give back to them for all they have done for us. In the daily battles of life, these senior citizens can be very helpful. One may wonder how. The biggest advantage of senior citizens is that they have time and experience to offer. The younger generation has neither of the two. So, in reality, the two could fit together like a perfect jigsaw puzzle. It can be synergetic. Let us consider a practical example that I recently came across. There was an orphanage where children longed for the love of parents. Right across the road was a home for the aged, neglected parents of well-off children. The children wished they had the love of parents and grandparents. And the senior citizens longed to have their children and grandchildren with them. A brilliant social worker came up with the idea of merging the orphanage with the home for the elderly. Imagine the transformation that took place. Senior citizens were surrounded by children, who were active and vibrant. They found joy once again in their lives. And the children were fed and taken care of by the elders, who became their parents and grandparents. This concept embodies —association with elders. They take care of us much beyond our expectations. Elders have nothing to expect from life. The next generation, on the other hand, has a long life ahead. But, when the elderly come forward to guide the next generation, they create a win-win situation. It is important not to neglect senior citizens in one's house and family. Our generation needs them as much as the elderly need the youngsters. There will always be some difference of opinion between generations. This is natural. However, love is what keeps a human society going. With love we can fight the biggest battles of life. A person without a family has already lost half the battle. Members of a family make sure that each one is taken care of and emerges as a winner.

15.3   WHEN DEALING WITH THE POWERFUL, KEEP IN TOUCH WITH A HIGHER POWER

There is always a frustration when we have to deal with a difficult boss. Those who have gone through it know what I am talking about. If not, let's try and imagine the situation of a person who works day in and day out, for years, in the same office. And at the end of the hard work he puts in, all he gets is a message of dissatisfaction from his boss. There are countless people who face this in workplaces all over the world. They work eight to ten hours every day under such pressure for a senior who never seems satisfied with the work done. Even their best effort goes unrecognized. Every day is a battle. A battle that will last as long as the employee retains the job, or the boss remains in his seat of superiority. So what is the solution? The easy way out is to resign and find another job. Is there an alternative, though? The softer way is to accept it as a part of life and continue working. Listen to the senior's opinion from one ear and let it go out from the other, as they say. At least, the employee is drawing a salary and there is monetary happiness at the end of the month. But there is a solution that Chanakya offers as well. That is, to think through the situation and find out what makes the boss a boss after all. Is it not that she or he is more powerful than the employee in designation and salary? The boss has more decision-making power than the employee. Now, what we need to remember is to learn how to crack the power of the boss. We must realize that even the boss has a boss. So, if we understand the higher power, we can deal with the lower seat of power easily—this actually gives us a strategic advantage. Chanakya says, 'While dealing with a strong king, take a stronger king on your side.' Automatically, due to fear of the higher power, the person we are dealing with comes under our control. Some people take the route of the court of law. When we have legal power on our side, our strength increases. So, if we have a superior harassing us, we must never lose confidence. We must take some advice and hit back hard. Let us think of the #MeToo movement that gained such momentum in recent times. The victims gave it back. Of course, some people misused it to settle petty, personal scores. But overall, most women benefited by giving it back to their bosses and other oppressors, using the might of social media. I have a friend who had worked in a company for fifteen years. When a new boss came in, he started troubling my friend. Frustrated, my friend asked me, 'How do I deal with him? After all, he is the director of our company. Do you have a Chanakya strategy I could use?' I smiled at him and asked, 'Who is higher than this boss of yours who is the director?' His reply was quick. 'The chairman of the company to whom my boss reports.' I suggested, 'Your boss is powerful. But do you have access to the highest power—the chairman?' He thought for a while and said, 'Yes, I have been working in this company for a long time and the chairman knows me personally. 'Before I could speak further, he said, 'But this immediate boss of mine will not allow me to go to the chairman. And even if I do, he will come to know of it and he will give me more mental agony.' I thought for a while before suggesting, 'Ok. So let's access the highest power indirectly then. Is there any advisor whom your chairman listens to, whom you know?' His eyes lit up. 'Yes, of course. Our chief accountant. He is a school friend of mine and we stay in the same colony . . .' 'There lies the solution,' I said and smiled. 'Talk to your friend and communicate the same to the chairman.' Relieved, he put the idea into action. Thus, my friend solved the problem. Let us remember never to be afraid of power. There is always a higher power that we can access. If not directly, we can try the indirect route to success.

15.4   WAR IS A MIND GAME

Henry Ford once said, 'If you think you can, or if you think you cannot—either way you are right.' Chanakya would also give similar advice. Most of us do not lose the war on the battlefield, but a lot earlier. War is always a mind game and, therefore, Chanakya would prepare the minds of the warriors first before sending them to war. It has been proven by research that winners in all fields actually visualized it even before they attained victory. Be it the sportspersons who won Olympic gold medals, or business tycoons who became billionaires, or those who became presidents or prime ministers of nations. All of them motivated themselves first. Therefore, it is essential that in your mind you are clear about winning. The rest will follow. Where the mind is not conditioned or blocked by the negatives of failures, one will get fresh ideas required to fight the daily battles of life. A common example comes to mind. Whenever there is a public transport strike in Mumbai where I live, when trains, buses or taxis do not ply, many commuters avoid going to offices. They feel it is not possible to go since their regular transportation is on strike. They do not think of any alternatives. Interestingly, it is precisely that day it is easiest to reach office, a lot earlier than the usual time. In case cabs are not working, the government decides to put extra buses on the road. The roads are empty, and this sight evokes fear, so many people do not come out of their houses. The smarter people, though, see a strategic advantage here. They set out of their houses and take the first available ride and reach office faster. Usually, such a day is the most productive day too, as fewer people turn up and one can focus on one's key priorities and be effective at the workplace. Once we take the first step towards our goal, the rest is easy. After all, we have reached the goal inside our mind. The rest is just a matter of time.

15.5   ADVISORS CAN MAKE YOU OR BREAK YOU

In daily life, we have to be mentally alert. We must be aware that we are receiving various thoughts and opinions from different people. Apart from human beings, we are constantly being bombarded with information from the Internet, social media, radio, newspapers, television, books and other mediums. Such information overload becomes dangerous after a point. We get thoroughly confused with contradictory views on a particular matter. To take a simple everyday instance, while some say that ghee, which is a traditional component of Indian cuisine, is good for health, others say it's saturated fat. What does one do in such situations? First things first. Gathering too much information is not good. We need to be selective in what we read and watch. We get into discussions that really do not matter to us. How does it matter if X sportsperson gets married to Y cinema star? It's ok to add our bit to some social updates happening around. But it is not worth thinking too much about such matters. A happy person keeps her/his mind free of stupid and irrelevant thoughts. We must choose our ideas and thoughts carefully, consciously. The same applies to the choice of our friends. We need to be discriminating in selecting the books we read. Most importantly, we must choose our advisors carefully. Advisors can make or break us. If we get stupid advice, it can ruin our whole life and career. In the most important moments of our life, where decisions are critical, it is vital to have good advisors on our side. When we have to choose a career path, or join a new educational program, let us ask for the right guidance from the right teacher and not just from our friends who may be equally confused. The most important decision a person makes in her/his life is marriage. It involves choosing the person with whom we will be spending the rest of our life. Here, too, sound advice, in the form of a good matchmaker, marriage counsellor and family support, is required. Chanakya suggests we choose our advisors with care. They should be mature and wise. They should have the necessary experience and they must also look at our wellbeing as the top priority. He also suggests that one should not have just one advisor, but about two or three of them. Not too few, not too many. When we take expert advice in any matter from three good sources, we gain access to better choices while taking a decision. We must make a list of experts in every field, persons who will guide us in our career, education, married life, financial dealings and everything that is important to us. Such people will help us win the battles of life. Such wise people also help us avoid the pitfalls that we may come across. They are the safety net we have provided for ourselves.

15.6 LIFT YOUR PEOPLE TO THE NEXT LEVEL

This is the advice given to people in power. We saw an example of how to deal with people who are more powerful than us. But what if we are the one in power and hold an authoritative position? There is a problem in being powerful. Either we can look higher to see who are more powerful than us, and seek to aim higher, or we can look below and see how many people are looking up to us, since we are in the position of authority. A true leader is not one who wants to scale the ladder of authority. A true leader, according to Chanakya, is one who takes care of his people. Such a person, who looks at the welfare of his subordinates, automatically, by default, rises higher up the ladder of leadership. So, if we are blessed with a certain level of leadership and authority, let us lift our people to the next level. Let us not keep the people below us confined to only the lower levels. We can train them, educate them, give them some bigger responsibilities, and looking at their capacity and capabilities, even promote them. A true leader is one who creates more leaders. In daily life, let us remember we are fighting a battle. But the reality is that on a daily basis, we are also preparing for the bigger battle of the future. So when the war finally arrives, our team should be ready to fight for us. They should take up the challenges and come along with us. If we do not train our people and equip them with better skills, weapons and education, how will they face the bigger wars? So, let's lift our people. Build their morale. Give them some freedom. Empower them with more trust. And slowly, each of the team members will shine to give their best. That is how, slowly, on a regular basis, we can build our team. Spend time with them. Guide them. Talk and discuss matters with them. Attend to their problems immediately. If we care and show it, they will reciprocate. Shivaji, who built the huge Maratha Empire within one generation, knew of this strategy of Chanakya. His ministers were empowered and they fought the battles for their leader. When they won the battles, the ministers were put in charge of the newly conquered territories. The ministers then became kings in those respective regions. If Shivaji did not have a team of good and trusted ministers, how would he have expanded his base? One single person is not enough. A team is required. And the team should be trained by the leader itself. We must think about it every day. Are we a true leader? Are we supporting, helping and empowering our juniors? Chanakya has written about this in detail in the Arthashastra.

15.7   STUDY EVERY DAY (SWADHYAYA)

One faces problems every day. From the moment one gets up in the morning to the moment one goes to sleep at night, one has something or the other to do. Daily life involves many unplanned and routine activities. At times, we feel everything is fine, while at other times, we feel life slipping away. Chanakya recommends a technique to keep the mind in control. He suggests that the best way to handle everyday problems is to study every day. Chanakya is suggesting not just academic study. He is indicating something higher, also called swadhyaya. This includes worldly as well as spiritual study. The highest form of study is the study of scriptures.

When we read them regularly on a daily basis, we acquire a direction for our lives. We develop moral values and we also get inspiration from the wisdom of great people before us. A daily study of the scriptures is akin to consuming a daily capsule of nutrients. While nutritious foods and supplements give us energy for the body, the scriptures give us energy for our mind and intellect. They give us direction and help us solve the challenges we have to face. Gandhiji used to say, 'When disappointment stares me in the face and all alone I see not one ray of light, I go back to the Bhagavadgita. I find a verse here and a verse there, and I immediately begin to smile in the midst of overwhelming tragedies—and my life has been full of external tragedies— and if they have left no visible or indelible scar on me, I owe it all to the teaching of Bhagavadgita.' This is the power of swadhyaya, the study of scriptures on a daily basis. Every country, religion, tradition has some books of wisdom. Studying them regularly helps gather the right momentum for the required direction. Like an unknown power, it comes to our rescue during the most difficult situations we face in life. It gives us a road map when all paths seem stuck. Chanakya made sure that in the daily timetable followed by a king, there were at least a few hours dedicated to swadhyaya.

15.8 KNOW THE STRENGTH AND WEAKNESS OF THE OPPONENT

Some people are born smart, some acquire smartness along the way, some others remain ordinary, and the rest die as fools. Having a strategic mindset is an important skill one should be able to develop. A smart person is one who is able to accurately judge others. He is constantly studying and analyzing, trying to understand what is going on in the mind of the person in front of him. There are various methods Chanakya has suggested in the training of a leader. One of them is 'deh vidya', or what we call 'body language' today. The body has its own language. Most of us know about verbal communication—what a person says. But there is non-verbal communication as well. If we can study the body language of a person, we can understand what is going on in the mind of the person. The same goes for the methods used by Chanakya in his war strategies. He is continuously studying the opponent. The enemy is being scanned minutely by Chanakya. Can this technique be used in our daily lives? Yes, of course. We can observe people around us—when we take a walk in any public place, be it a garden, railway station or bus stand, the marketplace or when we are at a café or bar where people hang out. Let us look at the way people move about and that can tell us a lot about what they are thinking. If we practice this, we will be able to develop the art of observation.

15.9 HONOUR SCHOLARS AND THINKERS

There is a basic problem we face in our generation. Teachers are a part of our lives only during the days when we formally study in schools, colleges and universities. However, this was not the case in the previous generations. Students were connected with their teachers, lifelong. Tutors were a part of their lives on a regular basis. One major advantage this had over today was that the students had a perpetual guide by their side during any trouble they came across in life. These gurus, teachers and acharyas knew their students personally and guided them accordingly. It was like having a family physician. This doctor was not just a physician; he was a friend, philosopher and guide. The teacher knew the student's problem well before time. He also knew what would work for his student. At times, the problem was not at a physical level; it was psychological. So he would suggest treatment accordingly. Each solution was tailor-made for the individual, as what may work for one may not work for another. The teacher, at times, simply lent an ear. This simple act can sometimes make all the difference. A patient hearing is all that a person requires at times. This is no ordinary family doctor; obviously, he's more of a strategist. We must take time to think whether we have access to a teacher of this kind in our life. This is someone who has been a lifelong mentor, a friend, philosopher and guide in every stage we have crossed. Those who already have one are lucky. For the others, it is important to look for such a mentor.

Then no mountain or obstacle in life will be insurmountable. Such mentors will be our daily inspiration. One of the best ways to start looking for such a master is by respecting scholars and thinkers. Chanakya himself was a scholar and a thinker. Because he was respected by the students, he made them kings and emperors. We can all see the transformation he brought about with Chandragupta Maurya. From an ordinary student, Chandragupta was molded into one of the greatest leaders in the land. Chanakya also trained his students to respect other scholars and thinkers. If a scholar ever wanted to meet the king, it became a priority. The king even offered his throne for teachers to sit upon. In return, their guidance helped him rule the kingdom more effectively. It is easy to seek the company of scholars, teachers and thinkers. Readers can easily find them at schools, colleges or universities they have attended. It is important to keep their company lifelong. Let us help them a bit by doing some service, and they will guide us multiple times. Once we have a thinker on our side, battles can be won easily. Once we have a teacher on our side, she or he will be our strategist in the daily battles of life.

15.10   TEACH CHILDREN TO BE MATERIALLY AND SPIRITUALLY SUCCESSFUL

Expecting our children to be successful is a natural feeling for any parent. But what kind of success do we want children to pursue? Unfortunately, the definition of success has changed. Success has become limited to children doing well in career and financially. There is no doubt that being materially successful is important as far as worldly achievements are concerned. But are we neglecting another important aspect of success—the spiritual side? There is a story in the Upanishads. Swetaketu, a brilliant boy, came back home after his studies from the gurukul. He had been away for twelve years. And when he reached home, his father, a great rishi himself, asked, 'Do you know everything? Have you studied everything?' When the answer was negative, he was sent back to learn again. This back and forth between the gurukul and home went on until

Swetaketu attained enlightenment. This is what great parents do to their children. They want their children to be materially successful, but also learn the spiritual sciences and become enlightened. Do we impart such training to our kids? For that to happen, we ourselves need to understand the value of spiritual knowledge. Only then can we pass it on to our children. Chanakya had trained his students to be brilliant rulers of large kingdoms and empires. But he also wanted them to know that a day would come when they would have to fight the biggest war—the challenge of giving up their power and position. It is not at all easy. If one has been in the seat of power for a long time, one gets attached to it. Yet, the greatest winner is one who can let go of that power. And if we are willingly able to let go, we have truly won the ultimate war—the war of winning over ourselves and our ego. This is the ultimate war we need to win. The right time to learn spirituality is here and now. Let us take the first step, and the rest will follow. We can read a spiritual book, attend a spiritual discourse (satsang), meet a spiritual master, or visit an ashram. On a daily basis, we can measure the progress of our children's spiritual growth. Impart to them values, moral and ethics. Teach them to be strong from the inside. The foundations of life have to be spiritual. Let this be the start of a journey within. Let all of us seek that winning mentality—the conquering of the ego and the ability to let go. Such a person can never be defeated. He is an eternal winner in every stage of life. He has won over himself— he has won the ultimate war.

CHAPTER 16

LEGACY OF CHANAKYA

16.1 LESSONS TO BE LEARNT FROM CHANAKYA'S PERSONALITY

Chanakya is widely regarded as one of the most influential thinkers in Indian history and his teachings continue to be studied and followed to this day.

Following qualities of Chanakya that you must have in order to succeed in life:

(i) **Visionary:** Chanakya was a visionary who always looked beyond the present and had a clear idea of what he wanted to achieve. He had a long-term perspective and was able to anticipate future trends and developments. To be successful, you must also have a clear vision of what you want to achieve and be able to plan accordingly.

(ii) **Strategist:** Chanakya was a master strategist who was able to devise clever plans and tactics to achieve his goals. He was able to use his intelligence and creativity to outsmart his opponents and achieve victory. To be successful, you must also be a good strategist and be able to think creatively to find solutions to problems.

(iii) **Intelligent:** Chanakya was a highly intelligent person who had a deep understanding of human nature and the world around him. He was able to use his intelligence to come up with innovative ideas and solutions. To be successful, you must also be intelligent and have a thirst for knowledge.

(iv) Courageous: Chanakya was a courageous person who was not afraid to take risks and stand up for what he believed in. He was able to face challenges and overcome obstacles with courage and determination. To be successful, you must also have the courage to take risks and pursue your dreams.

(v) Disciplined: Chanakya was a disciplined person who followed a strict routine and was committed to his goals. He believed in hard work and perseverance and was able to achieve his goals through discipline and dedication. To be successful, you must also be disciplined and committed to your goals.

(vi) Ethical: Chanakya was an ethical person who believed in doing the right thing and following moral principles. He believed in honesty, integrity, and fairness, and his teachings emphasized the importance of ethical behaviour. To be successful, you must also be ethical and follow moral principles in your personal and professional life.

(vii) Adaptable: Chanakya was an adaptable person who was able to adjust to changing circumstances and environments. He was able to change his plans and strategies as needed to achieve his goals. To be successful, you must also be adaptable and flexible, and be able to adjust to changing circumstances.

(viii) Persevering: Chanakya was a persevering person who never gave up on his goals, even in the face of adversity. He was able to overcome setbacks and obstacles through sheer determination and perseverance. To be successful, you must also be persevering and never give up on your dreams.

(ix) Strategic thinker: Chanakya was a strategic thinker who was able to see the big picture and plan accordingly. He was able to identify the key drivers of success and focus on them to achieve his goals. To be successful, you must also be a strategic thinker and be able to see the big picture.

(x) Humble: Chanakya was a humble person who did not seek fame or fortune for himself. He believed in serving the greater good and was always willing to help others. To be successful, you must also be humble and have a spirit of service, and be willing to help others without seeking personal gain.

16.2   LEADERSHIP LESSONS FROM CHANAKYA'S ARTHASHASTRA

One of the greatest minds in leadership and strategy is Chanakya. Chanakya, also known as Kautilya or Vishnugupta, was the Prime Minister in the court of Chandragupta Maurya, the founder of the Mauryan empire. He was also a teacher, philosopher, and possibly the very first economist of India.

His is also the author of Arthashastra, the ancient Sanskrit treatise on statecraft, military strategy, and economic policy. Arthashastra is considered to be a training manual transforming Chandragupta from a normal citizen into a monarch. Just like empires, many companies are built, and many close down with time. Arthashastra also provides invaluable lessons on governance, management, and leadership. While written in ancient India, its principles continue to offer practical leadership applications for the modern workplace.

In our experience, effective leaders exhibit a blend of strategic thinking, ethical governance, and people-centric leadership — all of which are deeply rooted in Chanakya's philosophy. Whether you are a first-time manager or a seasoned executive, understanding these leadership lessons can help build leadership capacity and navigate today's complex business world.

Remember, some companies create history. They last for ages and carve a unique identity for themselves. The secret behind their success is great leadership. Great business leaders strike the right balance between business foresight, character, and performance. Some of the management principles in Chanakya's Arthashastra may be up for study. However, the leadership lessons are relevant even today for business leaders running their business empires from their corporate offices.

Let's explore some of the key leadership lessons from Chanakya's Arthashastra and how they align with modern leadership skills.

16.2.1   Leadership Insights for a High Performance Team

1.   Visionary Leadership: The Importance of Strategy

Chanakya was a firm believer in long-term vision and strategic planning. In the Arthashastra, he emphasizes that a leader should always anticipate future challenges and prepare accordingly.

How is this applicable for the corporate world today? In today's corporate world, agile leadership is essential. A leader must be proactive rather than reactive, thinking ahead and making data-driven decisions. Organizations that succeed are those where leaders develop a strategic vision while remaining adaptable to change.

In our experience, some of the best leaders we've worked with focus on building leadership skills through structured planning, risk analysis, and decision-making frameworks.

Leadership Tip-1:

To build your leadership skills, start by setting clear goals, conducting SWOT analyses, and preparing contingency plans.

2.   Ethics & Accountability in Leadership

Chanakya believed that a king (leader) must uphold the highest ethical standards. His teachings emphasize that a ruler should act with integrity, fairness, and responsibility to earn the trust of his subjects.

How is this applicable for the corporate world today? The importance of accountability in the workplace cannot be overstated. Leaders who take personal accountability and create a culture of transparency and fairness inspire loyalty and productivity.

We have noticed that companies that invest in accountability training for leaders tend to have higher employee engagement and better organizational outcomes.

Leadership Tip-2:

Implement accountability training for employees by setting clear expectations, offering constructive feedback, and leading by example.

3. People-Centric Leadership: The Role of Empathy

Chanakya advocated for treating people with respect and fairness, emphasizing that a kingdom (or company) thrives when its people are happy and motivated.

How is this applicable for the corporate world today? In today's world, leadership is not just about power — it's about influence and empathy. Great leaders understand the importance of psychological safety, open communication, and emotional intelligence.

In our experience, teams perform best when leaders prioritize mentorship, team development, and active listening.

Leadership Tip-3:

Develop people-centric leadership by practicing active listening, regular one-on-one check-ins, and recognizing achievements.

4. Training & Development: Building Future Leaders

Chanakya emphasized training and education as critical aspects of leadership. A ruler's success depended on the continuous growth of his ministers and advisors.

How is this applicable for the corporate world today? Leaders today must focus on developing their teams through coaching, mentorship, and continuous learning programs. Basic leadership training should be available for all employees, helping them build leadership skills progressively.

We have noticed that companies with strong leadership development programs tend to have higher retention rates and stronger leadership pipelines.

Leadership Tip-4:

Implement a basic leadership training module to help employees transition into leadership roles smoothly.

5.   Delegation & Trust: The Art of Empowering Others

Chanakya firmly believed that a king should delegate responsibilities to trusted ministers to ensure smooth governance. He argued that a leader who tries to do everything alone will inevitably fail.

How is this applicable for the corporate world today? A leader's strength lies in empowering their team. Delegation not only improves efficiency but also builds trust and confidence among team members.

In our experience, managers who effectively delegate and empower employees foster innovation and stronger team collaboration.

Leadership Tip-5:

Start building leadership capacity by identifying strengths in your team and assigning tasks that align with their skills.

6.   Business Ethics & Decision-Making

Chanakya's Arthashastra stresses ethical leadership and warns against corruption and exploitation. He believed that a leader must set an example of honesty, integrity, and fairness.

How is this applicable for the corporate world today? Business ethics and leadership go hand in hand. Leaders who uphold strong ethical standards not only maintain credibility but also create a culture of trust.

We have noticed that companies that prioritize business ethics leadership experience higher levels of employee satisfaction and customer loyalty.

Leadership Tip-6:

Make ethical decision-making a priority in your organization by establishing clear ethical guidelines and fostering an open, transparent workplace.

7. Your People Come First

"In the happiness of his subjects lies the King's happiness, in their welfare his welfare. He shall not consider as good only that which pleases him but treat as beneficial to him whatever pleases his subjects."

Chanakya believed that a King should always put his subjects before himself. The common man creates the King. Hence, the very existence of a King depends upon the happiness and well-being of his subjects.

Similarly, business leaders of today should put their people at the forefront and not themselves when making decisions. A good leader's top priority is his peers and subordinates. Every person matters in an organisation. No job is small or insignificant. These are basic principles that are taught in modern-day Business Schools, but Chanakya followed it back then. He was a man ahead of his time.

It is important to give due importance to every person in an organisation as the growth of the organisation depends on it. Very often, leaders get enamoured by their titles and privileges so much that they start ignoring their people.

Leadership-7:

One of the keys to becoming a successful business leader is to put your people's needs before yourself. Remember, happy employees create happy customers.

8. People In Power Must Be Accessible

"When in the court, he shall never cause his petitioners to wait at the door, for when a king makes himself inaccessible to his people and entrusts his work to his immediate officers, he may be sure to engender confusion in business and to cause thereby public disaffection, and himself prey to his enemies."

It is not uncommon for a King to be surrounded by his ministers and noblemen. However, if he does not listen to and is not accessible to his subjects, he endangers not just his kingdom but also himself. Likewise, business leaders at the top of the hierarchy are often not accessible to the people at the bottom. It is a common complaint in today's corporate world that leaders do not listen to their people. They only listen to those higher up or equal in rank.

Sometimes the best ideas come from the least expected places. Your employees are in direct contact with the customers and understand their needs and preferences much better than anyone else. Keeping communication open with your frontline employees may give you the ideas that can take you way ahead of other competitors in the market.

What sets apart great business leaders from the rest is that they keep communication channels open-both horizontally and vertically. A good business leader values the importance of good communication and takes time to answer people's queries and explain their deliverables.

Leadership Tip-8:

It is important to bridge the distance between you and your people through better communication and sometimes direct contact.

9. Hold People Accountable For their work

"Whoever imposes severe punishment becomes repulsive to the people; while he who awards mild punishment becomes contemptible. But whoever imposes punishment as deserved becomes respectable. For punishment when awarded with due consideration, makes the people devoted to righteousness and works productive of wealth and enjoyment; while punishment, when ill-awarded under the influence of greed and anger or owing to ignorance, excites fury even among hermits and ascetics dwelling in forests, not to speak of householders."

Chanakya believed that rewarding those who are performing well motivates them to continue doing their best. It is important to hold people accountable for their work – both good and bad. The ones performing well must be encouraged and rewarded. The underperformers must be put on the spot. Rewarding your best performers motivates them to do even better. It also sets them up as an example that others would want to follow.

However, business leaders must be wary of overburdening the good performers.

Leadership Tip-9:

Often, good performers are given additional responsibility, whereas underperformers get by doing just the minimum. If you overburden your best performers, resentment is bound to creep in.

10. Don't Delay Your Decisions – Do the Right Thing at the Right Time

"All urgent calls he shall hear at once, but never put off; for when postponed, they will prove too hard or impossible to accomplish."

Chanakya understood that a good King did his duties the right way and most importantly, at the right time. That is the only way that a King can expand his empire. After all, time and tide wait for no man. A good King understands the value of time. He understands that time, once lost, can never be gained back. A good business leader knows the importance of time management and how crucial it is to the success of an organisation. Delayed decision making can slow down organisational growth. When you do not solve problems on time, they often snowball into larger problems that are hard or cannot be solved.

Why does decision-making take time in most organisations? One of the likely reasons is that key decisions are only made by the higher-ups creating a bottleneck. Outdated processes are another reason why decision making becomes slow. If the same problem crops up over and over, an effective leader will see to it that the process is, redesigned. Fast and effective decision making is the sign of a great leader.

Leadership Tip-10:
Leaders should not delay the decisions – Do the right thing at the right time.

Chanakya's teachings offer a timeless blueprint for leadership success. From visionary strategy and accountability to people-centric leadership and ethics, his lessons remain deeply relevant in today's fast-paced business world.

The ancient wisdom of Chanakya is every bit relevant today as it was hundreds of years ago. We try and emulate the leading business leaders of the world today.

Chanakya's teachings were ahead of their time and are relevant even today. It is time that we start valuing them. Which leadership lesson from Chanakya resonates with you the most.

16.3 KAUTILYA (CHANAKYA) IN INDIA'S FOREIGN POLICY

In the 21st century, there is a need to interpret and follow Kautilya's policy as per current needs.

The revival of the 2003-ceasefire agreement in February 2021 between India and Pakistan show signs of a thaw in the relationship between India and Pakistan after years of tense relations. It is speculated that it is the result of the backchannel talks of officials and pushed by United Arab Emirates (UAE). There is a need to understand this normalisation in the context of India's current tense (Galwan Valley clash of 2020) relationship with the northern neighbour i.e., China.

The above-mentioned scenario provides a great guide regarding the approach of the current Indian regime's foreign policy. India's foreign policy clearly shows the reflection of Kautilyan notion of foreign policy.

16.3.1   Mandal Siddhant and Shadgunya Siddhant

Kautilya has given the Mandal Siddhant, which is concentric circles showing different mandals., circles. It is based on the view that neighbours are natural enemies. Since land is the source of material welfare, neighbours aim to acquire the same piece of land.

In the case of India, Pakistan and China, all aim to acquire the territory of Kashmir by virtue of its abundant resources as well as its strategic location. Hence there is bound to be war between India-Pakistan and India-China.

In the case of China, Arunachal Pradesh can also be added with its claims as its own.

Now, as per Kautilya, neighbours are natural enemies hence they are to be subdued. To achieve that aim, Kautilya has given a strategy of SHADGUNYA SIDDHANT (**six-fold policy**), which is to be used as per the situation.

It includes strategies as follows:

Sandhi (treaty), Vigraha (break a treaty and start a war), Asan(stationing of forces near enemy), Yaan (mobilisation of troops), Samashraya (joining hand with those having similar aims), and lastly Dwaidbhava (Dual policy i.e, friendship with one enemy for time and enmity with other).

16.3.2 Reflection of Kautilya in India's Policy

Now if we jump back to a time when India was having tensed relations with Pakistan during (2015-2020), we can analyse the trend of our foreign policy. During that period, we ensured peaceful relationship with other neighbours specifically China. It can also be remembered that even during the Doklam valley stand-off, where Indian and Chinese soldiers came face to face, conflict was not allowed to exacerbate by both sides, particularly by the Indian side. Prime Minister Modi made an informal visit to China, which led to the emergence of the Wuhan Spirit, to ensure peace at the border. It was taken forward by the visit of China's President Xi Jinping to India, which furthered the relations.

During the same time the relation with our western neighbour i.e, Pakistan was at a nadir. It saw the Pulwama terror attack, India's Balakot airstrike and so on.

Here in the above scenario, we can see the application of Kautilya's policy, more specifically of Dwaidbhava (Dual policy i.e, friendship with one enemy for time and enmity with other).

The same can be said about a recent thaw in our relations with Pakistan and increasing tensions with China. Though disengagement at Pangong-Tso-lake has taken place, other contested points are yet to see a withdrawal agreement.

Indian regime at one point or other have applied Kautilya's Shadgunya Siddhant in foreign policy. Be it conducting of a military exercise in Arunachal Pradesh, troops mobilisation and so on etc.,

16.3.3 In Indo-Pacific

In the current emerging geopolitical scenario, the Indo-Pacific region has acquired centrality. Its importance is due to the shift of the centre of gravity of geopolitics as well as geoeconomics. Here as well, from the Indian side, we see an application of Shadgunya Siddhant.

In this region, we are seeing increasing aggression on the part of China. Be it in the South China Sea (claim of 9-Dash line), construction of artificial island, manoeuvre in Indian Ocean region etc., India due to its asymmetry in conventional warfare with China, has favoured Kautilyan approach of Samashraya (joining hand with those having similar aims). Its reflection can be found in the revival of Quadrilateral Security dialogue and also India's cooperation with other South East Asian nations like Vietnam, Philippines etc.,

When Kautilya prescribed the above policy he also included the internal dimension with it. He envisioned uniting India (Akhand Bharat) to fight foreign aggression. In the 21st century, there is a need to interpret and follow Kautilya's policy as per current needs.

It can also be understood from the example of China. Deng Xiaoping's policy of hiding strength and biding our time attempted to strengthen China internally till about 2013 when Xi Jinping took over as President. Once it became powerful internally (economic, social, political, military etc.,) it started showing aggression.

India needs to have a similar kind of approach, certainly not to invade any country but to defend ourselves.

Currently, our condition vis-a-vis China is not so inspiring. We are approaching to become a $3 trillion economy while China is reaching $15 trillion, about to overtake the USA with the current growth rate. Also, huge poverty, distressed agriculture, unskilled labour force, huge unemployment, divided society, communal politics and so on weaken us further. Unless we emerge stronger, we cannot fight the external enemy.

To fight the dragon which is spewing fire, our elephant must also spew more powerful fire or else risk losing the existence. We should also remember that though we are increasing strategic closeness with the USA, we should not let ourselves be used to contain China by the USA's policy of buck-passing or blood-letting.

Ultimately, it is we, Indians who have to protect and defend ourselves. We also need allies, not at cost of our sovereignty. For that India's fundamentals in all dimensions must be stronger. Hence, we should develop holistic policy i.e, domestic as well as foreign that includes the vision to make India one of the most powerful nations, which is more than capable of defending and promoting its interests.

16.4   ESSENCE OF CHANAKYA NEETI FOR SUCCESS

Key Messages from Chanakya Neeti

These are applicable to modern day leaders & organizations.

16.4.1   Effective Communication

Chanakya quotes- "When in the court, he shall never cause his petitioners to wait at the door, for when a king makes himself inaccessible to his people and entrusts his work to his immediate officers, he may be sure to engender confusion in business, and to cause thereby public disaffection, and himself a prey to his enemies."

In most organizations, leaders get caught in the entrapments of their titles and entitlements. The higher they are in the organization, the less accessible they become to the very people who at the end of the day are responsible for delivering results.

According to Chanakya, Leaders need to understand that sending people to a communication skills workshop does not improve communication in the organization. Communication improves when the channels of communication are kept open both vertically and horizontally. When leaders are willing to answer people's queries and take the time to explain the deliverables – that's when people learn the value of good communication and practice it themselves.

16.4.2 Decision Making

Chanakya quotes- "All urgent calls he shall hear at once, but never put off; for when postponed, they will prove too hard or impossible to accomplish".

The most malignant of corporate diseases is delayed decision making. There are several reasons why decision making is slow in so many organizations.

(i)   A lack of empowerment across levels is one reason why all decisions seem to get passed up the hierarchy which results in a bottleneck.

(ii) Processes are at times followed more in letter than spirit.

(iii) Decision making is centralized or rather in the custody of key personnel in the organization and these people are always busy.

Chanakya says a good leader should never postpone decisions and should make swift and effective decisions.

16.4.3 Addressing the Needs of the Organization and Keeping employees Happy

Chanakya quotes- "In the happiness of his subjects lies his happiness; in their welfare his welfare; whatever pleases himself he shall not consider as good, but whatever pleases his subjects he shall consider as good".

According to Chanakya, a good leader realizes that his/her whims and preferences come secondary to the real needs and issues of the organization. He should give due consideration to the needs of his employees and keep them happy. An Organization with happy employees usually leads to happy customers.

16.4.4 Accountability

Chanakya quotes- "Whoever imposes severe punishment becomes repulsive to the people; while he who awards mild punishment becomes contemptible. But whoever imposes punishment as deserved becomes respectable. For punishment when awarded with due consideration, makes the people devoted to righteousness; while punishment, when ill-awarded under the influence of greed and anger or owing to ignorance, excites fury even among hermits and ascetics dwelling in forests, not to speak of householders".

According to Chanakya, holding people accountable for their results is one of the most important tools of a leader. Unfortunately, in today's corporate world, we see time and again through many instances that performance becomes punishing and non-performance becomes rewarding. Those who perform well are burdened with more and more responsibility and by contrast those whose performance is not up to the mark seem to get away with minimal work – simply because we do not trust them enough with the responsibility. But what it does is create bitterness in the high performers, as they see themselves being burdened with more and more work while the non-performer seems to be slacking off. Chanakya tells us to reward the high performers and give due punishment to the under performers.

The modern-day kings and queens do not reside in palaces but are found in boardrooms across the globe and just as the words of this ancient wisdom of Chanakya were relevant thousands of years ago, they still hold true in this present day and age.

16.5   RELEVANCE OF CHANAKYA IN THE MODERN TIMES

Chanakya, was an ancient Indian philosopher, teacher, and political advisor. His treatise, the Arthashastra, is considered a masterpiece of political science and economics and has been widely studied for its insights into governance, statecraft, and diplomacy. Despite being written over 2,000 years ago, Chanakya's teachings are still relevant in the modern era and can be applied to various aspects of life, from leadership and management to conflict resolution and diplomacy.

One of the key principles that Chanakya emphasized was the **importance of education**. He believed that acquiring knowledge and skills was crucial for success in life and advocated for individuals to be well-educated in various fields, such as economics, politics, and warfare. This

idea is still relevant today, as a good education is considered a critical factor in personal and professional growth and success.

Another aspect of Chanakya's teachings that is still relevant today is his **understanding of human nature and his ability to judge people's strengths and weaknesses.** He emphasized the importance of being able to identify people's character and intentions and believed that understanding human nature was crucial for effective communication and leadership. This idea is still applicable in today's world, as effective leaders and communicators are often those who are able to understand the motivations and behavior of others.

In addition to his insights into education and human nature, Chanakya's teachings on **strategic thinking and diplomacy** are still highly relevant in the modern era. He provided strategies for building and maintaining power, as well as for using diplomacy to resolve conflicts and negotiate disputes. These teachings can be applied to modern-day negotiation and conflict resolution, as well as to building and maintaining power in business and politics.

Another key principle of Chanakya's teachings is the importance of **ethics and morality** in leadership and governance. He believed that a ruler must possess moral and ethical values in order to maintain the support of the people. In the modern era, this principle can be applied to leadership in both government and corporate settings, as ethical and responsible leadership is essential for building trust and credibility with stakeholders.

Furthermore, Chanakya also emphasized the importance of **financial stability and wealth management.** He believed that a ruler must have a strong financial base in order to maintain the stability of the state. In today's world, this principle can be applied to personal finance and wealth management, as having a solid financial foundation is essential for personal stability and security.

Finally, Chanakya's ideas about **good governance and balancing economic development with social justice** are still relevant today. He believed in the importance of providing for the welfare of the people, and his ideas about balancing economic growth with social equality are still applicable in today's world. Good governance and administration can be improved by incorporating these principles, ensuring that the needs and welfare of the people are taken into account.

Despite being written over 2,000 years ago, the teachings of Chanakya are still relevant in the modern era. From education and human nature to strategic thinking and good governance, his insights provide valuable lessons that can be applied to various aspects of life. However, it is important to understand the historical and cultural context in which his teachings were written and to apply them with a nuanced and critical perspective.

16.6 DIPLOMATIC LEGACY OF CHANAKYA

Chanakya, is one of the most celebrated figures in Indian history. His ideas and strategies laid the foundation for governance and diplomacy in ancient India, and they continue to resonate even today. Living during the 4th century BCE, Chanakya played a pivotal role in the establishment of the Maurya Empire. As the chief advisor to Emperor Chandragupta Maurya, his wisdom and guidance helped unify a fragmented India under a strong central government. His writings, especially the Arthashastra, remain a treasure trove of knowledge on politics, economics, and strategy.

16.6.1 Understanding Chanakya's Era

To fully appreciate Chanakya's genius, it's important to understand the turbulent times he lived in. The Indian subcontinent was divided into multiple kingdoms, each vying for dominance. The threat of foreign invasions, particularly after Alexander the Great's incursion into the region, further destabilized the political landscape. In this chaotic environment, Chanakya envisioned a unified India led by a strong ruler who could safeguard its sovereignty and promote prosperity.

Chanakya's rise was not accidental but a testament to his strategic brilliance. Recognizing the potential in Chandragupta Maurya, he mentored the young leader and orchestrated a series of plans to overthrow the Nanda dynasty, which was then ruling much of northern India. Through careful planning, alliances, and strategic warfare, the foundation of the Maurya Empire was laid, marking the beginning of a new era.

16.6.2   Cornerstones of Chanakya's Diplomacy

(i)   The Mandala Theory

One of Chanakya's most famous contributions to the art of diplomacy is the Mandala Theory. According to this theory, neighboring states are natural adversaries, while those farther away are potential allies. Chanakya advocated for forming alliances with distant powers to counterbalance immediate threats. This pragmatic approach to foreign relations is strikingly similar to modern strategies, where nations often align themselves with others based on shared interests rather than proximity.

(ii)   Intelligence and Espionage

Chanakya was a firm believer in the importance of intelligence. He emphasized the need for a well-organized network of spies who could provide critical information about rival kingdoms, internal dissent, and potential threats. His approach to espionage wasn't limited to gathering information; it also included spreading misinformation to destabilize adversaries.

The relevance of this strategy is evident even today, as nations heavily invest in intelligence agencies to safeguard their interests.

The role of agencies like the CIA, MI6, or RAW mirrors Chanakya's emphasis on the power of information in shaping the outcomes of conflicts and negotiations.

(iii) The Art of Negotiation

Chanakya's diplomatic strategies often prioritized dialogue over warfare. He believed in resolving conflicts through negotiations, leveraging economic and political incentives to achieve favorable outcomes. For instance, he advocated for matrimonial alliances and trade agreements as tools for fostering peace and cooperation.

This reliance on soft power reflects modern diplomatic practices, where economic partnerships and cultural exchanges often play a more significant role than military might in maintaining international relations.

(iv) Pragmatism and Morality in Governance

Critics often label Chanakya as ruthless, citing his emphasis on pragmatism over morality. However, his actions were guided by a deep sense of responsibility toward the state and its people. For Chanakya, the ultimate goal was the welfare of the kingdom, even if it meant making morally ambiguous decisions.

His philosophy aligns with the realist school of thought in international relations, which argues that the pursuit of national interest should take precedence over ideological considerations. Chanakya's teachings remind us that leadership often involves navigating complex ethical dilemmas where the greater good must be prioritized.

16.6.3 Lessons in Administration and Strategy

(i) Centralized Governance

Chanakya's vision for governance revolved around a centralized system where efficiency and accountability were paramount. He stressed the importance of meritocracy in administrative appointments and advocated for a fair taxation system to ensure economic stability. By promoting agricultural productivity and trade, he laid the groundwork for a prosperous and self-sufficient state.

These principles are remarkably relevant today, where governments strive to balance economic growth with social equity. Chanakya's insights into anti-corruption measures and fiscal discipline offer valuable lessons for contemporary policymakers.

(ii) Military Strategy

Chanakya's approach to warfare was as much about strategy as it was about strength. He believed in weakening adversaries through non-military means such as economic blockades, fostering internal dissent, and forming strategic alliances. Only when all other options were exhausted did he advocate for direct confrontation.

A notable example of his strategic acumen is the way he orchestrated the downfall of the Nanda dynasty. By exploiting internal weaknesses and rallying support from disaffected factions, he ensured a relatively swift and decisive victory for Chandragupta Maurya.

(iii) Economic Policies

Chanakya's economic vision was centered on wealth creation and equitable distribution. He recognized the importance of a strong economy in ensuring political stability and advocated for policies that encouraged trade, agricultural growth, and innovation. His emphasis on public welfare, including building infrastructure and providing social safety nets, underscores his holistic approach to governance.

(iv) Relevance in the Modern World

Chanakya's teachings transcend time and geography, offering valuable insights for contemporary leaders and diplomats. His Mandala Theory, for instance, finds parallels in the foreign policies of modern nations that seek to balance regional power dynamics through strategic alliances. Similarly, his focus on intelligence and economic strength underscores the importance of non-military tools in achieving national objectives.

India's current foreign policy, which emphasizes strategic autonomy and leveraging economic partnerships, reflects many of Chanakya's principles. His ideas also resonate in the broader context of global diplomacy, where pragmatism and adaptability are often key to navigating complex international challenges.

The legacy of Chanakya is a testament to the enduring relevance of his insights into governance, diplomacy, and strategy. His ability to blend pragmatism with ethical considerations provides a roadmap for effective leadership, both in ancient and modern contexts. By studying his life and works, we not only gain a deeper understanding of India's rich political heritage but also uncover timeless lessons that can guide us in addressing today's challenges.

As we navigate an increasingly interconnected and volatile world, Chanakya's wisdom serves as a beacon, reminding us of the importance of adaptability, foresight, and a relentless commitment to the greater good.

16.7 RELEVANCE OF CHANAKYA FOR INDIA

Various economists around the globe have named the 21st century as India's century. In the post-pandemic period, India has been among the world's fastest-growing economies. It has occurred at a time when most global economies, including those of developed nations, have witnessed economic slowdown. This is merely a glimpse of India's extraordinary potential. The current momentum shows no signs of slowing down. The Indian government aims to develop the country in a way that places it uniquely ahead of the world. To bring about the actualization of this aim, the government has set a target to place India among the ranks of the developed nations of the world by 2047, which would also mark a hundred years since the country's independence. To achieve these targets, the country needs an all-round development from all fronts.

It is remarkable that Chanakya's theories possess such profound relevance for a country like India. Integrating his strategic ideologies and theories with the current policy formulation can lay the groundwork for the developmental trajectory that India aims to achieve in the long run. In fact, some of his theories and ideas have already been adopted by India in the past.

At the time of independence, a major task in front of the Indian decision-makers was to find a way to integrate India and prevent the newly formed Pakistan from gaining control over key strategic locations across India. At that time, Sardar Vallabhbhai Patel played a pivotal role in ensuring that Pakistan's attempts to take over various areas in India remained unsuccessful. Using his intelligent foresight, he made use of the **four upayas**, or the ways to resolve a conflict, proposed by Chanakya to accomplish his mission. **The first one is Sama,** conciliation. According to Chanakya, peaceful and friendly dialogue should be used as the first resort. Patel skillfully blended diplomacy with friendly dialogue and managed to convince the rulers of several princely states to join India. For example, by engaging in amicable conversations with the rulers of several princely states, such as Travancore (present-day Kerala), he convinced them to join India.

The second way is Dana, or Dama, which means price, or paying the value. It means the use of gifts and other forms of compensation to lure the opposition into an agreement. A large number of princely states did not agree to join India after initial conversations. Therefore, in order to convince them, the Indian government offered them a fixed annual payment called **'Privy Purse'**. It acted like a financial compensation for the rulers of these princely states in exchange for them relinquishing their ruling powers over their respective states. It played a crucial role in the integration of states like Bhopal and Baroda with India.

The next way to resolve a conflict is **Bheda**, the use of logic or trickery to get things done in one's desired manner. It involves the use of methods like persuasion, propaganda, and taking advantage of the rivalries existing between different subgroups in the same unit. The success of the previous methods resulted in over 550 princely states agreeing to join India. Therefore, the use of this method was rendered unnecessary.

According to Chanakya, if the first three methods fall short, the final course of action is **Danda**, the use of force, violence, and punishment to get things done. The first three methods had not worked with the **Nawab of Junagadh and the Nizam of Hyderabad**. Therefore, the Indian armed forces had to intervene militarily. Through a combination of economic pressure and military forces, these states were merged with India and the integration of India was completed.

Circling back to the present, Chanakya's views on governance, leadership, economic policies, national security, and foreign policies step into the spotlight. Chanakya laid great emphasis on the need of a powerful leader who follows an ethical route to bring about the development of his kingdom. A good leader should always focus on promoting welfare and set a good example for the masses. The current government headed by Honorable Prime Minister Narendra Modi has taken several dynamic decisions such as demonetization, implementation of GST, etc. **which align well with Chanakya's policies.** However, many argue that public opinion should be considered before going ahead with such steps.

Chanakya's Arthashastra explores his views on taxation, resource management, infrastructure development, investment, and international trade. He believed in fair and equitable tax systems which do not prove to be an overburden on the taxpayers. In his words, taxes should be collected from individuals just like a bee collects nectar from a flower without causing any damage to it. India follows a progressive tax paying structure, with higher rates of taxes being imposed on individuals with elevated incomes.

Moreover, Goods and Service Tax (GST) was introduced to promote simplification of indirect tax structure. However, there is a need to address concerns like tax evasion and other inefficiencies to promote shared prosperity. Chanakya also emphasized the sustainable use of resources to prevent their overexploitation and promote their long-term benefits. Present-day global efforts to combat environmental degradation also focus on sustainability and long term-use of resources.

Although **Chanakya** is mainly lauded for his diplomacy, his understanding and views on trade were surprisingly impressive. He viewed trade and commerce as major players in promoting economic prosperity. He argued for a certain extent of state control over trade to ensure shared mutual benefits. After independence, the Indian government implemented several measures which were aimed at regulating the activities of domestic industries. Several industries were reserved exclusively for the state. Moreover, a licensing system was set up, under which firms had to take permission from the government for setting up a new industry, expanding an existing one, or diversifying into a new range of offerings. However, these measures proved to be counter-productive and the economy ran into an economic crisis in the 1980s. Therefore, liberalization and privatization were implemented as parts of the New Economic Policy in 1991. They were aimed at reducing the excessive amount of state control over trade. In a favorable turn of events, the economy recovered from the crisis, with positive trends of growth in the real GDP. Therefore, some measures proposed by Chanakya may not be entirely suitable in the contemporary society. There is a need to carefully evaluate them in the light of their current feasibility instead of demonstrating blind trust in them.

When it came to international trade, Chanakya prioritized national interest and mutual benefits. He felt that international trade can play an important role in promoting domestic business, attracting foreign investments and generating employment. Before 1990s, the Indian government discouraged international trade to protect the domestic industries from the well-established foreign industries.

When India decided to implement globalization, the Indian economy reaped the benefits of international trade, such as finding new markets for domestic produce and having better foreign relations. However, it is important to keep strategic considerations in mind. **According to Chanakya, trade ties with potential enemies should be limited to a particular extent as they could strengthen their economies.** Currently, India has kept limited trade ties with countries like Pakistan.

Chanakya was a staunch proponent on national security. His Saptanga theory is closely correlated to national defence. Under this theory, he describes seven elements of a state which are instrumental to safeguard it. According to him, diplomacy is essential to avoid unnecessary aggression and maintain peace. India has forged strong diplomatic ties with several countries across the world. Moreover, it has invested in the defence infrastructure by focusing on indigenous production of defence equipment. These moves have contributed to making India less dependent on western nations and promoted self-reliance.

Chanakya's perspectives on foreign policy were strategic and aimed at developing the economy and maintaining stability in the state. He believed that collecting useful intelligence about neighbouring or enemy states was essential to identify their weaknesses and potential threats. The Rajamandala Theory and the Shadgunya Siddhant are two of his most prominent theories in foreign policy.

16.7.1   The Rajamandala Theory

In his Rajamandala theory, he points out that it is possible to change one's friends, but it is impossible to change one's neighbors. This theory portrays a sequence of concentric circles which surround a central kingdom. The centre of these circles is known as the vijigishu, the state with ambitions and desires, usually the one which is being referred to. In the present context, India can be seen as a vijigishu, a country with goals, ambitions, and a vision. Chanakya states that geographically contiguous states are natural enemies.

India has a long history of animosity against Pakistan. Several territorial disputes, cultural and regional differences, and other geopolitical issues have contributed to the widening gulf between the two nations. A mitra is a friendly state. Such states serve as reliable economic partners, strategic allies, and security partners. Until lately, Bangladesh and Bhutan have been allies to India, and are, therefore, friendly states. But Bangladesh has recently adopted an anti-India policy; so it cannot be viewed as a friendly country anymore.

An arimitra is an enemy's friend. Chanakya advises to remain cautious when it comes to dealing with such states, because an enemy's friend is also an enemy. China is one of Pakistan's greatest allies. India has already run into disputes on various fronts with the country. An ariari is an enemy's enemy. The vijigishu should try and befriend such states, because an enemy's enemy is a friend. India has befriended Japan, which is China's enemy. The two countries have worked together on infrastructure development. Moreover, both nations hold deep respect for each other's culture. A parshnigraha is an enemy in the rear. There are several nations which aim to improve their standing in the global arena and may prove to be potential threats for developing countries like India. An akranda is defined as a friend in the rear, or a friend which is needed as a backup. Israel, France, and Russia have openly shown support to India on various geopolitical issues. These countries have also been dependable trade partners. India has also developed friendly relations with USA, which is an enemy to China.

16.7.2 Shadgunya Siddhant

Chanakya's Shadgunya Siddhant is a six-fold policy technique, which lays down six ways of dealing with internal and external dilemmas confronted by a state. The principle of sandhi, which means a treaty or an agreement to maintain harmony, involves the use of methods which promote peace. It involves developing diplomatic ties with foreign nations to foster mutual interests. India has actively been a part of various global groupings like BRICS, SAARC, etc. which aim to promote cooperation among group members. The principle of vigraha is the use of force by waging a war to achieve a goal.

For instance, in 1971, India intervened militarily to provide aid in Bangladesh's freedom struggle. Asana demonstrates the use of a neutral stance when dealing with certain complex situations. In the recent Russia-Ukraine war, India chose the path of neutrality, and avoided taking any sides. Yaan involves the execution of several diplomatic operations to gain an advantage over foes. The instances of the surgical strike and the Balakot airstrike undertaken by the Indian armed forces against terror camps in Pakistan as a response to the increasing terrorist activities serve as examples of the principle. The principle of samashraya refers to finding shelter for the purpose of forming strategic alliances and dealing with common threats. India has formed strong relations with USA and Japan to deal with the growing threat of China. Lastly, the principle of dwaidbhava implies the use of a dual policy approach which includes methods like creating discord to achieve diplomatic goals.

India's foreign policy has been applauded across the globe. In recent times, India has managed to maintain friendly relations with Russia and the West, despite the growing strain in relations between the West and Russia. It is a testament to India's growing international reputation and standing. The increasing growth rate and infrastructural development provide a strong base for India to propel itself among the ranks of the developed nations in the future. Some of Chanakya's ideas are questioned by critics. However, it is important to keep in mind that these ideas came up in ancient times and are considered to be relevant in those times. These ideas need to be appropriately bended to suit the modern era. For India, it is essential to not to lose focus. It is important to learn from the mistakes that other developed nations have committed, since there will never be enough time for India to commit those mistakes and then learn from them in the future. **By embracing Chanakya's ideas and teachings without blindly trusting them** and forming appropriate policies, India can map out a path to sustainable development in the long run and serve as a beacon for the world to emulate.

16.8   RELEVANCE OF CHANAKYA NEETI FOR BUSINESS

Chanakya Neeti is a collection of aphorisms that cover various aspects of life, including politics, economics, ethics, and personal conduct. These teachings emphasize pragmatism, foresight, & strategic thinking, making them highly relevant for modern-day business practices.

Here are a few fundamental principles from Chanakya Neeti and their business application:

(i)   Strategic Planning and Foresight

Chanakya emphasized the importance of planning and anticipating future challenges. This translates to strategic planning, risk management, & staying ahead of business trends. Companies that invest in thorough market research & develop long-term strategies are better equipped to navigate uncertainties and seize opportunities.

(ii)   Leadership and Governance

According to Chanakya, a leader should possess intelligence, integrity, & decisiveness. Influential business leaders inspire their teams, make informed decisions, & maintain ethical standards. Good governance ensures transparency, accountability, and sustainable growth within an organization.

(iii) Resource Management

Chanakya Neeti underscores the efficient utilization of resources. This involves optimizing human, financial, & material resources to achieve maximum productivity and profitability in a business context. Efficient resource management reduces waste & enhances operational efficiency.

(iv) Adapting to Change

Chanakya advised adaptability and flexibility in response to changing circumstances. Businesses must be agile and responsive to market dynamics, technological advancements, & customer preferences. Adapting to change is crucial for maintaining competitiveness and fostering innovation.

(v) Building Alliances

Forming strategic alliances and partnerships is crucial for businesses. Collaborations, joint ventures, & strong stakeholder relationships can lead to mutual growth and success. Align the company with the right people.

(vi) Ethical Conduct

Chanakya emphasized the importance of ethics and morality. Ethical conduct fosters trust and credibility in business, which is essential for long-term success. Companies that prioritize ethical practices and corporate social responsibility earn the loyalty of customers and employees.

In conclusion, Chanakya Neeti offers valuable insights that apply to modern business practices. By embracing these timeless principles, businesses can achieve sustainable growth, build strong leadership, and create a positive impact in their industries.

16.9 RELEVANCE OF CHANAKYA IN THE MODERN WORLD

Something great happening in the past has its use mainly if it can be applied in the present for the betterment of the future. Kautilya's Arthashashtra, the most famous of the works on statecraft produced in ancient Bharat, is a treatise comprehensively dealing with the political, economic and administrative concepts on which a king could do justice to his duties.

For a vast compendium on how to run a successful regime, produced in 300 BC, it is remarkable that the thematic points made by Chanakya retain their relevance for the world of today – many of these can be identified and examined by the strategic analysts for adoption by the modern State both, for governance at home as well as the handling of foreign relations.

Chanakya's first immutable principle precisely is the one that calls upon the ruler to be well informed about the situation within and outside of the empire. The State must have its channels for the information inflow and whatever was required to safeguard the sensitive information must be done. Functioning of the Intelligence agencies of the state is a sphere that was deeply examined by Chanakya. It was said that **'walls have ears'** and a specific advice Chanakya gave, therefore, was that communication of 'secret' information would be better done at the centre of a field of the size of today's football stadium. That the voice detection through censor technology can be done from remote locations now, does not detract from the importance that was laid then on the awareness of a possible covert interception of confidential communication by the enemy.

Perhaps the most important theory of governance of a State given out by Chanakya that stands the test of time is his emphasis on complete identification of the ruler with the State in terms of his having the required political will, no vested interest of a personal kind and the ability to provide a strong governance while at the same time maintaining a perfect balance between State management and people's welfare.

Chanakya laid the foundation for making Bharat the first welfare State when he ruled that 'in the happiness of his subjects lies the king's happiness'. He included even animals among the subjects – in all likelihood alluding to the cattle wealth of Bharat. With an exceptional farsightedness, Chanakya pronounced that 'security of State lies in the security of citizens' – he could see that an insecure citizen was vulnerable to outside influences.

Another point of focus for Chanakya that was in line with an absolutely modern concept of governance of the State was to recognise that the ruler had not only to provide a sound administration but also work for making the state prosperous. He could see the link between economy and security – the foundation of the contemporary thesis that 'national security was inseparable from economic security'.

Chanakya saw the obvious when he postulated that the strength of the State ultimately derived from its military power but in an astute recommendation that connected with reasons of economy of the State, he wanted this power to be a mix of a permanent segment, or the standing army and the part mobilized at short notice. For this, he favoured the idea of military training being imparted to all youth keeping in view the requirement of what would come to be known as 'conscription' later.

It is in the area of international relations that Chanakya's principles hold good today and even provide added strength to policymakers in the present. He called for a well-founded evaluation of friends and adversaries outside and further identification of the 'circle of contacts' of both. Chanakya, in his profound wisdom, makes a distinction between 'natural friends' and 'potential allies' and enunciates the concept of 'balance of power'. This later emerged as the prime mover of international relations in the years of Cold War and became relevant in the post-Cold War era too.

Bharat's foreign policy under Prime Minister Narendra Modi favoring bilateral and multilateral friendships based on mutuality of economic and security interests and upholding the cause of world peace without the baggage of 'isms', is in complete alignment with Kautilya's philosophy and is serving the nation well.

As already mentioned, Chanakya believed in the primacy of the State and supremacy of the political leadership ruling the State. He united Bharat in spite of the heterogeneity of race and region within the empire. Stability and security of the State was his prime mission. He was able to put the State above caste and class and, in fact, above religion by postulating the theory of Dharma as the guiding principle of the ruler in place of any theology-based approach. Dharma or 'right conduct' combined duty, social justice and responsibility.

According to Chanakya, whenever there is a conflict between the Shastras (religious law) and the written law based on Dharma, the written law shall prevail. The modern State would do well to emulate this conceptual framework of governance. Chanakya foresaw the importance of internal peace and security, recommended an egalitarian approach for the ruler pointing out that unequal treatment bred resentment and preferred the strategy of conciliation, concessions and perks to bring around belligerent groups before exercising the option of brutal power to suppress an insurgency or rebellion.

Kautilya's Arthashashtra was produced in an era preceding the advent of the Prophetic religions – particularly Islam with its exclusive claim on one and the only God – and it is a moot point how the political philosopher would have dealt with a situation where the empire housed religions contradicting each other and dividing people on grounds of faith. He kept the State above religion, race and regional loyalties – a legacy democratic Bharat has preserved to this day.

There is no gain saying the fact, however, that today's challenge of preserving the integrity and security of Bharat is beset with new complexities and what is needed the most is a determined effort of the State to put down forces that indulged in terrorist violence in the name of faith and subverted the unity of the nation by running minority politics.

There are two more epoch making changes of our times that distantly connect with Chanakya's thoughts but need an entirely new understanding and innovative application to serve the interests of the State. One is the rise of the phenomenon of **'proxy wars'**, particularly in the post-Cold War era as a substitute to 'open' military attacks. Terrorism is the new modern weapon of this asymmetric warfare which gives the enemy the advantage of deniability and remote control.

In Bharatiya context, the threat of terrorism is far more serious since it is rooted in faith-based motivation. Chanakya did envisage the concept of a 'pass' from the State authorizing the entry of foreigners but terrorism comes into play either after the terrorists are able to illegally infiltrate into the country or when the masterminds raise an indigenous module of agents to carry out the covert offensive. Chanakya's emphasis on internal security does provide the base on which to build counter-terror measures but the ancient statecraft might not answer all the problems and threat scenarios posed by the contemporary geopolitics.

The second is the new version of **'information warfare'** that is linked to the arrival of cyber age following the success of IT revolution in the closing decades of the 20th century. Rudimentarily mentioned by the Arthashastra, information warfare has been taken to an entirely new level of operation across geographical frontiers and air spaces and demanded new answers. Today social media is an instrument of combat and 'proxy politics' because of its capacity to influence people. Chanakya recognized the importance of sending out information to influence targeted population as also the enemy camp but information warfare presently is a different ball game.

CHAPTER 17

SOME FAMOUS CHANAKYA QUOTES EVERYONE CAN LEARN FROM

17.1 CHANAKYA QUOTES ON ADMINISTRATION

(i) Whoever imposes severe punishment becomes repulsive to the people; while he who awards mild punishment becomes contemptible. But whoever imposes punishment as deserved becomes respectable.

(ii) Punishment when awarded with due consideration, makes the people devoted to righteousness and to works productive of wealth and enjoyment.

(iii) No deliberation made by a single person will be successful; the nature of the work which a sovereign has to do is to be inferred from the consideration of both the visible and invisible causes. The clearance of doubts as to whatever is susceptible of two opinions, and the inference of the whole when only a part is seen is possible of decision only by ministers. Hence the king shall sit at deliberation with persons of wide intellect.

(iv) He shall despise none, but hear the opinions of all. A wise man shall make use of even a child's sensible utterance.

(v) The king shall singly deliberate over secret matters; for ministers have their own ministers, and these latter some of their own; this kind of successive line of ministers tends to the disclosure of counsels.

17.2   CHANAKYA QUOTES ON INTEGRITY

(i)   A person should not be too honest. Straight trees are cut first and honest people are screwed first.

(ii)   Before you start some work, always ask yourself three questions: why I am doing it, What the results might be and Will I be successful. Only when you think deeply and find satisfactory answers to these questions, go ahead.

(iii)   Once you start working on something, don't be afraid of failure and don't abandon it. People who work sincerely are the happiest.

(iv)   The biggest guru-mantra is: Never share your secrets with anybody. If you cannot keep a secret with you, do not expect that others will keep it? It will destroy you.

(v)   The king shall lose no time when the opportunity waited for, arrives.

(vi)   If a king is energetic, his subjects will be equally energetic. If he is reckless, they will not only be reckless likewise, but also eat into his works.

(vi)   The fragrance of flowers spreads only in the direction of the wind but the goodness of a person spreads in all directions.

(vii)   A man is great by deeds, not by birth.

(viii)One whose knowledge is confined to books and whose wealth is in the possession of others can use neither knowledge nor wealth when the need for them arises.

(ix)   Time perfects men as well as destroys them.

(x)   We should not fret for what is past, nor should we be anxious about the future; men of discernment deal only with the present moment.

(xi)   There is no austerity equal to a balanced mind, and there is no happiness equal to contentment; there is no disease like covetousness, and no virtue like mercy.

17.3   CHANAKYA QUOTES ON EDUCATION

(i)   Books are as useful to a stupid person as a mirror is useful to a blind person.

(ii)   Education is the best friend. An educated person is respected everywhere. Education beats the beauty and the youth.

(iii) Learning is like a cow of desire. It, like her, yields in all seasons. Like a mother, it feeds you on your journey. Therefore learning is a hidden treasure.

17.4   CHANAKYA QUOTES ON DAILY LIFE

(i)   He who is overly attached to his family members experiences fear and sorrow, for the root of all grief is attachment. Thus one should discard attachment to be happy.

(ii)   A man is born alone and dies alone; and he experiences the good and bad consequences of his karma alone; and he goes alone to hell or the Supreme abode.

(iii) The wise man should restrain his senses like the crane and accomplish his purpose with due knowledge of his place, time and ability.

(iv)   Purity of speech, of the mind, of the senses, and of a compassionate heart are needed by one who desires to rise to the divine platform.

(v)   He who lives in our mind is near, though he may actually be far away; but he who is not in our heart is far, though he may really be nearby.

(vi)   The happiness and peace attained by those satisfied by the nectar of spiritual tranquility, is not attained by greedy persons restlessly moving here and there.

(vii) There is some self-interest behind every friendship. There is no friendship without self-interests. This is a bitter truth.

(viii) The earth is supported by the power of truth; it is the power of truth that makes the sun shine and the winds blow; indeed all things rest upon truth.

(ix) Do not reveal what you have thought before doing, but by wise council keep it secret being determined to carry it into execution.

(x) As a single withered tree, if set aflame, causes a whole forest to burn, so does a rascal son destroy a whole family.

(xi) A man attains greatness by his merits, not simply by occupying an exalted seat. Can we call a crow an eagle, simply because he sits on the top of a tall building?

(xii) We should always speak what would please the man of whom we expect a favor, like the hunter who sings sweetly when he desires to shoot a deer.

17.5   CHANAKYA QUOTES ON RELIGION

(i) God is not present in idols. Your feelings are your god. The soul is your temple.

(ii) A man is born alone and dies alone; and he experiences the good and bad consequences of his karma alone; and he goes alone to hell or the Supreme abode.

(iii) He who nurtures benevolence for all creatures within his heart overcomes all difficulties and will be the recipient of all types of riches at every step.

(iv) All the creatures are pleased by loving words; and therefore we should address words that are pleasing to all, for there is no lack of sweet words.

(v) Sinfully acquired wealth may remain for ten years; in the eleventh year it disappears with even the original stock.

(vi) He who wears unclean garments, has dirty teeth, is a glutton, speaks unkindly and sleeps after sunrise – although he may be the greatest personality — will lose the favour of Lakshmi.

(vii) Eschew wicked company and associate with saintly persons. Acquire virtue day and night, and always meditate on that which is eternal forgetting that which is temporary.

(viii) He who is prepared for the future and he who deals cleverly with any situation that may arise are both happy; but the fatalistic man who wholly depends on luck is ruined.

(ix) Even as the unborn baby is in the womb of his mother, these five are fixed as his life destiny: his life span, his activities, his acquisition of wealth and knowledge, and his time of death.

(x) Who realizes all the happiness he desires? Everything is in the hands of God. Therefore one should learn contentment.

(xi) By means of hearing one understands dharma, malignity vanishes, knowledge is acquired, and liberation from material bondage is gained.

(xii) The poor wish for wealth; animals for the faculty of speech; men wish for heaven; and godly persons for liberation.

(xiii) Learning is a friend on the journey; a wife in the house; medicine in sickness; and religious merit is the only friend after death.

17.6 CHANAKYA QUOTES ON WISDOM

(i) The man who remains a fool even in advanced age is really a fool, just as the Indra-Varuna fruit does not become sweet no matter how ripe it might become.

(ii) The cuckoos remain silent for a long time (for several seasons) until they are able to sing sweetly (in the Spring) so as to give joy to all.

(iii) We should not feel pride in our charity, austerity, valour, scriptural knowledge, modesty, and morality for the world is full of the rarest gems.

(iv) Drop the idea that attachment and love are one thing. They are enemies. It is attachment that destroys all love.

(v) Wealth, a friend, a wife, and a kingdom may be regained; but this body when lost may never be acquired again.

(vi) Poverty, disease, sorrow, imprisonment and other evils are the fruits borne by the tree of one's own sins.

(vii) There are three gems upon this earth; food, water, and pleasing words — fools consider pieces of rocks as gems.

(viii) As a calf follows its mother among a thousand cows, so the (good or bad) deeds of a man follow him.

(ix) He who forsakes his own community and joins another, perishes as the king who embraces an unrighteous path.

(x) Generosity, pleasing address, courage and propriety of conduct are not acquired, but are inbred qualities.

(xi) A learned man is honoured by the people. A learned man commands respect everywhere for his learning. Indeed, learning is honoured everywhere.

(xii) Beauty is spoiled by an immoral nature; noble birth by bad conduct; learning, without being perfected; and wealth by not being properly utilized.

(xiii) Moral excellence is an ornament for personal beauty; righteous conduct, for high birth; success for learning; and proper spending for wealth.

(xiv) Our bodies are perishable; wealth is not at all permanent and death is always nearby. Therefore we must immediately engage in acts of merit.

(xv) Those base men who speak of the secret faults of others destroy themselves like serpents that stray onto anthills.

(xvi) Low class men desire wealth; middle class men both wealth and respect; but the noble, honour only; hence honour is the noble man's true wealth.

(xvii) He who has wealth has friends and relations; he alone survives and is respected as a man.

(xviii) Accumulated wealth is saved by spending just as incoming fresh water is saved by letting out stagnant water.

(xix) Swans live wherever there is water, and leave the place where water dries up; let not a man act so — and comes and goes as he pleases.

(xx) The power of a king lies in his mighty arms; that of a brahmana in his spiritual knowledge; and that of a woman in her beauty youth and sweet words.

(xxi) He who gives up shyness in monetary dealings, in acquiring knowledge, in eating and in business, becomes happy.

(xxii) Time perfects all living beings as well as kills them; it alone is awake when all others are asleep. Time is insurmountable.

(xxiii) The learned are envied by the foolish; rich men by the poor; chaste women by adulteresses; and beautiful ladies by ugly ones.

(xxiv) She is a true wife who is clean, expert, chaste, pleasing to the husband, and truthful.

(xxv) When one is consumed by the sorrows of life, three things give him relief: offspring, a wife, and the company of the Lord's devotees.

(xxvi) As long as your body is healthy and under control and death is distant, try to save your soul; when death is imminent what can you do?

(xxvii) Do not keep company with a fool for as we can see he is a two-legged beast. Like an unseen thorn he pierces the heart with his sharp words.

(xxviii) At the time of the pralaya (universal destruction)the oceans are to exceed their limits and seek to change, but a saintly man never changes.

(xxix) He who befriends a man whose conduct is vicious, whose vision impure, and who is notoriously crooked, is rapidly ruined.

(xxx) Avoid him who talks sweetly before you but tries to ruin you behind your back, for he is like a pitcher of poison with milk on top.

(xxxi) Even if a snake is not poisonous, it should pretend to be venomous.

(xxxii) Never make friends with people who are above or below you in status. Such friendships will never give you any happiness.

(xxxiii) As soon as the fear approaches near, attack and destroy it.

BIBLIOGRAPHY

Chanakya. "Chanakya Neeti: with Complete Sutras", Grapevine India Publishers, 2018.

Chaturvedi, B.K. " Chanakya Neeti (Chanakya's Aphorism on Morality), Diamond Pocket Books, 2013.

Hammad, "Life and Legacy of Chanakya: Who was Chanakya?", Chegg, March 2025.

Kangle, R.P. " The Kautilya Arthasastra: 3 Volumes" Motilal Banarsidass, 2019.

Olivelle, Patrick. "King, Governance, and Law in Ancient India: Kautilya's Arthashastra", Oxford University Press' 2013.

Pillai, Radhakrishnan. "Chanakya and the Art of War", Penguin Books / India Portfolio, 2019.

Rangarajan, L.N. "The Arthashastra (Introduction)", Penguin Books, 2016.

Shamasastry, Dr. R. "Kautilya's Arthashastra", Mysore Printing and Publishing House, 8th edition, 1967.

Trautmann, Thomas R. "Arthashastra: The Science of Wealth", Penguin Books, 2016.

Vittal, Vinay. "Kautilya's Arthashastra: A Timeless Grand Strategy", Graduation Thesis, School of Advanced Air and Space Studies, Alabama, June 2011.